Prentice Hall

WRITING and GRAMMAR

Communication in Action

Silver Level

Grammar Exercise Workbook

Prentice
Hall

Upper Saddle River, New Jersey
Glenview, Illinois
Needham, Massachusetts

Student Edition

ISBN 0-13-043473-6

5 6 7 8 9 10   05 04 03 02

Contents

Note: This workbook supports Chapters 14–27 (Part 2: Grammar, Usage, and Mechanics) of *Prentice Hall Writing and Grammar.*

Chapter 20: Phrases and Clauses

Chapter 21: Effective Sentences

Chapter 25: Using Modifiers

Chapter 26: Punctuation

14.1 Nouns (People, Places, and Things) • Practice 1

People, Places, and Things   A noun is the name of a person, place, or thing.

People	Places	Things
carpenter	auditorium	*Those You Can See*
students	Grant's Tomb	hedgehog marigold
cheerleader	art gallery	ambulance blouse
Dr. Nelson	fish markets	*Those You Cannot See*
technician	Lincoln Center	warmth generosity
Canadians	Wrigley Building	sickness noise

▶ **Exercise 1**   **Recognizing People, Places, and Things.**   Put the words below in the proper columns.

EXAMPLE:

	People	Places	Things	
			shoes	

dictionary	Stephanie	garage	umbrella	health
witness	mall	meadow	Eisenhower	envelope
sister	helicopter	dinosaur	principal	Babe Ruth
success	capitol	peanut	office	restroom

People   Places   Things

_____   _____   _____

_____   _____   _____

_____   _____   _____

_____   _____   _____

_____   _____   _____

_____   _____   _____

▶ **Exercise 2**   **Using Nouns.**   Fill in the blank in each sentence with the kind of word indicated in the parentheses.

EXAMPLE: For Christmas I got a new ____calculator.____ (thing)

1. My favorite _____ will arrive from Atlanta today. (person)

2. When will you finish your _____? (thing)

3. The Supreme Court is located in _____. (place)

4. Until now my grandfather has always been in good _____. (thing)

5. You will find many reference books in the _____. (place)

6. Because of my poor handwriting, I need a _____. (thing)

7. Her _____ is appreciated by everyone. (thing)

8. My _____ makes the best chocolate cake. (person)

9. I always buy new CD's at _____. (place)

10. I believe the most important scientist was _____. (person)

14.1   Nouns (People, Places, and Things) • Practice 2

▶ **Exercise 1**   **Classifying Nouns.**   All the words in the following list are nouns. Place each word in the correct column.

EXAMPLE: People   Places   Things
                                    carrot

1. teacher   6. uprising   11. Maine   16. Mary Stuart
2. grizzly bear 7. Frank   12. fable   17. vegetables
3. sadness   8. ranch   13. flower   18. silliness
4. city   9. heroism   14. justice   19. Atlantic Ocean
5. basketball 10. newspaper   15. countryside 20. truth

People   Places   Things
_____   _____ _____
_____   _____ _____
_____   _____ _____
_____   _____ _____
_____   _____ _____
_____   _____ _____
_____   _____ _____
_____   _____ _____

▶ **Exercise 2**   **Classifying Nouns in Sentences.**   Complete each sentence by writing a noun in the blank. Then write the noun in the proper column below.

EXAMPLE: An encyclopedia is an excellent reference book.
             People Places Things
                           encyclopedia

1. Fourteen _____ signed up for soccer tryouts.

2. For their vacation, the Jeffersons went to _____.

3. The _____ needs to be cleaned.

4. Please pick up some _____ at the store.

5. Jamie's _____ are coming to her house for a sleep-over.

6. Would you like to eat lunch at the _____?

7. Inez needs some new _____ for those pictures.

8. The _____ broke when Alice dropped it.

9. Let's invite _____ over for dinner.

10. Josh and Frankie went swimming in the _____.

People   Places   Things
_____   _____ _____
_____   _____ _____
_____   _____ _____
_____   _____ _____
_____   _____ _____

14.1 Nouns (Collective and Compound Nouns) • Practice 1

Collective Nouns   A collective noun is a noun that names a group of individual people or things.

COLLECTIVE NOUNS		
squad	flock	crew
company	team	orchard

Compound Nouns   A compound noun is made up of two or more words.

COMPOUND NOUNS	
workshop	Getty Museum
ice age	father-in-law

▶ **Exercise 1**   **Recognizing Collective Nouns.**   In each blank below, write the collective noun from the sentence.

EXAMPLE: The entire clan gathered in the hall. ____clan____

1. An angry crowd assembled in front of the church. _____
2. My uncle hopes to raise a flock of sheep. _____
3. Our class voted to have a spring picnic. _____
4. Melissa applauded the performance of the orchestra. _____
5. What did you think about the reaction of the audience? _____
6. A company of dancers will entertain us first. _____
7. The jury voted to acquit the defendant. _____
8. Later, the trio played three interesting numbers. _____
9. A squadron of soldiers surrounded the building. _____
10. The bill was sent to a committee for further study. _____

▶ **Exercise 2**   **Recognizing Compound Nouns.**   In each blank below, write the compound noun from the sentence.

EXAMPLE: We definitely need a new football. ____football____

1. My father wants to build new bookshelves. _____
2. Visit the Smithsonian Institution in Washington. _____
3. How late is the post office open on Saturday? _____
4. Her outlook is always positive. _____
5. How did your cousin like her new junior high school? _____
6. Paul Simon is my favorite songwriter. _____
7. To improve, we will need a lot of teamwork. _____
8. No medicine is a complete cure-all. _____
9. This cartridge uses an advanced magnetic tape. _____
10. We are going to assemble a new mailing list. _____

14.1 **Nouns** (Collective and Compound Nouns) • **Practice 2**

▷ **Exercise 1** **Recognizing Collective Nouns.** Underline the nouns in the following sentences. Circle the collective nouns.

EXAMPLE: Marie shocked the (audience) with her final words.

1. A panel of scientists debated the probability of life on other planets.
2. An outlandish sketch of an imaginary Martian amused the audience.
3. The performance of the team improved tremendously after the speech given by the coach.
4. Pickett led his brigade in a daring charge at Gettysburg.
5. William Shakespeare wrote his plays for one particular company of actors.
6. A pair of swans swam lazily around the lake.
7. The captain ordered new uniforms for the crew.
8. Christopher wants to join the army when he is eighteen.
9. Tony hired a jazz trio to play at the party.
10. An interesting speaker gave a presentation for the assembly today.
11. The entire herd had to be checked for disease.
12. An unruly mob moved quickly toward the jailhouse.
13. Members of the union were marching with signs in front of the store.
14. The singer approached the microphone, and the band began to play.
15. Melanie and her seven musical friends formed an octet.

▷ **Exercise 2** **Recognizing Compound Nouns.** Underline each compound noun in the following paragraph.

EXAMPLE: There is no way their high school can beat ours this year.

(1) Yesterday in homeroom, Bob and I discussed sports in our junior high school. (2) We agreed that our victory in volleyball was the highlight of the year. (3) Bob said he couldn't wait to go to high school, where we will be able to play basketball, water polo, and baseball. (4) I myself would like to be a linebacker on the football team.

▷ **Exercise 3** **Writing Sentences With Compound Nouns.** Write a sentence of your own that uses the type of compound noun given in parentheses. Then underline the compound noun.

EXAMPLE: (hyphenated words) *Mel's great-grandmother likes to ski.*

1. (separate words) _____
2. (hyphenated words) _____
3. (combined words) _____
4. (separate words) _____
5. (hyphenated words) _____
6. (combined words) _____
7. (separate words) _____
8. (hyphenated words) _____
9. (combined words) _____
10. (separate words) _____

Nouns (Common and Proper Nouns) • **Practice 1**

Common and Proper Nouns   A common noun names any one of a class of people, places, or things. A proper noun names a specific person, place, or thing.

Common Nouns	Proper Nouns
soldier	General Eisenhower
theater	Globe Theater
opera	*Porgy and Bess*

▶ **Exercise 1**   **Recognizing Common and Proper Nouns.**   In the sentences below, underline each proper noun and circle each common noun.

EXAMPLE: Bruce Springsteen is an outstanding (performer) .

1. Charles Dickens is easily my favorite British author.
2. The touring cast of *South Pacific* arrived early.
3. Did you know that Robert F. Kennedy once served as attorney general?
4. My math teacher at Sarah J. Hale High School is very interesting.
5. Recently, Thanksgiving was voted the most popular holiday.
6. Long ago, Rome was the largest city.
7. The library on Weldon Lane will be closed tomorrow.
8. Euripides, the tragic poet, was born in 485 B.C.
9. Andrew Carnegie built a very elaborate mansion.
10. In soccer, Mia Hamm was peerless.

▶ **Exercise 2**   **Changing Common Nouns Into Proper Nouns.**   In the spaces provided below, supply a proper noun that illustrates the common noun.

EXAMPLE: A famous highway ____*Pennsylvania Turnpike*____

Common Noun	Proper Noun
1. A favorite book	_____
2. A former president	_____
3. A noted composer	_____
4. A baseball team	_____
5. A beautiful river	_____
6. A famous actor	_____
7. A news magazine	_____
8. A senator	_____
9. An exciting museum	_____
10. A famous bridge	_____

14.1 Nouns (Common and Proper Nouns) • Practice 2

▶ **Exercise 1** **Identifying Common and Proper Nouns.** Place a *C* after each common noun and a *P* after each proper noun. Write a proper noun that gives an example of each common noun. Then, write a common noun that gives an example of a class to which each proper noun belongs.

EXAMPLE: Mars ____*P planet*____

1. writer_____
2. Chicago_____
3. Zeus_____
4. river_____
5. street_____
6. Louisa May Alcott_____
7. Jamaica_____
8. horse_____

9. automobile_____
10. Blondie_____
11. state_____
12. singer_____
13. Rockies_____
14. relative_____
15. team_____

▶ **Exercise 2** **Distinguishing Between Common and Proper Nouns.** Each of the following items contains three nouns, one of which is a proper noun that has not been capitalized. Underline each proper noun.

EXAMPLE: lion   leo   kitten   <u>Leo</u>

1.	car	convertible	studebaker
2.	state	district	dade county
3.	lake erie	ocean	river
4.	magazine	bible	pamphlet
5.	nation	ghana	country
6.	singer	songwriter	john lennon
7.	aunt sally	relative	woman
8.	character	tom sawyer	boy
9.	cartoon	movie	bambi
10.	poet	writer	emily dickinson

▶ **Writing Application** **Writing Sentences With Nouns.** Write five sentences of your own using each of the different types of nouns listed below. Underline these nouns.

EXAMPLE: a compound noun
The carpenter constructed a <u>bookshelf</u> for my room.
_____

1. a noun that names a place

_____

2. a noun that names a person

_____

3. a noun that names a thing you can see

_____

4. a noun that names an idea

_____

5. a collective noun

_____

14.2 Pronouns (Antecedents of Pronouns, Personal Pronouns) • Practice 1

Antecedents of Pronouns   A pronoun is a word used to take the place of a noun. The noun for which it substitutes is called an antecedent.

PRONOUNS AND ANTECEDENTS
ANTECEDENT   PRONOUN   PRONOUN Bill raised his trophy in triumph and he smiled. PRONOUN   ANTECEDENT   PRONOUN Waving her hand, the actress greeted her fans.

Personal Pronouns   Personal pronouns refer to (1) the person speaking, (2) the person spoken to, or (3) the person, place, or thing spoken about.

First Person	Second Person	Third Person
I, me, my, mine we, us, our, ours	you, your, yours	he, him, his, she, her, hers, it, its, they, them, their, theirs

▶ **Exercise 1**   **Recognizing Pronouns and Antecedents.**   Underline the personal pronoun in each sentence. Then circle its antecedent.

EXAMPLE: The (players) brought their lunches to the game.

1. Because of her illness, the singer was unable to appear.
2. At the party, Bob asked his friend's sister for a dance.
3. When Betsy read *Romeo and Juliet* for the first time, she cried.
4. With their tickets in hand, the three sisters approached the gangplank.
5. Jean, will you read this poem aloud?
6. In spite of their accident, the actors arrived on time.
7. The lion snarled, opened its mouth, and roared.
8. Beethoven wrote his famous *Ninth Symphony* when he was deaf.
9. Grabbing his knee, the tackle collapsed on the grass.
10. Had she wanted, Sylvia could have won the first prize.

▶ **Exercise 2**   **Using Personal Pronouns in Sentences.**   Fill in each blank with an appropriate personal pronoun.

EXAMPLE: Of all ____*his*____ operas, Verdi liked *Macbeth* the best.

1. Susan called _____ mother as soon as dancing class was over.
2. Without _____ helmets, the football team could not play.
3. Shakespeare returned to _____ home in Stratford often.
4. These flowers are so beautiful I wish _____ would bloom all year.
5. The wingspan of the frigate bird is the largest in proportion to _____ body.
6. Were you able to get _____ autographs?
7. I want you to ask for _____ passports now.
8. Marie and _____ have no spare time.
9. Have you prepared _____ welcoming speech yet?
10. I don't think I can take _____ coin collection with us.

14.2 Pronouns (Antecedents of Pronouns, Personal Pronouns) • Practice 2

▶ **Exercise 1** **Recognizing Antecedents.** In each of the following sentences, a pronoun is underlined. Find the antecedent of each pronoun and circle it.

EXAMPLE: Somehow (Jeff) managed to lose his tuba.

1. A zoo in Arkansas is interesting because it trains and houses a remarkable group of animals.
2. Visitors at the zoo can see such marvels as Bert Backquack and his all-duck band.
3. The zoo also includes among its residents a roller-skating parrot.
4. The trainers there believe that most animals behave intelligently if they are treated with respect.
5. Davy Crocket's tales made him a legend in his own time.
6. Davy went to Congress claiming that he had wrestled grizzly bears as a child.
7. Fashionable people found themselves competing for Davy's attention at parties.
8. As children, the Brontës created their own private world.
9. To avoid the prejudice against women writers, Brontë sisters used pen names on their books.
10. Charlotte called herself Currer Bell, and her sister Emily became Ellis Bell.

▶ **Exercise 2** **Identifying Personal Pronouns and Their Antecedents.** Each of the following sentences contains two personal pronouns. Underline each personal pronoun and circle its antecedent.

EXAMPLE: (Jim), you forgot your hat.

1. Mom, you forgot to call your sister.
2. "I tried to repair my CD player," said Carlos.
3. Since Meg moved, she has called her friends once a week.
4. Now, boys, you have to clean up your own mess.
5. James tried to reach the doctor, but she was not in her office.
6. The brothers quit the team when they found that their grades were suffering.
7. Marge, yesterday you promised to lend your album to Judy.
8. The book is not as exciting as its jacket suggests, but it has one suspenseful chapter.
9. The McCurdys said that they would volunteer some of their time.
10. Uncle Dan gave his favorite watch to his oldest nephew.

▶ **Writing Application** **Writing Sentences That Contain Personal Pronouns.** Write a short sentence using a personal pronoun that fits each description. Underline the pronoun you use.

EXAMPLE: third person, plural pronoun   *I folded the sheets and put them into the closet.*

1. first person, singular pronoun

_____

2. third person, singular, masculine pronoun

_____

3. first person, plural pronoun

_____

4. a different first person, plural pronoun

_____

5. third person, singular, feminine pronoun

_____

14.2 Four Special Kinds of Pronouns
(Demonstrative and Relative Pronouns) • Practice 1

Demonstrative Pronouns A demonstrative pronoun points out a specific person, place, or thing. There are four demonstrative pronouns, two singular and two plural.

DEMONSTRATIVE PRONOUNS	
Singular	**Plural**
this	these
that	those

Relative Pronouns A relative pronoun begins a subordinate clause and connects it to another idea in the same sentence. There are five relative pronouns.

RELATIVE PRONOUNS				
that	who	whose	which	whom

▶ **Exercise 1** **Recognizing Demonstrative and Relative Pronouns.** Circle the demonstrative or relative pronoun in each sentence. At the end of the sentence use a *D* to identify the pronoun as demonstrative or an *R* to identify it as relative. Note that the pronoun *that*, depending on use, can be either type.

EXAMPLE: (This) article is not correct. _____D_____

1. Unfortunately, these are now overripe tomatoes. _____
2. Picasso is the painter whom I most admire. _____
3. Are those your books? _____
4. The book that you reserved has not yet arrived. _____
5. Is this the map of Antarctica? _____
6. The woman who is in charge just left. _____
7. That is the last piece of chicken. _____
8. Of all her photos, those are the most original in concept. _____
9. Where is the man whose dog was found? _____
10. Father decided this was the most practical van. _____

▶ **Exercise 2** **Using Demonstrative and Relative Pronouns in Sentences.** Fill in each blank with an appropriate demonstrative or relative pronoun.

EXAMPLE: I wonder _____whom_____ we will meet at the dance.

1. You must walk the dog each morning. _____ is your responsibility.
2. Where is the cake _____ she chose?
3. _____ has not worked properly for some time.
4. Do you know _____ the speaker will be?
5. You really have no choice. _____ are the rules.
6. Is Mary the girl _____ grandfather is visiting?
7. Take _____ and store them in the garage.
8. Is Sandy the girl _____ he likes?
9. Give us the design _____ the manager selected.
10. The senator, _____ will present the award, has just arrived.

14.2 # Four Special Kinds of Pronouns
(Demonstrative and Relative Pronouns) • **Practice 2**

▶ **Exercise 1**   Recognizing Demonstrative Pronouns.   Underline the demonstrative pronouns.

EXAMPLE: <u>That</u> is not the CD I would have chosen.

1. Those are the most expensive dresses in the store.
2. Of all the Beatles' records, these are their best.
3. I brought a dictionary, and that has helped improve my spelling.
4. These are the three most popular exhibits.
5. Of all his ideas, those are the strangest.
6. This is the artist I want you to meet.
7. You may help by peeling carrots. That is your first chore.
8. He raises bromeliads. These are a kind of exotic plant.
9. That seems to be their busiest time of the year.
10. This was all she said before leaving: "I'll be back."
11. "Is this the first time you've been here?" asked the guide.
12. "I'd like to try a taste of that," said Amy, pointing to the pie.
13. These are the times that try men's souls.
14. Those were the days, my friend.
15. My advice to you is this: Calm down.
16. Are these your shoes?
17. If you lose that, you can find another one in the top drawer.
18. Holding out a bunch of daffodils, Daisy said, "I brought you these."
19. "That is not what I meant," said Prufrock.
20. "May I please see those?" asked Fran, looking into the display case.

▶ **Exercise 2**   Recognizing Relative Pronouns.   Underline the relative pronouns.

EXAMPLE: The person <u>who</u> left has just volunteered.

1. A leader whom our nation will never forget is Lincoln.
2. She chose a hat that matched her gown.
3. I will spend the summer vacation with my cousin who lives in Kingston.
4. The pipe that had leaked for a month finally burst.
5. The woman who was chosen scientist of the year works as a biochemist.
6. We joined the club whose introductory offer was the best.
7. The experimental car, which runs on batteries, does not pollute the air.
8. The pupil who gets the scholarship must excel in mathematics.
9. The dancer whom we admired most performed two solos.
10. Can you find a button that matches the others?
11. The birds that we saw at the zoo were flamingoes.
12. This hat, which I use when I go out into the snow, keeps my ears warm.
13. Cara, who will be here in an hour, is bringing the dessert.
14. Denise, whom we invited at the last minute, cannot come.
15. Albert is the boy whose bike you borrowed.

14.2 Four Special Kinds of Pronouns
(Interrogative and Indefinite Pronouns) • Practice 1

Interrogative Pronouns   An interrogative pronoun is used to begin a question. There are five interrogative pronouns.

INTERROGATIVE PRONOUNS
what   which   who   whom   whose

Indefinite Pronouns   Indefinite pronouns refer to people, places, or things, often without specifying which ones. There are many indefinite pronouns, some singular, some plural, and some either singular or plural.

INDEFINITE PRONOUNS			
Singular		**Plural**	**Singular or Plural**
anyone	neither	both	all
each	no one	few	any
either	one	many	more, most
everything	other	others	none
everyone	somebody	several	some

▶ **Exercise 1**   **Recognizing Interrogative and Indefinite Pronouns.**   Circle the interrogative or indefinite pronoun. Identify interrogative pronouns with *int.* and indefinite pronouns with *ind.*

EXAMPLE: (No one) really knows our secret. _____*ind.*_____

1. Who was chosen as our Homecoming Queen? _____
2. Both of the suggestions are extremely helpful. _____
3. Amazingly, Uncle Burt knew everyone at the dinner. _____
4. The junior prom committee accepted one of our ideas. _____
5. I found my jacket. Whose is still in the closet? _____
6. My father knows somebody at the licensing bureau. _____
7. Either of their choices is acceptable to the principal. _____
8. Have you tried some of these fabulous desserts? _____
9. Which is the shortest route to the stadium? _____
10. Many of our friends will be going on the field trip. _____

▶ **Exercise 2**   **Using Interrogative and Indefinite Pronouns.**   Fill in each blank with an appropriate interrogative or indefinite pronoun.

EXAMPLE: I finally asked _____*someone*_____ to help us.

1. _____ is the eighth-grade assistant principal?
2. The committee will examine _____ of their proposals.
3. _____ of these books are too expensive for us.
4. Can _____ enter this restricted area?
5. There are several photographs. _____ is the best?
6. Your information was wrong. _____ has to pay an entry fee.
7. _____ of the original buildings still stand on Main Street.
8. You know that _____ of H. G. Wells's predictions came true.
9. With _____ do you expect to go to the party?
10. _____ in the hall was delighted with Bill's performance.

14.2 Four Special Kinds of Pronouns
(Interrogative and Indefinite Pronouns) • Practice 2

▶ **Exercise 1** **Recognizing Interrogative Pronouns.** Underline each interrogative pronoun.

EXAMPLE: Which of the colors goes best with this sweater?

1. Which of Ernest Hemingway's novels takes place during the Spanish Civil War?
2. One President of the United States served as Chief Justice of the Supreme Court after he left office. Who was this President?
3. What are the main differences between professional football and college football?
4. Which is your favorite Joni Mitchell song?
5. A special symbol is hidden in this painting. What is the symbol?
6. Whom did Tom Sawyer and Becky Thatcher see when they were lost in the cave?
7. Who pitched the only perfect game in the history of the World Series?
8. What did Dorothy do to escape from the Wicked Witch of the West?
9. Who was the first woman to be elected to the United States Congress?
10. For whom did Lewis Carroll write *Alice's Adventures in Wonderland*?

▶ **Exercise 2** **Recognizing Indefinite Pronouns.** Each of the following sentences contains at least one indefinite pronoun. Underline the indefinite pronoun or pronouns in each sentence.

EXAMPLE: Nobody went to see that movie.

1. Everyone applauded the winner of the marathon.
2. The coach asked all the girls to prepare thoroughly for the match.
3. Most of the students are interested in computers, but few know how they actually work.
4. Few of my classmates knew anything about Susan B. Anthony.
5. The auditorium was so dark that we could see nothing.
6. Did someone remember to turn on the lights?
7. Somebody has taken one of the dictionaries.
8. Neither wanted to go, but it was important for both to attend.
9. Little is known about the people who built Stonehenge.
10. No one knew why some of the pages had been torn from his diary.

▶ **Writing Application** **Writing Sentences With Pronouns.** Write five sentences of your own using each of the different types of pronouns listed below. Underline the pronouns.

EXAMPLE: *who* as a relative pronoun.   *The room was crowded with people who were cheering.*

1. a singular demonstrative pronoun

   _____

2. a plural demonstrative pronoun that comes after its antecedent

   _____

3. *that* as a relative pronoun.

   _____

4. *who* as a relative pronoun

   _____

5. *whose* as an interrogative pronoun

   _____

Name _____   Date _____

Visible and Mental Action   An action verb tells what action a person or thing is performing. Action verbs can express different kinds of actions. Some actions are visible and can be seen easily. Others are mental actions that can be seen only with difficulty, if at all.

Visible Action		Mental Action	
jump	travel	believe	dream
build	grow	know	think
jog	deliver	consider	understand

▶ **Exercise 1**   **Recognizing Action Verbs.**   Underline the action verb in each sentence below. In the space provided write *V* if it describes a visible action and *M* if it indicates a mental action.

EXAMPLE: The batter slid into third base. _____*V*_____

1. I wonder about my future almost every day. _____
2. The old locomotive pulled into the station. _____
3. Maria purchased a new wallet in the flea market. _____
4. After several hours at the beach, we drove home on the bus. _____
5. My grandmother remembers her childhood in Poland. _____
6. Some people worry almost all the time. _____
7. Cut the beef for the stew into small cubes. _____
8. This airline flies to Madrid twice weekly. _____
9. I considered my choices carefully. _____
10. After dinner, my parents opened their anniversary present. _____

▶ **Exercise 2**   **Using Action Verbs in Sentences.**   Fill in the blanks below with appropriate action verbs. Supply the kind of action verb indicated in the parentheses.

EXAMPLE: I often _____*wonder*_____ about the future. (mental)

1. A large delivery van _____ in front of our building. (visible)
2. I often _____ about my childhood on the farm. (mental)
3. Our committee strongly _____ about making some changes. (mental)
4. The Independence Day parade _____ early in the morning. (visible)
5. Christine _____ a leading role in *West Side Story*. (visible)
6. Our family _____ to take a vacation in August. (mental)
7. Finally, after mother's warning, I _____ my room. (visible)
8. I _____ exactly how to put it together. (mental)
9. After the big snow storm, Mark _____ the driveway. (visible)
10. Last night I _____ that I was walking down a long, dark corridor. (mental)

15.1 Action Verbs (Visible and Mental Action) • Practice 2

▶ **Exercise 1** **Recognizing Action Verbs.** Underline the action verb in each sentence. Then label each as *visible* or *mental*.

EXAMPLE: People once believed in goblins. _____*mental*_____

1. Jetliners fly quickly across the Atlantic. _____
2. For many weeks, Columbus and his crew worried about reaching land. _____
3. Juan dreamed of his family in Cuba. _____
4. The quarterback threw a long pass. _____
5. The receiver barely caught the ball. _____
6. Elizabeth Kenny developed a treatment for polio. _____
7. She considered warmth and exercise to be the best therapy. _____
8. He remembers many events from World War II. _____
9. Weeds suddenly sprouted all over our front lawn. _____
10. She believed in justice and freedom for all. _____
11. Paco rode his pony across the meadow. _____
12. Terry hoped for better days. _____
13. For several hours, Rita carefully prepared the feast. _____
14. Jean wrapped the gift in colorful paper. _____
15. With the approach of the storm, the sailors feared the worst. _____
16. Darlene appreciated her aunt's efforts. _____
17. Stan pushed his little sister on the swing. _____
18. After an hour of study, Maryanne understood the concept. _____
19. We drove to our little cabin in the mountains. _____
20. Wanda wondered about the meaning of Juan's actions. _____

▶ **Exercise 2** **Writing Sentences With Action Verbs.** Write a sentence for each action verb. Then write *V* if the action is visible and *M* if the action is mental.

EXAMPLE: listen: _____The birds listen for an answering call. V_____

1. ate _____
2. feared _____
3. slept _____
4. appreciated _____
5. understand _____
6. folded _____
7. wrote _____
8. wondered _____
9. drank _____
10. hoped _____

Action Verbs (Transitive and Intransitive Verbs)
• Practice 1

Transitive Verbs An action verb is transitive if the receiver of the action is named in the sentence. The receiver of the action is called the object of the verb.

TRANSITIVE VERBS
Meg *unwrapped* her present.
(unwrapped what?) present
Mother *likes* eggs.
(likes what?) eggs

Intransitive Verbs An action verb is intransitive if no receiver of the action is named in the sentence. A sentence with an intransitive verb will not have an object.

INTRANSITIVE VERBS
Both witnesses *agreed*.
(agreed what?) no answer
Nancy *spoke* to her doctor.
(spoke what?) no answer

▶ **Exercise 1** **Recognizing Transitive Action Verbs.** Underline the transitive action verb in each sentence below and circle its object.

EXAMPLE: I have your (ticket) for the football game.

1. Firemen pulled the child from the burning car.
2. After a long trip we finally reached Atlanta.
3. Judy left her jacket in her school locker.
4. After dinner I enjoy a rich dessert.
5. The sergeant ordered his troops to halt.
6. Each of us named our favorite rock group.
7. Our quarterback threw a long pass for a touchdown.
8. Much to my surprise, I knew the answer to the problem.
9. Father mailed your letter in the city.
10. Carefully explain your decision to the committee.

▶ **Exercise 2** **Recognizing Intransitive Action Verbs.** Underline the intransitive verb in each sentence below.

EXAMPLE: The young colt galloped alongside the fence.

1. Both my sisters sing in the church choir.
2. After listening to the charges, the manager resigned.
3. All the files burned in the fire.
4. My sister swam in the 100-meter freestyle event.
5. The United Nations delegate flew to Geneva for a conference.
6. In Babylonian legend, Gilgamesh ruled in the kingdom of Erech.
7. The two gray cats peacefully slept on the couch.
8. Our victorious team raced off the field.
9. Receiving an enthusiastic welcome, the speaker grinned broadly.
10. The park concert lasted for almost three hours.

15.1 Action Verbs (Transitive and Intransitive Verbs)
• Practice 2

▶ **Exercise 1** **Recognizing Transitive Action Verbs.** Draw an arrow from the transitive verb to its object.

EXAMPLE: Andy hit a home run on her first try.

1. Lightning struck the new building.

2. Later in the day, Beth prepared the entire report.

3. Congress bought its first two navy vessels on October 13, 1775.

4. The train reached the station two hours late.

5. According to legend, Lincoln wrote the Gettysburg Address while on his way to Pennsylvania.

6. Tom chopped enough wood to last through January.

7. At noon the flood waters reached the top of the barrier.

8. Jan put the groceries away.

9. Louise uses a kerosene heater in her room.

10. My parents planted various flowers near the entrance to our house.

▶ **Exercise 2** **Recognizing Intransitive Action Verbs.** Underline the intransitive action verbs.

EXAMPLE: He runs faster in the morning.

1. Her ring fell between the planks of the boardwalk.

2. My brother laughed for an hour at the joke.

3. The explorers traveled along the banks of the river.

4. We talked for hours after dinner.

5. Fort Pierre grew slowly from a small trading post near Bad River in Missouri.

▶ **Writing Application** **Writing Sentences With Action Verbs.** Use each of the five verbs in *two* sentences of your own, once as a transitive verb and once as an intransitive verb. Label your sentences *transitive* or *intransitive*.

EXAMPLE: read _____*He read the novel in a week. transitive*_____

_____*After lunch, he read until dinner. intransitive*_____

1. eat _____

_____

2. jump _____

_____

3. grow _____

_____

4. write _____

_____

5. visit _____

_____

15.2 Linking Verbs (Transitive and Intransitive Verbs)
• Practice 1

Forms of *Be*   A linking verb connects a noun or pronoun at or near the beginning of a sentence with a word at or near the end. The verb *be* is the most commonly used linking verb.

FORMS OF *BE*	
am	were being
are	can be
is	shall be
was	have been
were	should have been

Other Linking Verbs   A number of other verbs can be used as linking verbs.

OTHER LINKING VERBS		
appear	look	sound
become	remain	stay
feel	seem	taste
grow	smell	turn

▶ **Exercise 1**   **Recognizing Forms of *Be* as Linking Verbs.**   Underline the form of *be* in each sentence below.

EXAMPLE: With luck I would have been at the station.

1. Hazleton is an industrial city in central Pennsylvania.
2. Who will be at the airport to greet the candidate?
3. Because of the storm, the speaker may be late.
4. My assistant will be happy to help you.
5. Until today they have been early each morning.
6. My brother is being unusually stubborn.
7. The bus should have been on time.
8. Your umbrella must be in the hall closet.
9. Elizabeth Bishop was a fine American poet.
10. Yes, I am quite proud of my heritage.

▶ **Exercise 2**   **Recognizing Other Linking Verbs.**   Underline the linking verb in each sentence below.

EXAMPLE: The mushroom sauce tastes bitter.

1. Your fundraising plan sounds excellent.
2. The president becomes a private citizen in a month.
3. The cake in the oven smells delicious.
4. The actress looked older than her pictures.
5. Grandfather feels a little better this morning.
6. This new plan seems acceptable to everyone.
7. Without refrigeration, milk quickly turns sour.
8. This new cello sounds richer than my old one.
9. After the question, the congressman appeared angry.
10. In later life my aunt grew impatient with us.

15.2 Linking Verbs (Transitive and Intransitive Verbs)
• Practice 2

Exercise 1 **Recognizing Forms of *Be* as Linking Verbs.** Underline the form of *be* in each of the following sentences. Then draw a double-headed arrow connecting the words that are linked by the verb.

EXAMPLE: Edgar Allan Poe <u>was</u> a writer of great imagination.

1. Ringo Starr was the drummer for the Beatles.

2. The team League has been the winner in most recent All-Star games.

3. Edgar Allan Poe was for a short time a cadet at West Point.

4. The writer of supernatural tales might have been a strange general.

5. Marie Curie was the winner of two Nobel Prizes.

6. Your first choice should be the new jazz album.

7. Halley's Comet was visible from parts of the United States in 1986.

8. Americans were fearful and excited about its visit in 1910.

9. Ethel Barrymore was part of a famous theatrical family.

10. This family of actors had been successful on the stage before working in movies.

11. The hole in the donut's center was the invention of the Pennsylvania Dutch.

12. Before that invention, donuts were often very soggy inside.

13. I am sure of these facts.

14. Spoons are thousands of years older than forks.

15. Forks have been useful since the eleventh century.

Exercise 2 **Identifying Other Linking Verbs.** Underline the linking verb in each of the following sentences. Then draw a double-headed arrow connecting the words that are linked by the verb.

EXAMPLE: The chili <u>tastes</u> delicious.

1. The plant grew sturdy in the hothouse.

2. Gold coins seem a better investment.

3. Although far apart, the sisters remained good friends.

4. The new chorus sounds even better than the old.

5. Sometimes Alex feels weak and tired.

6. That plant turns brown in the fall.

7. The roast goose looks sensational.

8. At the moment he appears very unhappy.

9. Both sponges smell sour.

10. The noises from the empty house sound strange.

11. Marjorie stayed optimistic all those years.

12. This sandwich tastes stale.

13. The visitor became more and more demanding.

14. The argument turned more boisterous.

15. His destination remains a mystery.

15.2 Linking Verbs (Action Verb or Linking Verb?)
• Practice 1

Action Verb or Linking Verb?   To see whether a verb is a linking verb or an action verb, substitute *am, is,* or *are* for the verb. If the sentence still makes sense and if the new verb links a word before it to a word after it, then the original verb is a linking verb.

Linking	Action
The costume *looks* interesting. (The costume *is* interesting?) linking	My brother often *looks* for his little sister. (My brother often *is* for little sister?) not linking

▶ **Exercise 1**   **Distinguishing Between Action Verbs and Linking Verbs.**   Find and underline the verb in each sentence below. In the space provided, write *AV* for action verb or *LV* for linking verb.

EXAMPLE: At last the traveler grew tired.   *LV*

1. Our neighbor remained a close friend for years. _____

2. My mother felt my head often during my illness. _____

3. Your perfume smells too strong today. _____

4. Grandmother tasted our fresh bread. _____

5. After his defeat Father felt sad for a long time. _____

6. The new snow shovel looks sturdy. _____

7. Betsy appeared troubled at her interview. _____

8. We grew two varieties of tomatoes last summer. _____

9. Your new stereo speakers sound sensational. _____

10. The bright day suddenly turned cloudy. _____

▶ **Exercise 2**   **Using Action and Linking Verbs in Original Sentences.**   Use each verb below first as an action verb and then as a linking verb.

EXAMPLE: smell   (action)   _____I smell gas in the kitchen._____
                             (linking)   _____Our new roses smell magnificent._____

1. look   (action)   _____
2.   (linking)   _____
3. grow   (action)   _____
4.   (linking)   _____
5. feel   (action)   _____
6.   (linking)   _____
7. taste   (action)   _____
8.   (linking)   _____
9. sound   (action)   _____
10.   (linking)   _____

15.2 Linking Verbs (Action Verb or Linking Verb?)
• Practice 2

▷ **Exercise 1**   **Distinguishing Between Action Verbs and Linking Verbs.**   Underline the verb in each sentence. After each action verb write *AV* and after each linking verb write *LV*.

EXAMPLE: Lucy smells a rat. _____*AV*_____

1. My aunt in Iowa grows wheat and corn. _____
2. Just home from the hospital, my sister looked pale. _____
3. The ghost supposedly appears every night at twelve. _____
4. The guests stayed at the cottages near the lake. _____
5. For some reason he remains angry and depressed. _____
6. The apple and peach pies look absolutely delicious. _____
7. Lucinda remained at the convention in California for a full week. _____
8. Suddenly the valley became dark and misty. _____
9. The butter turned rancid. _____
10. Felix seems happy and rested. _____
11. Justin looked through the telescope. _____
12. The afternoon speaker appears very confident. _____
13. The children became restless and irritable. _____
14. After their swim, the boys felt very refreshed. _____
15. David smelled the flowers. _____
16. That sweater looks terrific on you. _____
17. Close to the fire, you can really feel the heat. _____
18. The old dresser smelled musty. _____
19. The entertainer appeared suddenly on the stage. _____
20. These vegetables taste very fresh. _____

▷ **Writing Application**   **Writing Sentences With Action and Linking Verbs.**   Use each of the following verbs in two sentences of your own. Use the verb as a linking verb in the first sentence and as an action verb in the second sentence.

EXAMPLE: sound   ___*Jenny sounds too happy this morning.*___
                        ___*The bell sounded over the loudspeakers.*___

1. smell _____
    _____

2. feel _____
    _____

3. appear _____
    _____

4. grow _____
    _____

5. taste _____
    _____

15.3 Helping Verbs • Practice 1

Recognizing Helping Verbs   Helping verbs are added before another verb to make a verb phrase. A helping verb can be one, two, or three words. Forms of the verb *be* are often used as helping verbs.

SELECTED HELPING VERBS			
is	are	was	were
has	have	had	
do	does	did	
would	should	could	
shall	will	can	may

Finding Helping Verbs in Sentences   Verb phrases are sometimes separated by such words as *not*, *often*, *slowly*, and *carefully*. In looking for helping verbs, do not include these words.

Typical Verb Phrases	Verb Phrases Separated
are growing	Jorge *has* certainly *been* helpful.
did open	Our friends *will* not *arrive* until evening.
have been taken	Dad *may have* already *started* dinner.
may have been found	
(helping verbs in italics)	

▶ **Exercise 1**   **Recognizing Helping Verbs.**   In the sentences below, underline the helping verbs.

EXAMPLE: I <u>could</u> easily <u>have</u> gone to the festival yesterday.

1. My parents have driven to Canton, Ohio, several times.
2. When are you going to the library?
3. Bill must have taken another route to the hospital.
4. She has been carefully prepared for this role.
5. My friends have often attended semipro hockey games.
6. Yes, I did explain my reasons for not going.
7. My father is not taking his vacation this year.
8. Marie could have been elected our secretary.
9. I have carefully wrapped both lamps for shipment.
10. Can you spend a couple of hours in the park with me?

▶ **Exercise 2**   **Using Helping Verbs in Sentences.**   Complete the sentences below by filling the blanks with appropriate helping verbs.

EXAMPLE: I _____*have*_____ _____*been*_____ able to find the earring.

1. We _____ listening to records all day.
2. Bruce _____ not _____ reached Boston yet.
3. My mother _____ speak to the principal tomorrow.
4. I _____ written my report last week.
5. _____ you asked your parents for permission to go?
6. By tomorrow, she certainly _____ had her audition.
7. We _____ not going to the state fair this year.
8. My mother _____ finished baking by now.
9. This poor paper _____ written over.
10. I _____ carefully prepared for this exam.

15.3 Helping Verbs • Practice 2

▷ **Exercise 1** **Supplying Helping Verbs.**   Each of the following sentences contains one or more blanks. Fill in each blank with an appropriate helping verb.

EXAMPLE: Ian ____should____ ____have____ ____been____ told not to ask that question.

1. Jose _____ decided to go away to college.
2. She _____ _____ waiting at the station for more than two hours.
3. _____ you chosen a topic for your report?
4. She _____ going to St. Louis on business tomorrow.
5. My brother _____ perform the leading role in the show next week.

▷ **Exercise 2** **Locating Helping Verbs.**   Underline the complete verb phrase in each of the following sentences. Include all parts of the helping verbs, but do *not* include any words that separate the parts of the verb phrase.

EXAMPLE: Patty did not leave until after four.

1. Uncle Bob should have reached Boston by now.
2. Have you ever wanted to ski at Mount Washington?
3. She had carefully arranged her plans a week in advance.
4. Sailboats are often seen on the lake in summer.
5. She probably would have given you her phone number later.
6. Traders would often exchange tools, weapons, and utensils for pelts of fur.
7. That book has been on the best-seller list for ten weeks.
8. Do you know the name of the first state?
9. You should not even have attempted that difficult somersault.
10. Those plants have not been watered in more than a week.

▷ **Writing Application** **Writing Sentences With Helping Verbs.**   Use each of the following verb phrases in a complete sentence. Underline all parts of the verb phrase in each sentence. If you wish you can put the word *not* or some other word between parts of the verb phrase.

EXAMPLE: have been   *My favorite books have always been about horses.*

1. will open

_____

2. could have been

_____

3. has been told

_____

4. can be reached

_____

5. have been talking

_____

16.1 # Adjectives as Modifiers (Adjectives With Nouns and Pronouns) • Practice 1

Adjectives With Nouns and Pronouns   An adjective is used to describe a noun or pronoun. Adjectives answer the questions *What kind? Which one? How many?* or *How much?* about the nouns or pronouns they modify.

ADJECTIVE QUESTIONS		
What Kind?	*white* fence	*unhappy* child
Which One?	*this* photo	*each* one
How Many?	*two* snacks	*many* others
How Much?	*enough* time	*more* pizza

▶ **Exercise 1**   **Recognizing Adjectives and the Words They Modify.**   In the sentences below underline each adjective, and circle the noun or pronoun it modifies.

EXAMPLE: A <u>hungry</u> (lion) stalked the <u>frightened</u> (animals).

1. Laura bought a blue blouse with white trimmings.
2. Several athletes complained about the old stadium.
3. The writer, tall and impressive, entered the auditorium.
4. Each one in the class will develop an original project.
5. I made three attempts to reach the local representative.
6. A gracious hostess greeted us at the flower show.
7. The branches, dry and peeling, showed the effects of the drought.
8. We packed the fragile glassware in a reinforced container.
9. The investigator hopes to get some answers from the lone witness.
10. The decorator suggested using three large paintings to cover the bare wall.

▶ **Exercise 2**   **Using Adjectives in Sentences.**   Complete the sentences below by filling in an appropriate adjective in each blank space.

EXAMPLE: My ____*foreign*____ car is equipped with ____*radial*____ tires.

1. A _____ teacher scolded the _____ student.
2. My mother just bought a _____ _____ suit.
3. Maxwell Elementary School, _____ and _____, will soon be closed.
4. _____ visitors waited to see the _____ prime minister.
5. The front of the house is painted _____ and _____.
6. This _____ edition of the book is _____.
7. Do you have _____ time to pay for the _____ bike?
8. _____ police cars followed the _____ van.
9. _____ one is by far the _____ version.
10. A _____, _____ crowd greeted the hero.

16.1 # Adjectives as Modifiers (Adjectives With Nouns and Pronouns) • Practice 2

▷ **Exercise 1** **Recognizing Adjectives and the Words They Modify.** In each of the following sentences, draw an arrow pointing from each underlined adjective to the noun or pronoun it modifies.

EXAMPLE: His sharp, witty remark was hardly appropriate.

1. The many rings of Saturn glowed in the blurry photograph.

2. The tired old man stumbled down the road.

3. Several books have been written about the last days of Roman power.

4. Willie Mays leaped for the high fly ball and made a brilliant catch.

5. Her third attempt was good, but on her fourth and final try, she broke a ten-year-old record.

6. The house, dreary and uninviting, has not been lived in for seventeen years.

7. Irving Berlin wrote many wonderful songs.

8. The feathery fins of the angel fish drifted in the clear blue water.

9. The marble statue was pale and dramatic against the dark velvet curtains.

10. The crusty little turtle crawled across the deserted parking lot.

▷ **Exercise 2** **Using Adjectives in Sentences.** Write a sentence for each pair of adjectives. Then underline the two given adjectives in the sentence, and draw an arrow from each adjective to the word it modifies.

EXAMPLE: colorful, yellow   The colorful flower garden features bright yellow marigolds.

1. energetic, young _____

2. dusty, quiet _____

3. valuable, costly _____

4. sweet, juicy _____

5. bright, shining _____

16.1 # Adjectives as Modifiers (Articles, Nouns Used as Adjectives) • Practice 1

Articles The definite article, *the*, refers to a specific person, place, or thing. The indefinite articles, *a* and *an*, refer to any one of a class of people, places, or things. *A* is used before consonant sounds. *An* is used before vowel sounds.

USING *A* AND *AN*	
Consonant Sounds	**Vowel Sounds**
a *c*old drink	an *e*nvelope
a *h*ammer (*h* sound)	an *h*onorary guest (no *h* sound)
a *o*ne-sided game (*w* sound)	an *o*boe (*o* sound)
a *u*nicorn (*y* sound)	an *u*nlikely event (*u* sound)

Nouns Used as Adjectives Nouns are sometimes used as adjectives. When a noun is used as an adjective, it comes before another noun and answers the question *What kind?* or *Which one?*

Nouns	Used as Adjectives
river	river bank (*What kind* of bank?)
bottle	bottle opener (Which opener?)

▷ **Exercise 1** **Using the Indefinite Articles *A* and *An* Correctly.** In the space provided, place the article *a* or *an*.

EXAMPLE: _____*an*_____ old person _____*a*_____ happy audience

1. _____ honest woman
2. _____ compound verb
3. _____ union meeting
4. _____ only child
5. _____ uneasy parent

6. _____ one-time experience
7. _____ horse trade
8. _____ egg salad sandwich
9. _____ helping hand
10. _____ uniform test

▷ **Exercise 2** **Recognizing Nouns Used as Adjectives.** In each sentence below underline the noun used as an adjective and circle the noun it modifies.

EXAMPLE: This is the only _____*food*_____ (market) for a while.

1. How often do you play table tennis?
2. Our village square is two blocks from here.
3. My older sister joined an exclusive supper club.
4. Speak to the organizers about making a rule change.
5. The producer was not pleased with the audience participation.
6. A new work order arrived this morning.
7. For my birthday my brother bought me a new desk lamp.
8. With this strobe light you can achieve special effects.
9. The basketball game was suddenly canceled.
10. Which radio station do you listen to the most?

16.1 Adjectives as Modifiers (Articles, Nouns Used as Adjectives) • Practice 2

▶ **Exercise 1**   **Distinguishing Between Definite and Indefinite Articles.**   In the blank write the article that will correctly complete each of the following sentences. The word in parentheses tells you which kind of article.

EXAMPLE: What _____*an*_____ unusual subject! (indefinite)

1. Did you see _____ mayor yet? (definite)

2. She bought _____ new dress and _____ umbrella. (indefinite)

3. Our history teacher mentioned _____ emperor. (definite)

4. _____ old man and _____ young woman slowly approached. (indefinite, indefinite)

5. She was given _____ once-in-a-lifetime opportunity. (indefinite)

6. _____ road we must take to _____ bridge is blocked. (definite, definite)

7. He was eager to make friends because he was _____ only child. (indefinite)

8. Read _____ book on World War II, and then write _____ report. (indefinite, indefinite)

9. Where did you put _____ combination to _____ safe? (definite, definite)

10. Some say _____ apple a day keeps _____ doctor away. (indefinite, definite)

11. He devoted _____ entire first issue of the magazine to _____ story about motorcycles. (definite, indefinite)

12. That is _____ interesting observation on _____ state of our economy. (indefinite, definite)

13. _____ exhibition was financed by _____ wealthy woman from Mexico. (definite, indefinite)

14. For _____ low price of one dollar, you can have _____ taste of this incredible treat. (definite, indefinite)

15. "I am thinking of _____ island in the Pacific," said Irene, planning _____ vacation for her parents. (indefinite, indefinite)

▶ **Exercise 2**   **Identifying Nouns Used as Adjectives.**   Each of the following sentences contains one noun used as an adjective. Underline the modifying noun and circle the noun it modifies.

EXAMPLE: Fifteen baby (buggies) were blocking the path.

1. They brought a long grocery list to the market.

2. Did you attend the evening performance?

3. Guitar music soothes me.

4. Have the street lights been repaired yet?

5. The local bus will take you right to the train station.

6. The art show will run for three weeks.

7. Did you read the magazine article about Aspen, Colorado?

8. The child was a mirror image of her grandmother.

9. Tina and Terrie played catch near the baseball field.

10. With the scraps of fabric, Mona made some doll clothes.

16.1 Adjectives as Modifiers (Proper Adjectives, Compound Adjectives) • Practice 1

Proper Adjectives   A proper adjective is a proper noun used as adjective or an adjective formed from a proper noun.

Proper Nouns as Proper Adjectives	Proper Adjectives from Proper Nouns
Kennedy memoirs	Congressional elections
Brooklyn Bridge celebration	Shakespearean costumes
Chicago meeting	Indian customs

Compound Adjectives   A compound adjective is an adjective made up of more than one word.

Hyphenated Compound Adjectives	Combined Compound Adjectives
three-piece suit	newspaper reporter
full-time job	schoolwide project

▶ **Exercise 1**   **Recognizing Proper Adjectives.**   Underline the proper adjective in each sentence below and circle the noun it modifies.

EXAMPLE: A <u>Kansas</u> (tornado) destroyed three towns.

1. The Senate committee adjourned the hearing.
2. My uncle just recorded a Beethoven symphony.
3. Our Canadian relatives will arrive next week.
4. Did you see the last Super Bowl special?
5. My social studies report is on Victorian traditions.
6. This new restaurant features American favorites.
7. A Chicago group wants to purchase land in our area.
8. I found that *Newsflash Magazine* article fascinating.
9. The Russian ballet will appear in Los Angeles soon.
10. The general manager canceled the Monday meeting.

▶ **Exercise 2**   **Recognizing Compound Adjectives.**   Underline the compound adjective in each sentence below and circle the noun it modifies.

EXAMPLE: <u>Hyperactive</u> (children) sometimes need treatment.

1. Have you ever taken a multiple-choice test?
2. We invited a professional football player to visit us.
3. Our next guest will be a well-known actress.
4. When do we change to daylight-saving time?
5. My talented aunt is designing a crisscross pattern.
6. We have just formed a cleanup squad.
7. Our inept team actually scored a first-quarter touchdown.
8. I have two nearsighted brothers.
9. We have planned a life-size statue of Winston Churchill.
10. People are afraid he will be a rubber-stamp legislator.

16.1 Adjectives as Modifiers (Proper Adjectives, Compound Adjectives) • Practice 2

▶ **Exercise 1** **Recognizing Proper Adjectives.** Underline the proper adjective in each sentence and circle the noun it modifies.

EXAMPLE: Some Victorian (antiques) are rather ugly.

1. My brother is studying Jacksonian democracy in his history class.
2. Indian jewelry made of silver is very popular.
3. The weather bureau predicts a February blizzard.
4. My uncle has four rolls of silver Washington quarters.
5. Reporters watch the first Presidential primaries very carefully.

▶ **Exercise 2** **Recognizing Compound Adjectives.** Underline the compound adjective in each sentence and circle the noun it modifies.

EXAMPLE: Do you think that (story) is old-fashioned?

1. Joanne was an unusually sweet, bright-eyed baby.
2. The Parents Council planned a schoolwide festival.
3. Joe Louis was a popular heavyweight champion.
4. My mother sees well, but my father is farsighted.
5. The hit-and-run driver was later captured by the police.
6. An offside penalty cost our team five yards.
7. A four-inch steel latch protects the office safe.
8. She tells funny stories about her absentminded friend.
9. That region of New Hampshire has several mountains with snow-covered peaks.
10. Achilles drove his spear into Hector's bloodstained armor.

▶ **Writing Application** **Writing Sentences with Adjectives.** Rewrite the following paragraph, adding two or more adjectives to each sentence. Use at least one noun as an adjective, one proper adjective, and one compound adjective. Then underline the adjectives that you have added.

(1) While traveling along the coast one day, I saw a beach covered with rocks and shells. (2) Scores of seagulls circled the beach, their cries echoing in the air. (3) Each time a gull spotted a fish under the water, it dove toward the water and brought out a fish within its beak. (4) I found a spot among the rocks from which to watch the battle between birds and fish. (5) On the highway behind me, trucks and cars raced by, their drivers unaware of the events that were happening just off to their right.

_____
_____
_____
_____
_____
_____
_____
_____
_____
_____
_____

Name _____ Date _____

 16.1 # Pronouns Used as Adjectives (Possessive and Demonstrative Adjectives) • Practice 1

Possessive Adjectives   A pronoun is used as an adjective if it modifies a noun. A personal pronoun used as a possessive adjective answers the question *Which one?* about a noun that follows it.

POSSESSIVE ADJECTIVES			
my	his	its	their
your	her	our	

Demonstrative Adjectives   The four demonstrative pronouns—*this, that, these,* and *those*—can also be used as demonstrative adjectives.

DEMONSTRATIVE ADJECTIVES

I want *this* one.

She chose *that* car.

These apples are sour.

Did you read *those* notes?

▷ **Exercise 1**   **Recognizing Possessive and Demonstrative Adjectives.**   Underline the possessive or demonstrative adjective in each sentence below, and circle the noun it modifies.

EXAMPLE: The committee chose those (colors).

1. Have you explained their responsibilities to them?

2. Everyone found his report terribly upsetting.

3. Unfortunately, those cartons are blocking the main entrance.

4. This short story by Pearl Buck has a surprise ending.

5. Did you speak to your grandmother last night?

6. Maureen has wanted that jacket for a long time.

7. If you are interested, I will show you my camera.

8. All of these recipes are sugar-free.

9. I really wanted to give them our opinion first.

10. I think her graphic will certainly win a prize.

▷ **Exercise 2**   **Using Possessive and Demonstrative Adjectives in Sentences.**   Fill in the blank in each sentence below with an appropriate possessive or demonstrative adjectives.

EXAMPLE: We explained _____*our*_____ idea to them.

1. _____ manual explains what you have to do.

2. Later, I told them _____ plans for the new theater.

3. Have you found _____ glasses yet?

4. I suggest that you study _____ charts carefully.

5. Paula described _____ frightening experience to us.

6. You can redeem _____ coupons in the supermarket.

7. Before they left, they paid for _____ tickets.

8. My father asked me to send you _____ best wishes.

9. All of _____ cars have diesel engines.

10. _____ explanation seems to be incorrect.

16.1 # Pronouns Used as Adjectives (Possessive and Demonstrative Adjectives) • Practice 2

▶ **Exercise 1**   **Identifying Possessive Adjectives.**   In each of the following sentences, a possessive adjective is underlined. Write the underlined word in the first column. Then find the noun it modifies and its antecedent and put them in the second and third columns.

EXAMPLE: Lincoln gave his life for his country.

Possessive Adjective   Noun Modified   Antecedent
his   *life*   *Lincoln*

1. Dori finished washing the dishes and then worked on her report.
2. Leaving his office, Mr. Cruz took a cab to the station.
3. Mary Louise will exhibit some of her watercolors in the village library.
4. My friends were late and could not keep their appointment.
5. Grabbing their lunches, the twins raced from the house.
6. Daniel put on his running shoes and ran around the track.
7. Testing her new key, Gilda opened the front door.
8. Donald and Tim plan to finish their report on ancient Egypt this weekend.
9. Alicia, is this your bracelet?
10. Trish said, "I hope you can come to my party."

	Possessive Adjective	Noun Modified	Antecedent
1.	_____	_____	_____
2.	_____	_____	_____
3.	_____	_____	_____
4.	_____	_____	_____
5.	_____	_____	_____
6.	_____	_____	_____
7.	_____	_____	_____
8.	_____	_____	_____
9.	_____	_____	_____
10.	_____	_____	_____

▶ **Exercise 2**   **Recognizing Demonstrative Adjectives.**   Find the word *this, that, these,* or *those* in each of the sentences and underline it. If it is used as a pronoun, write *pronoun* on the blank. If it is used as an adjective, write the noun it modifies.

EXAMPLE: That is her decision. _____*pronoun*_____

1. This room is always light and airy. _____
2. After thinking it over, he took those. _____
3. Have you read that article yet? _____
4. These photos are among the best I've seen. _____
5. I just can't believe that. _____

16.1 Pronouns Used as Adjectives (Interrogative and Indefinite Adjectives) • Practice 1

Interrogative Adjectives   Three interrogative pronouns—*which, what,* and *whose*—can be used as interrogative adjectives.

INTERROGATIVE ADJECTIVES
Which member of the team scored the most points? *What* kind of hiking boots did you buy? *Whose* composition was read aloud in class?

Indefinite Adjectives   Some indefinite pronouns can also be used as indefinite adjectives. Some indefinite adjectives can be used only with singular nouns, some only with plural nouns, and some with both.

INDEFINITE ADJECTIVES
Used with Singular Nouns: another, each, either, neither *Used with Plural Nouns:* both, few, several, many *Used with Singular or Plural Nouns:* all, any, more, most, other, some

▶ **Exercise 1**   **Recognizing Interrogative and Indefinite Adjectives.**   Underline the interrogative or indefinite adjective in each sentence below, and circle the noun it modifies. Then write whether the pronoun is indefinite or interrogative.

EXAMPLE: Each (visitor) was given a souvenir. _____*Indefinite*_____

1. Both singers gave outstanding performances tonight. _____
2. Whose report did you like the best? _____
3. I still expect to read another book this week. _____
4. There are many explanations for her absence. _____
5. Chris suggested many ideas that could work. _____
6. Several doctors attended the patient. _____
7. Most visitors to the country fair were pleased with the exhibits. _____
8. Have you developed some new styles recently? _____
9. All indications point to a glorious victory. _____
10. What excuse will the principal offer the students? _____

▶ **Exercise 2**   **Using Interrogative and Indefinite Adjectives in Sentences.**   Fill in the blank in each sentence below with an appropriate interrogative or indefinite adjective.

EXAMPLE: I just can't give them _____*other*_____ topics.

1. _____ countries would you like to visit this summer?
2. My guess is that there are only a _____ possibilities.
3. _____ contestant will sing two numbers.
4. I know _____ students who will participate.
5. Bill asked _____ friends to go to the junior high dance.
6. _____ movie is fine with me.
7. _____ dictionary did she borrow?
8. _____ explanation is better than none.
9. We waited _____ hours for them to arrive.
10. _____ sport will rival basketball at our school?

16.1 Pronouns Used as Adjectives (Interrogative and Indefinite Adjectives) • Practice 2

▶ **Exercise 1** **Recognizing Interrogative Adjectives.** Underline the word *which, what,* or *whose* in each of the sentences. If the word is used as a pronoun, write *pronoun* in the blank. If it is used as an adjective, write the noun it modifies.

EXAMPLE: What are you going to do? _____*pronoun*_____

1. Which route did he decide to take? _____

2. What can be done now to stop them? _____

3. At whose house shall we have the party? _____

4. What movie do you want to see this weekend? _____

5. Which of the routes is the fastest to your house? _____

▶ **Exercise 2** **Recognizing Indefinite Adjectives.** Underline the indefinite pronoun or adjective in each of the following sentences. If the word is used as a pronoun, write *pronoun* in the blank. If it is used as an adjective, write the noun it modifies.

EXAMPLE: Both children adored playing in the mud. _____*children*_____

1. Several people phoned the police after the accident. _____

2. Both appeared at the hotel for the contest. _____

3. More apples in the bushel have spoiled. _____

4. Few winners claimed their prizes. _____

5. Neither of the choices was acceptable. _____

6. After eating one sandwich, Albert helped himself to another. _____

7. Each child received a box of crayons and a coloring book. _____

8. The judges chose neither of the contestants from Albany. _____

9. Many magazines were scattered on the living room floor. _____

10. Most of the students attended the pep rally. _____

▶ **Writing Application** **Writing Sentences With Pronouns Used as Adjectives.** Write five sentences of your own. In each sentence use one of the following words to modify a noun. Then draw an arrow pointing from each adjective to the word it modifies.

EXAMPLE: that

Bobby will never get *that* role in the play. _____

1. this

_____

2. whose

_____

3. both

_____

4. her

_____

5. which

_____

Name _____ Date _____

 16.2 # Adverbs as Modifiers (Modifying Verbs)
• Practice 1

Adverbs Modifying Verbs   Adverbs modify verbs, adjectives, or other adverbs. An adverb modifying a verb will answer one of four questions about the verb: *Where? When? In what manner?* or *To what extent?*

ADVERBS MODIFYING VERBS	
Where?	**When?**
jogged *here*	arrive *tonight*
signaled *left*	will speak *soon*
In What Manner?	**To What Extent?**
smiled *happily*	*hardly* know
willingly gave	explained *completely*

▶ **Exercise 1**   **Recognizing Adverbs That Modify Verbs.**   Underline the adverb in each sentence. In the space provided, indicate which question the adverb answers: *where? when? in what manner?* or *to what extent?*

EXAMPLE: They <u>nearly</u> had an accident. ____*to what extent?*____

1. I arrive early at school on Fridays. _____

2. To reach the mall, turn left at the light. _____

3. Everyone reacted sadly to the news. _____

4. My brother will be going away to college. _____

5. Do you thoroughly understand your task? _____

6. Bring all the reference books here. _____

7. I opened the door to the barn cautiously. _____

8. Nina is barely acquainted with them. _____

9. I will drive tomorrow at the festival. _____

10. The train suddenly jolted to a halt. _____

▶ **Exercise 2**   **Writing Original Sentences with Adverbs.**   Use each adverb below in an original sentence. Make certain that the adverb modifies the verb.

EXAMPLE: nearly ____*My grandmother nearly slipped on the ice.*____

1. quickly _____

2. here _____

3. completely _____

4. soon _____

5. away _____

6. easily _____

7. tomorrow _____

8. almost _____

9. quietly _____

10. hardly _____

16.2 Adverbs as Modifiers (Modifying Verbs)
• Practice 2

▶ **Exercise 1** **Recognizing Adverbs That Modify Verbs.** Find the adverb in each sentence and write it in the appropriate column.

EXAMPLE: The dog slept quietly by the stove.

Where?	When?	In What Manner?	To What Extent?
		quietly	

1. The bus traveled rapidly into the night.
2. Does he fully understand what is expected?
3. She immediately described the accident to a police officer.
4. The guests arrived late but found nobody at home.
5. Silently, the detective climbed the stairs to the attic.
6. Bud has almost finished his model.
7. Do you expect to move away from Albuquerque?
8. He is always creating problems.
9. The shopping center has nearly been completed.
10. My sister quickly cleaned the cage.

Where?	When?	In What Manner?	To What Extent?
_____	_____	_____	_____
_____	_____	_____	_____
_____	_____	_____	_____
_____	_____	_____	_____

▶ **Exercise 2** **Using Adverbs in Sentences.** Use each adverb below in a sentence, making certain that the adverb modifies a verb. Then circle the verb that the adverb modifies.

EXAMPLE: slowly
           The roast (cooked) slowly in the oven.

1. patiently _____
2. there _____
3. yesterday _____
4. completely _____
5. eagerly _____
6. nearly _____
7. courageously _____
8. closer _____
9. now _____
10. immediately _____

16.2 Adverbs as Modifiers (Modifying Adjectives and Other Adverbs) • Practice 1

Adverbs Modifying Adjectives   An adverb modifying an adjective answers the question *To what extent?*

ADVERBS MODIFYING ADJECTIVES	
often ready	*extremely* helpful
too late	*scarcely* prepared

Adverbs Modifying Other Adverbs   An adverb modifying another adverb also answers the question *To what extent?*

ADVERBS MODIFYING ADVERBS	
moves *quite* rapidly	visits *less* regularly
drives *more* carefully	speaks *very* slowly

▶ **Exercise 1**   **Recognizing the Words Adverbs Modify.**   On the blank, write whether each underlined adverb modifies an adjective or another adverb.

EXAMPLE: Her coat appears <u>rather</u> short. ____*adjective*____

1. Bob should learn to speak <u>more</u> clearly. _____
2. The senator was <u>nearly</u> late for his meeting. _____
3. The patient's reactions seem <u>rather</u> slow. _____
4. Her explanation is <u>perfectly</u> correct. _____
5. The doctor arrived <u>very</u> quickly at the scene of the accident. _____
6. Yes, I am <u>somewhat</u> embarrassed at his actions. _____
7. My best friend is <u>often</u> absent from school. _____
8. For my taste she plays <u>too</u> rapidly. _____
9. We receive a new shipment <u>almost</u> weekly. _____
10. At her audition Carrie seemed <u>slightly</u> upset. _____

▶ **Exercise 2**   **Adding Adverbs to Sentences.**   Fill in the blank in each sentence with an adverb that answers the question *To what extent?* Circle the word it modifies.

EXAMPLE: This road is ____*often*____ (deserted) at night.

1. Richard seemed _____ disturbed at the news.
2. _____ early in her speech, she began to stumble.
3. My older sister swims _____ rapidly.
4. The federal agents approached the building _____ cautiously.
5. John played his clarinet _____ well.
6. After the trip my grandmother looked _____ tired.
7. Response time to fires is now _____ more rapid.
8. Finally, the family is _____ ready to go.
9. Tom plays shortstop _____ awkwardly.
10. This salesman is _____ late for appointments.

16.2 Adverbs as Modifiers (Modifying Adjectives and Other Adverbs) • Practice 2

Exercise 1 **Recognizing Adverbs That Modify Adjectives.** Underline the adverb in each sentence. Then circle the adjective it modifies.

EXAMPLE: She was very (happy) with the results.

1. We examined an almost new tape recorder.

2. He was somewhat unwilling to answer our questions.

3. Sue was very glad to accept his invitation.

4. These baked potatoes are especially good.

5. He made the whipped cream too sweet.

Exercise 2 **Recognizing Adverbs That Modify Other Adverbs.** In each sentence, find an adverb that modifies another adverb by answering the question *To what extent?* Underline this adverb and circle the adverb it modifies.

EXAMPLE: The movers arrived too (early) in the day.

1. She worked too slowly to finish in time.

2. After his experience, he climbed trees rather cautiously.

3. The train should pull into the station quite soon.

4. After living for years in Japan, the child had almost totally forgotten how to speak English.

5. The vase was almost completely uncracked.

6. Do you think you can talk less rapidly?

7. My best friend has moved far away.

8. Although he lost, the knight fought very bravely.

9. He has been told that he speaks Spanish extremely well.

10. She was only slightly tired after the long race.

Writing Application **Writing Sentences With Adverbs.** Write five sentences using an adverb that fits each description below. Underline the adverb and draw an arrow from it to the word it modifies.

EXAMPLE: an adverb that modifies a verb and answers the question *To what extent?*

 The driver of the car narrowly avoided an accident.

1. an adverb that modifies a verb and answers the question *Where?*

_____

2. an adverb that modifies a verb and answers the question *When?*

_____

3. an adverb that modifies a verb and answers the question *In what manner?*

_____

4. an adverb that modifies an adjective

_____

5. an adverb modifying another adverb

_____

16.2 Adverbs Used in Sentences • Practice 1

Finding Adverbs in Sentences   Adverbs can be located in almost any part of a sentence: at the beginning or end of a sentence; before, after, or between the parts of a verb; before an adjective; and before another adverb.

FINDING ADVERBS	
Suddenly, they appeared.	My cousin smiled *happily*.
I am *not* surprised.	She is *rather* tall.

Adverb or Adjective?   Some words can be either adverbs or adjectives. Remember that an adverb modifies a verb, an adjective, or another adverb. An adjective modifies a noun or a pronoun.

Adverbs	Adjectives
Our team plays *hard*.	We also use a *hard* ball.
She exercises *daily*.	We have a *daily* drill.

> **Exercise 1**   **Finding Adverbs in Sentences.**   Locate the adverbs in these sentences. Underline the adverbs and circle the words they modify.

EXAMPLE: At the debate you (must speak) clearly.

1. I almost finished my homework in a hour.

2. I have often wondered about her past.

3. We have changed our minds completely.

4. Our new math teacher is extremely pleasant.

5. The gymnast performed all her tasks smoothly.

6. Unfortunately, the bad weather prevented the picnic.

7. On Saturdays, Bill and Phil thoroughly clean their apartment.

8. Gloria has not forgotten the insult.

9. My dance teacher always agrees to perform for us.

10. After a little work, the engine purred smoothly.

> **Exercise 2**   **Distinguishing Between Adjectives and Adverbs.**   In the space provided, write whether the underlined word is an *adjective* or an *adverb*.

EXAMPLE: We have a weekly conference.   *adjective*

1. On the day of the fair Sandy awoke early. _____

2. My sister has always been a fast eater. _____

3. I have an uncle who sings beautifully. _____

4. We bought Mom a lovely present for her birthday. _____

5. Our insurance salesman works late twice a week. _____

6. Make certain to give the squad leader an early signal. _____

7. Our Spanish teacher speaks too fast. _____

8. For breakfast I usually eat a hard roll. _____

9. My friend lives close to the racetrack. _____

10. Sam had an extremely close call this morning. _____

16.2 Adverbs Used in Sentences • Practice 2

▶ Exercise 1 **Locating Adverbs in Sentences.** Each of the following sentences contains one or two adverbs. Underline the adverbs. Then draw arrows from the adverbs to the words they modify.

EXAMPLE: The poet has happily inserted the perfect word.

1. She tearfully told us about the accident.

2. Suddenly the whistle sounded, and the train slowly left.

3. Bobby has almost finished his piano practice.

4. He has never asked for help.

5. My mother moved the couch slowly to the left.

▶ Exercise 2 **Distinguishing Between Adverbs and Adjectives.** In the blank indicate whether the underlined word in each of the following sentences is an adverb or an adjective.

1. My grandfather was a kindly man who always helped his grandchildren. _____

2. Aunt Millie drives regularly to Los Angeles to shop. _____

3. I always work hard on my class reports. _____

4. Mother had a hard time reaching the doctor. _____

5. The senator bitterly criticized his opponents. _____

6. My science teacher is an unusually friendly person. _____

7. Does the early bird catch the worm? _____

8. I jog daily. _____

9. Taking a coffee break is a daily practice in our company. _____

10. Has the engine been running smoothly? _____

▶ Writing Application **Writing Sentences With Adverbs.** Write five sentences of your own using the adverbs in the following list. After writing each sentence, draw an arrow pointing from the adverb to the word or words that the adverb modifies.

EXAMPLE: not

    She has not given us her answer.

1. slowly _____

2. amazingly _____

3. never _____

4. soon _____

5. almost _____

17 Prepositions (Words Used as Prepositions, Prepositional Phrases) • Practice 1

Words Used as Prepositions   Prepositions are words such as *in, at, from, ahead of,* and *next to*. A preposition relates the noun or pronoun following it to another word in the sentence.

PREPOSITIONS
Traffic was halted ⎰ at ⎱ the bridge.   near   in back of

Prepositional Phrases   A prepositional phrase is a group of words that includes a preposition and a noun or pronoun called the object of the preposition.

PREPOSITIONAL PHRASES	
Prepositions	**Objects of the Prepositions**
across	the *street*
between	*us*
next to	the old *statue*

▶ **Exercise 1**   **Identifying Prepositions.**   Underline each preposition in the sentences below. Some sentences have more than one.

EXAMPLE: <u>Without</u> oxygen she will never make it <u>to</u> the hospital.

1. I placed the lawn mower in a corner of the garage.
2. During the spring I often visit a flower show.
3. A man from the IRS called father at home.
4. She finally agreed in spite of her original protests.
5. Father is not terribly worried about them.
6. You will find extremely poor construction behind the wall.
7. Is this complicated project beyond them?
8. The invading army marched into the valley without warning.
9. The book is underneath the pillow near the headboard.
10. She almost never leaves her clothes on the floor.

▶ **Exercise 2**   **Identifying Prepositional Phrases.**   Place parentheses around each prepositional phrase. Underline each preposition and circle its object. Some sentences have more than one prepositional phrase.

EXAMPLE: (<u>In</u> the ⟨morning⟩) we left (<u>for</u> ⟨San Diego⟩).

1. From the meeting we strolled into the restaurant.
2. We listened intently throughout the manager's presentation.
3. A group of students demonstrated in front of the building.
4. As of this morning, the game was cancelled.
5. At dawn we attempted to swim across the river.
6. The investigators from the police station found evidence under the bridge.
7. We raced through the enemy town at great speed.
8. Instead of hamburgers, we had salads for lunch.
9. The road marker is some distance in front of the chalet.
10. According to the travel agent, we should arrive about noon.

17 Prepositions (Words Used as Prepositions, Prepositional Phrases) • Practice 2

▶ **Exercise 1** **Recognizing Prepositions.**   Find the preposition in each of the following sentences and underline it. Then rewrite the sentence using a different preposition.

EXAMPLE: They left the house at dawn.
            They left the house before dawn.

1. The florist left a box outside the house.

    _____

2. After breakfast I walk the dogs.

    _____

3. The baby crawled under the table.

    _____

4. He warned us of the danger.

    _____

5. The taxi drove in front of the delivery truck.

    _____

6. There is a round window near the entrance.

    _____

7. She hid her bicycle in back of the fence.

    _____

8. What are those flowers growing on the hillside?

    _____

9. Put these papers on top of my desk.

    _____

10. Three deer loped through the woods.

    _____

▶ **Exercise 2** **Identifying Prepositional Phrases.**   Underline the prepositional phrase appearing in each of the following sentences.

EXAMPLE: She opened the gate in the fence.

1. She waited all morning near the store.
2. In the morning Mom and Dad prepare breakfast and pack our lunches.
3. He put the bowls in the cabinet.
4. Uncle Steve brought a present for me.
5. According to Mr. Wilson, the math test has been postponed.
6. After much excitement we reached the airport five minutes early.
7. I stored my gear inside my best friend's locker.
8. In front of my house stands a stately blue spruce.
9. When is she coming home from school?
10. Edith planted flowers in front of the shrubs.

17 # Prepositions (Preposition or Adverb?) • Practice 1

Preposition or Adverb?   Some words can be either prepositions or adverbs, depending on how they are used. A preposition will always be followed by a noun or pronoun used as an object. Adverbs modify verbs and have no objects.

Prepositions	Adverbs
She peered *across* the *lake*.	Mary will look *across*.
The note is *inside* the *box*.	Please wait *inside*.
The car streaked past *us*.	The prisoner slipped *past*.

▶ **Exercise 1**   **Distinguishing Between Prepositions and Adverbs.**   Write whether the underlined word in each sentence is a *preposition* or an *adverb*.

EXAMPLE: My cousin wriggled and tried to slide <u>through</u>. _____*adverb*_____

1. I casually strolled <u>through</u> the entrance. _____
2. <u>Around</u> our house we always have excitement. _____
3. We were told to travel <u>along</u> this road for two miles. _____
4. From the bridge Susan tried to look <u>underneath</u>. _____
5. Do you think you can walk <u>past</u> the guards? _____
6. <u>Behind</u> the closet is a secret passageway. _____
7. After ten hours of work Tom was finally <u>through</u>. _____
8. Walk <u>around</u> to see if you can spot mother. _____
9. An angry crowd surged <u>near</u> the governor. _____
10. Pass <u>along</u> until you reach the sentry at the gate. _____

▶ **Exercise 2**   **Adding Prepositions and Adverbs to Sentences.**   The sentences below are grouped in pairs. For each pair, select a word that fits appropriately and write it in the spaces provided. Label the adverb *A* and the preposition *P*.

EXAMPLE: Walk *over*. _____*A*_____
              Throw the ball *over* the fence. _____*p*_____

1. a. Your best friend is _____ the phone. _____
    b. Keep your jacket _____. _____

2. a. Please come _____. _____
    b. We have a canopy _____ the window. _____

3. a. Keep searching. You will find the recipe _____. _____
    b. The emergency hose is _____ the radiator. _____

4. a. I hope to see them _____. _____
    b. The curio shop happens to be _____ the corner. _____

5. a. Don't forget to turn the lights _____. _____
    b. Paint has begun to chip _____ the wall. _____

17 Prepositions (Preposition or Adverb?) • Practice 2

▶ **Exercise 1** **Distinguishing Between Prepositions and Adverbs.**   In each of the following pairs of sentences, one sentence contains a word used as a preposition and the other contains the same word used as an adverb. Find that word in each pair of sentences and circle it. If the word acts as a preposition, underline the prepositional phrase. If the word acts as an adverb, write *adverb* in the blank.

EXAMPLE: We found the keys ⟨in⟩ the car. _____
  They came ⟨in⟩ and dinner began.   *adverb*

1. The rabbit would not come near. _____
  The rose bush is near the white fence. _____

2. You will find the house if you continue past the traffic light. _____
  The old man would often walk past in the evening. _____

3. Turn the lights on before it gets dark. _____
  The shopping center is two blocks farther on the right. _____

4. Several vultures soared around gracefully. _____
  Go completely around the traffic circle. _____

5. He and his baggage were thrown out the door. _____
  We all went out to celebrate our parents' anniversary. _____

6. When I saw him, I just walked on by. _____
  The packages were left by the back door. _____

7. Please plan to get here before noon. _____
  Have you ever been here before? _____

8. We walked to the meadow and strolled about for an hour. _____
  It has been about three hours since I talked to Ted. _____

9. The kite quickly rose above the trees. _____
  "I live in the apartment above," said Jason. _____

10. "Move along quickly now," said the guard. _____
  The daffodils were planted along the sidewalk. _____

▶ **Writing Application** **Writing Sentences With Prepositional Phrases.**   Write five sentences of your own, each containing a prepositional phrase that begins with one of the prepositions listed below. Underline the preposition and circle its object.

EXAMPLE: instead of
  Voters elected a newcomer instead of the ⟨incumbent⟩ .

1. against

  _____

2. ahead of

  _____

3. among

  _____

4. because of

  _____

5. beneath

  _____

18.1 Conjunctions (Coordinating and Correlative Conjunctions) • Practice 1

Coordinating Conjunctions   Coordinating conjunctions connect similar words. They connect two or more nouns, adjectives, or verbs. They can also connect larger groups of words, such as phrases, or even sentences.

COORDINATING CONJUNCTIONS			
and	for	or	yet
but	nor	so	

Correlative Conjunctions   Correlative conjunctions come in pairs. They connect the same kinds of similar words or groups of words as do coordinating conjunctions.

CORRELATIVE CONJUNCTIONS		
both ... and	not only ... but also	neither ... nor
either ... or		whether ... or

▷ **Exercise 1**   **Identifying Coordinating and Correlative Conjunctions.**   Find and circle the conjunctions below. Write *C* for each coordinating conjunction and *COR* for correlative conjunctions.

EXAMPLE: (Both) Sylvia (and) I will participate.   *COR*

1. Neither my brother nor my sister is eager to go. _____

2. I would like to buy a new stereo, but I can't afford to. _____

3. For our surprise party the entire family cooked and baked. _____

4. Either Stan or Bobby will run the final lap in the race. _____

5. Not only was I surprised, but I was also disappointed. _____

6. Marie kept working, for she knew her deadline was close. _____

7. We intend to visit both Toronto and Ottawa. _____

8. Whether Diane or Annette represents us is unimportant. _____

9. My brother will sing or play the saxophone. _____

10. Our old car is large yet economical. _____

▷ **Exercise 2**   **Writing Original Sentences Using Conjunctions.**   Use each conjunction below in an original sentence. Remember that you can connect nouns, verbs, adjectives, phrases, or sentences.

EXAMPLE: nor _____*I won't drive, nor will I take a train.*_____

1. but _____

2. both ... and _____

3. or _____

4. either ... or _____

5. yet _____

6. whether ... or _____

7. and _____

8. neither ... nor _____

9. for _____

10. not only ... but also _____

18.1 Conjunctions (Coordinating and Correlative Conjunctions) • Practice 2

Exercise 1 **Recognizing Coordinating Conjunctions.** Circle the coordinating conjunction in each of the following sentences. Then underline the word or groups of words connected by the conjunction.

EXAMPLE: We nibbled on cheese (and) crackers.

1. We bought a small yet comfortable car.
2. The experiments are conducted in the morning and in the evening.
3. The actor was handsome but untalented.
4. I must catch the train at noon, for I have a doctor's appointment in the city.
5. The eagle soared, swooped, and landed on its nest.
6. You cannot go to the movie, nor can you go to Fred's house.
7. Darryl's art was the best, so he won the prize.
8. Pam will ask Dorothy, Amy, or Anna to go with her.
9. Isabel bought a ticket, but she missed the train.
10. I need more paint, for the room is much larger than I thought.
11. Carol has not called, nor has she written.
12. The flowers are tiny yet fragrant.
13. Would you like to go to Micky's or Sue's?
14. The jacket was too small, so Sylvia gave it away.
15. Harry had no money, nor did Alfie.

Exercise 2 **Recognizing Correlative Conjunctions.** Circle the correlative conjunction in each of the following sentences. Then underline the two words or the two groups of words connected by the conjunction.

EXAMPLE: I can ask (neither) my father (nor) my mother for permission.

1. I don't care whether Marla or Lisa represents us.
2. She trains for the marathon both in the morning and in the afternoon.
3. Not only was he a fine athlete, but he was also a fine student.
4. Neither Michael nor she could explain the strange noises.
5. Grandfather was either reading or napping.
6. Both Sally and Harry enjoy this restaurant.
7. This hat belongs to either Joe or Bob.
8. The fault was neither Jack's nor Rosa's.
9. This car is not only attractive but also very efficient.
10. We're leaving, whether you want to or not.
11. Lee belongs to both the Spanish Club and the French Club.
12. I would like either a banana or an apple with my sandwich.
13. Bill likes neither purple nor green as a color for walls.
14. These sunglasses not only look good but also protect your eyes.
15. Whether you help me or Marsha helps me does not matter.

18.1 Conjunctions (Subordinating Conjunctions)
• Practice 1

Subordinating Conjunctions   Subordinating conjunctions connect two ideas by making one idea less important than the other.

FREQUENTLY USED SUBORDINATING CONJUNCTIONS			
after	as though	since	until
although	because	so that	when
as	before	than	whenever
as if	even though	though	wherever
as soon as	if	unless	while

▶ **Exercise 1**   **Recognizing Subordinating Conjunctions.**   Circle the subordinating conjunction in each sentence below. Then underline the dependent idea that follows it.

EXAMPLE: (When) I received the package, I jumped for joy.

1. Mother entered the store while everyone else waited in the car.
2. Although I understand his reason, I cannot accept his poor behavior.
3. Unless I hear from the committee tomorrow, I will change my plans.
4. Uncle Bob always phones whenever he is in town.
5. I can't go to the concert because I have to study for my finals.
6. Even though I enjoy some of the new musical groups, I don't think any group can replace the Beatles.
7. Unless we notify the book club, we will continue to get a new book each month.
8. Melody will bring us the tomato plants as soon as she returns from Boston.
9. Mother wants a new car so that she can drive herself to work.
10. Our team can win the championship if it continues to train hard.

▶ **Exercise 2**   **Writing Sentences Using Conjunctions.**   Fill in the blanks with words that will complete each sentence. All three kinds of conjunctions are included below.

EXAMPLE: ____I will polish the car____ since ____Father needs it tomorrow____ .

1. When _____, _____ .
2. _____ so that _____ .
3. Either _____ or _____ .
4. _____ , but _____ .
5. Unless _____ , _____ .
6. Both _____ and _____ .
7. _____ even though _____ .
8. If _____ , _____ .
9. _____ , or _____ .
10. Whenever _____ , _____ .

18.1 Conjunctions (Subordinating Conjunctions)
• Practice 2

▶ **Exercise 1**   **Recognizing Subordinating Conjunctions.**   Circle the subordinating conjunction in each of the following sentences. Then underline the dependent idea following the conjunction.

EXAMPLE: (If) he asks my permission, I will grant it.

1. Since they want to join our club, I will nominate them.

2. They all went fishing while their father slept.

3. The stamps will be available whenever you wish to pick them up.

4. As if she didn't have enough trouble, she has lost her wallet.

5. As long as I can remember, we have spent part of the summer in Vermont.

6. She went home as soon as she heard the news.

7. I sometimes eat more than I should.

8. He lost his way because he forgot to take a map.

9. I can do it if you help me.

10. You look as though you need a rest.

▶ **Exercise 2**   **Writing Sentences Using Conjunctions.**   Fill in the blanks with words that will complete each sentence. Use as many words as necessary to complete each thought, but keep each conjunction in the position shown.

EXAMPLE: _____ as though _____.
           She acted as though she didn't really want to go.

1. Both _____ and _____.

2. If _____, _____.

3. _____ because _____.

4. Although _____, _____.

5. Not only does she _____, but she also _____.

6. _____, but _____.

7. When _____, _____.

8. Either _____ or _____.

9. _____ even though _____.

10. While _____, _____.

▶ **Writing Application**   **Writing Original Sentences With Conjunctions.**   Write sentences of your own using each of the following conjunctions.

EXAMPLE: both ... and
           Both Irving and Poe wrote short stories.

1. unless _____

2. or _____

3. when _____

4. neither ... nor _____

5. although _____

18.2 **Interjections • Practice 1**

Using Interjections   An interjection expresses feeling or emotion and functions independently of a sentence. It is set off from the rest of the sentence with an exclamation mark or a comma.

EXPRESSING EMOTION WITH INTERJECTIONS	
Emotion	**Interjection**
Surprise	*Gee*, I never expected to see you today.
Joy	*Hurray!* We won.
Pain	*Ouch*, I hurt my finger.
Impatience	*Darn*, I missed my train.
Hesitation	We, *uh*, think you're wrong.

▶ **Exercise 1**   **Recognizing Interjections.**   Underline the interjection in each sentence. In the space provided, write which emotion the interjection conveys.

EXAMPLE: <u>Wow!</u> I never expected a fur coat. _____*surprise*_____

1. Hey! Keep your hands off that camera. _____

2. "Goodness, " exclaimed Grandmother. "I never expected to see you all today." _____

3. Darn, Alice is late again. _____

4. Gee, I won a prize in the lottery. _____

5. Uh, I'm afraid I've forgotten your name. _____

▶ **Exercise 2**   **Using Interjections in Sentences.**   Use the following interjections with commas or exclamation marks in sentences of your own.

EXAMPLE: hey
      _____*Hey, watch where you are parking!*_____

1. whew _____

2. oh _____

3. ouch _____

4. ugh _____

5. hurray _____

6. wow _____

7. goodness _____

8. darn _____

9. well _____

10. golly _____

18.2 Interjections • Practice 2

▶ **Exercise 1** **Recognizing Interjections.** Rewrite each of the following sentences, using an appropriate interjection in place of the feeling shown in parentheses.

EXAMPLE: (Anger) I wanted to watch the football game.
　　　　　Darn! I wanted to watch the football game.

1. (Surprise) I never expected this.

_____

2. (Impatience) We have to catch the train.

_____

3. (Dislike) I don't like that hat at all.

_____

4. (Pain) I caught my finger in the door.

_____

5. (Joy) We're all thrilled you came.

_____

6. (Annoyance) Please get this cat away from me.

_____

7. (Anger) I've told you not to do that.

_____

8. (Relief) I thought that lecture would never end.

_____

9. (Joy) I'm so glad to see you.

_____

10. (Surprise) I thought you'd forgotten my birthday.

_____

▶ **Writing Application** **Using Interjections in Sentences.** Use the following interjections with commas or exclamation marks in sentences of your own.

EXAMPLE: ___*uh*___　*My excuse is, uh, not what you might expect.*___

1. ouch _____

2. gee _____

3. oh _____

4. goodness _____

5. whew _____

6. wow _____

7. darn _____

8. ah _____

9. ugh _____

10. hey _____

The Basic Sentence • Practice 1

The Two Basic Elements of a Sentence   All sentences must contain two basic elements—a subject and a verb. The subject answers the question *Who?* or *What?* before the verb. The verb tells what the subject does, what is done to the subject, or the subject's condition.

SUBJECTS AND VERBS

Dogs of all kinds were enrolled in the obedience class.
Carefully, he removed the painting from the crate.
Lara has not been practicing the piano regularly.

The Need to Express a Complete Thought   A sentence must express a complete thought. A group of words with a subject and verb expresses a complete thought if it can stand by itself and still make sense.

COMPLETE THOUGHTS

Incomplete Thought: The senator from New Jersey
Complete Thought: The senator from New Jersey raced to the airport to catch a plane.

Exercise 1   **Recognizing Subjects and Verbs.**   Underline each subject once and each verb twice in the sentences below.

EXAMPLE: In the morning we began our trip.

1. An angry principal addressed the student body.

2. Hannibal was one of the greatest generals of all time.

3. A halfback with great speed is the dream of every coach.

4. In a glass tube, neon emits an orange glow.

5. My bad ankle is bothering me once again.

6. A bottle of shampoo just broke.

7. A rolltop oak desk is one of our family's heirlooms.

8. My sister just bought three new record albums.

9. Nehru became prime minister of India in 1947.

10. The road to the battleground is winding and dangerous.

Exercise 2   **Recognizing Complete Sentences.**   Only five of the following groups of words are sentences. If the sentence is complete, write a *C*. If the group of words is not a complete sentence, write *NC*.

EXAMPLE: If the fire department does not come at once. _____*NC*_____

1. Leslie borrowed two reference books from the library. _____

2. Whenever I go to the movies with my friends. _____

3. We decided to prune all the rose bushes. _____

4. Vincenzo Bellini is a famous Italian operatic composer. _____

5. At the end of the road near the Graham Bridge. _____

6. Because she wanted to do well on the test. _____

7. Bobby and Marie decided to shovel the snow. _____

8. A long report about problems in the environment. _____

9. Since I am very much interested in biology. _____

10. We cannot depend any longer on our old car. _____

19.1 The Basic Sentence • Practice 2

▷ **Exercise 1** **Recognizing Subjects and Verbs.** Underline each subject once and each verb twice in the sentences below.

EXAMPLE: One Greek hero spent ten years trying to reach home.

1. The ferry crosses the river twice a day.
2. Our teacher has been more than fair with us.
3. My sister bakes delicious vanilla cookies.
4. The old bridge creaks occasionally under a heavy load.
5. The book describes the causes of the Great Depression.

▷ **Exercise 2** **Correcting Incomplete Thoughts.** None of the following groups of words expresses a complete thought. Correct each one by adding whatever words are needed to make a sentence.

EXAMPLE: Three angry ducks in search of corn.
Three angry ducks in search of corn waddled by.

1. on top of the shelf in the kitchen
   _____

2. in the garage near the old newspapers
   _____

3. the clerk behind the counter
   _____

4. a police officer at the top of the hill
   _____

5. because of all the wrong answers
   _____

▷ **Exercise 3** **Recognizing Sentences.** If a group of words is a sentence, write *sentence*. If a group of words expresses an incomplete thought, add whatever words are needed to make a sentence. Then underline the subject once and the verb twice in each new sentence.

EXAMPLE: The suitcases from the plane.
The suitcases from the plane were unloaded.

1. She asked me about the next edition of the newspaper.
   _____

2. The room in the back of the house.
   _____

3. In the desert, tall cactuses.
   _____

4. We understood her reasons.
   _____

5. From the observation deck at the rim of the canyon.
   _____

19.2 Complete Subjects and Predicates

• Practice 1

Finding Complete Subjects and Predicates   Every sentence can be divided into two parts—a complete subject and a complete predicate. The complete subject consists of the subject and any words related to it. The complete predicate consists of the verb and any words related to it.

Complete Subject	Complete Predicate
Most <u>clerks</u>	answer questions.
Most <u>clerks</u> in the City Hall	answer questions cheerfully about taxes and unpaid bills.

> **Exercise 1**   **Recognizing Complete Subjects and Complete Predicates.**   Underline the subject once and the verb twice. Then draw a vertical line between the complete subject and the complete predicate.

EXAMPLE: The <u>mayor</u> of the city | <u><u>addressed</u></u> the civics club.

1. Our gnarled apple tree was destroyed in the storm.
2. Ribbons of water cascaded down the mountainside.
3. Our new teacher explained her requirements for a notebook.
4. The Chicago Cubs for many years played only in daylight.
5. A colorful Thanksgiving Day parade always brings out a crowd.
6. Our new uniforms were lost somehow during the summer.
7. The computer in mother's office has an expensive printer.
8. The background of the flag of Nova Scotia is white.
9. Some news photos remain in your mind for years.
10. A brilliant sunset filled the sky with a splash of reds, yellows, and oranges.

> **Exercise 2**   **Adding Complete Subjects or Complete Predicates.**   Each item below contains either a complete subject or a complete predicate. Supply the missing part.

EXAMPLE: _My old friend Dave_   entered the supermarket.

1. The throne in the center of the stage _____.
2. _____ welcomed the incoming class.
3. Our football coach _____.
4. _____ was extremely difficult to explain.
5. My favorite experiment in science _____.
6. _____ is much greater than before.
7. Our local post office _____.
8. _____ is a book I will never forget.
9. Next year in the spring I _____.
10. _____ should win a championship.

19.2 # Complete Subjects and Predicates
• Practice 2

▶ **Exercise 1** **Recognizing Complete Subjects and Predicates.** For each of the following sentences, underline the subject once and the verb twice. Then draw a vertical line between the complete subject and the complete predicate, as shown in the example.

EXAMPLE: The <u>man</u> in gray | <u><u>paced</u></u> in front of the statue.

1. A sudden storm swept across the prairie.
2. Two old cargo ships collided in the harbor.
3. Bruce described his nervousness about the history test.
4. The lilac bushes in our front yard burst into flower overnight.
5. Rosalyn sews all her own clothing.
6. A rather strange event occurred off the coast of Maine.
7. Small white spots appeared on the leaves of our plants.
8. He described the accident in detail.
9. The local museum sits on an acre of land near the river delta.
10. Many of the new telephones have caller ID.
11. Leroy laughed as he ran after the frisky puppy.
12. Our lives as flower growers changed after the hurricane.
13. Red, pink, yellow, and white roses grew in Maisie's backyard.
14. The stern judge was not pleased with the skater's performance.
15. That shampoo advertisement was one of the first on TV.
16. Some species of birds can imitate human speech.
17. The chattering monkey pointed at the red-haired girl.
18. A large bronze sculpture stands in the courtyard of the tall building.
19. The palm fronds were splattered with sparkling raindrops.
20. Mary and Elizabeth enjoyed their day at the ceramics studio.

▶ **Writing Application** **Developing Complete Subjects and Predicates.** The first word in each of the following items is a noun or pronoun that can be used as a subject. The second word is a verb. Develop each item into a complete subject and predicate by adding details to the subject and verb. Write the new sentences.

EXAMPLE: tree   fell
        The tree in our back yard fell during a storm last night.

1. river   flows
   _____

2. comedians   tried
   _____

3. everyone   is
   _____

4. result   was
   _____

5. storm   lasted
   _____

19.3 Compound Subjects and Verbs • Practice 1

Compound Subjects   A compound subject is two or more subjects that have the same verb and are joined by a conjunction such as *and* or *or*.

COMPOUND SUBJECTS
History and science are my favorites.
Judy, David, and Charles will travel to Philadelphia.

Compound Verbs   A compound verb is two or more verbs that have the same subject and are joined by a conjunction such as *and* or *or*.

COMPOUND VERBS
Uncle Steve will fly or drive to the wedding.
My grandmother still bakes, cooks, and sews as much as ever.

▶ **Exercise 1**   **Recognizing Compound Subjects.**   In each sentence below underline the compound subject.

EXAMPLE: A bus or train will get you to Memphis.

1. Jo Ann and I often do our research together.
2. Sketching paper and pencils can be purchased here.
3. In the accident Bob and Billy were slightly injured.
4. Ice cream, cookies, or pie will make excellent desserts.
5. In our English class, spelling and grammar are not popular.
6. Snakes, spiders, and assorted rodents infest this forest.
7. His neck and my neck are about the same size.
8. Boston, Philadelphia, and New York are all historic cities.
9. My parents, my grandparents, and my Aunt Sue will spend the summer together.
10. A high fever and a strange rash were the principal symptoms.

▶ **Exercise 2**   **Recognizing Compound Verbs.**   In each sentence below underline the compound verb twice.

EXAMPLE: The book opens and closes with a battle scene.

1. My brother sketches or paints almost every day.
2. The child opened the package and reached inside.
3. We walked to the beach, sat for a while in the sun, and took several cold dips.
4. The eagle soared in the sky and then suddenly dove after a prey.
5. The tin roof shook and rattled all night during the storm.
6. My friends bought several albums and had lunch in a hamburger place.
7. The main highway continues this way and then narrows into two lanes.
8. The President will arrive at nine and enter the convention hall a short time later.
9. After school, I do my homework, finish my chores, and watch TV.
10. Mom searched for her slippers and found them under the couch.

19.3 Compound Subjects and Verbs • Practice 2

▶ **Exercise 1** **Recognizing Compound Subjects.** Underline the compound subjects.

EXAMPLE: Red, white, and blue are popular colors for flags.

1. Skaters and cyclists crowd the park each weekend.
2. After the dance Joan and I stopped for a milk shake.
3. All day wind and rain lashed the tiny island.
4. The coach, the team, and the cheerleaders boarded the bus for the game.
5. Both gorillas and orangutans are in danger of extinction.
6. Along the road daisies, buttercups, lilies, and dandelions grew in profusion.
7. Either the principal or the superintendent will introduce the speakers.
8. Adjectives and adverbs are modifiers.
9. Utah, Colorado, New Mexico, and Arizona touch borders at the same point.
10. San Marino and Monaco are two of the smallest nations.

▶ **Exercise 2** **Recognizing Compound Verbs.** Underline the compound verbs.

EXAMPLE: Carol looked around and then laughed uproariously.

1. Our kite dipped suddenly and wrapped itself around a tree.
2. The workers first dug a hole and then carefully lowered the new shrub into it.
3. The dog turned around three times, settled into its bed, and yawned.
4. The coin slipped from my hand, rolled along the pavement, and dropped into a sewer drain.
5. My parents sold the station wagon and bought a new compact car.
6. I either left my door keys at home or lost them at school.
7. The conductor turned to the orchestra and conducted Beethoven's Fifth Symphony.
8. The snake recoiled and then struck.
9. Jan finished her homework, prepared for bed, and settled down to her favorite TV show.
10. We gathered the corn and put it in bushel baskets.

▶ **Exercise 3** **Recognizing Compound Subjects and Verbs.** Each of the following sentences contains a compound subject, a compound verb, or both. On the line, write the compound subjects and the compound verbs. Then label each compound subject and compound verb as in the example.

EXAMPLE: He and she are good friends. _____He, she   compound subject_____

1. Our old magazines and newspapers are stored in the attic.

   _____

2. She opened the door and rushed out of the lobby.

   _____

3. My mother and father either walk or drive to the station.

   _____

4. The top spun for a minute, teetered, and finally fell.

   _____

5. Trains, buses, and taxis are three popular means of transportation in urban areas.

   _____

19.4 Special Problems with Subjects (Subjects in Orders, Directions, and Questions) • Practice 1

Subjects in Orders and Directions In sentences that give orders or directions, the subject is understood to be *you*.

ORDERS AND DIRECTIONS

(You) Chew your food slowly.
Frank, (you) sit down!
After jogging, (you) take a shower.

Subjects in Questions In questions the subject often follows the verb or part of the verb.

QUESTIONS

Is the package ready?
Have you found your ring?
When will the senator speak ?

Exercise 1 **Recognizing Subjects That Give Orders or Directions.** Underline the verb in each sentence with a double line. Write the subject in the space provided. (Three of the sentences do not give orders or directions.)

EXAMPLE: Open the package quickly. _____*you*_____

1. Turn right at the traffic light near the mall. _____
2. Jennie, try to concentrate now. _____
3. In the morning Alice often sunbathes. _____
4. After changing the baby, warm up her milk. _____
5. Please wait for the light to change. _____
6. Remember to get a fresh loaf of bread and a bag of potatoes. _____
7. The radio slipped off the counter and broke. _____
8. Every morning brush your teeth carefully. _____
9. Dr. Slovak, phone your office now. _____
10. The name of the hotel was recently changed. _____

Exercise 2 **Finding the Subject in Questions.** Underline the subjects in the questions below.

EXAMPLE: Whom did the reporter meet?

1. Has the principal entered the auditorium yet?
2. Who is the governor of Arizona?
3. What do you expect to happen tomorrow?
4. Can the vegetables survive a three-week drought?
5. Have Dick and Lucy visited the exhibit?
6. Why have they attempted to stop our demonstration?
7. When did the second message reach you?
8. Which chapter of the book is the best?
9. Did both teams arrive simultaneously?
10. Is this the way to spell her name?

19.4 Special Problems with Subjects (Subjects in Orders, Directions, and Questions) • Practice 2

▷ **Exercise 1**   **Recognizing Subjects That Give Orders or Directions.**   Write the subject of each of the following sentences. Ten of the sentences give orders or directions. The other five are ordinary sentences in normal word order.

EXAMPLE: David, remember to turn out the lights. _____*you*_____

1. Wash your face with soap and water. _____
2. Tell us what happened, Frank. _____
3. Marie, open the window about an inch. _____
4. Paul tried to remove the splinter from Sue's finger. _____
5. After raking the leaves, spread an even coat of lime on the lawn. _____
6. Girls, help us carry these packages into the house. _____
7. Measure the amount of rain that falls each morning. _____
8. The bread jammed the toaster and burned. _____
9. Get the doctor at once! _____
10. She bought a portable radio. _____
11. Toss me the football, Harvey. _____
12. Peel the apples while I prepare the crust. _____
13. Mark selected only the juiciest oranges. _____
14. Dawn used all the hot water for her shower. _____
15. Peter, pick up some figs at the store. _____

▷ **Exercise 2**   **Finding the Subject in Questions.**   Underline the subject in each of the following sentences.

EXAMPLE: Which Dickinson poem do <u>you</u> like best?

1. When did she call from her office?
2. Which book did Billy choose?
3. Has Roberto left for college yet?
4. Were the flowers delivered on time?
5. Which team has won the trophy?
6. How did they accept the news?
7. Where is the signature on this check?
8. Are you certain about the record?
9. Who took my pencil?
10. Why has he objected to the title of the play?
11. How long ago did they leave?
12. Which of the three sisters is your friend?
13. Is that your final answer?
14. Who ordered this pizza?
15. Why are you so unhappy?

19.4 Special Problems with Subjects (Subjects in Sentences Beginning with *There* or *Here*, Subjects in Sentences Inverted for Emphasis) • Practice 1

Subjects in Sentences Beginning with *There* or *Here*   *There* or *here* is never the subject of a sentence. Sentences beginning with *there* or *here* are in inverted word order. The subject will come after the verb.

SENTENCES BEGINNING WITH *THERE* OR *HERE*
There are two telegrams in your office.
Here is the message.

Subjects in Sentences Inverted for Emphasis   There are also other sentences with inverted word order. In these sentences the subject follows the verb in order to receive greater emphasis.

OTHER SENTENCES IN INVERTED WORD ORDER
In her eyes was fear.
At the fork is a police station.

▶ **Exercise 1**   **Recognizing Subjects in Sentences with Inverted Word Order.**   Underline the subject once and the verb twice in each sentence below.

EXAMPLE: Near the beach is an old bathhouse.

1. There is a lesson to be learned from this.
2. At the top of the hill stands an impressive statue.
3. Here are the keys to the car.
4. From the burning building came a shout of a child.
5. There is too much confusion about your plan.
6. With her was a girl from college.
7. Out of the backfield raced Bob with the ball.
8. Here was a striking bit of evidence.
9. In the center of the ceiling was a listening device.
10. There should be a box of tools in the cellar.

▶ **Exercise 2**   **Writing Original Sentences in Inverted Word Order.**   Write sentences that begin with the words below. Make certain that the verb comes before the subject.

EXAMPLE: There _____
           There *is your lost ring.*

1. Here _____
2. Near the top of the hill _____
3. With them _____
4. There _____
5. In this story _____
6. Over there _____
7. Under my bed _____
8. Near the railroad station _____
9. In the truck _____
10. In her wallet _____

19.4

Special Problems with Subjects (Subjects in Sentences Beginning with x or *Here*, Subjects in Sentences Inverted for Emphasis) • Practice 2

▶ **Exercise 1** **Finding the Subject in Sentences Beginning with *There* and *Here*.** Underline the subject in each of the following sentences.

EXAMPLE: Here is the missing piece.

1. Here are the notes on the trip.
2. There were three steps to follow in the recipe.
3. There is a new sporting goods store in town.
4. There are the magazines on boating.
5. Here are three good mystery novels to read.
6. There is a bad winter storm approaching us.
7. There on the hill are the ruins of the ancient temple.
8. There can be only one choice.
9. Here sat the ambassador from Zimbabwe.
10. Here are your assignments for the next week.

▶ **Exercise 2** **Finding the Subject in Inverted Sentences.** Underline the subject in each of the following sentences.

EXAMPLE: Far in the distance came the first roar of thunder.

1. High atop the tree on a dead branch perched a vulture.
2. All about the neighborhood lay the debris from the tornado.
3. Suddenly, into the clearing came three deer.
4. On that hill once stood a one-room schoolhouse.
5. Not far from the cabin was a clear, cold stream.

▶ **Writing Application** **Writing Sentences with Subjects in Various Positions.** Write original sentences according to the following directions. Add any missing subjects, using parentheses. Then underline the subject in each.

EXAMPLE: Begin a sentence with *Were they*.
　　　　　Were they really lost on a desert island?

1. Begin a sentence with *There are*.

_____

2. Begin a sentence with *Choose*.

_____

3. Begin a question with *What have*.

_____

4. Begin a sentence with *How*.

_____

5. Begin a sentence with *Here*.

_____

19.5 Direct Objects (The Direct Object, Compound Direct Objects) • Practice 1

The Direct Object   A direct object is a noun or pronoun that receives the action of a transitive verb.

```
DIRECT OBJECTS
                        DO                    DO
Marge often drinks  milk .    I will ask  him  later.
```

Compound Direct Objects   A compound direct object is two or more nouns or pronouns that receive the action of the same transitive verb.

```
COMPOUND DIRECT OBJECTS
                        DO           DO
Bill needs a new  sweater  and  tie .
                   DO                    DO
I read a  newspaper  and a  magazine  each day.
```

▶ **Exercise 1**   **Recognizing Direct Objects.**   Circle the direct object or the compound direct objects in each sentence.

EXAMPLE: Jay told (Carol) and (her) about it.

1. We will plan the project for the fair carefully.
2. The next morning Sally took her driving test.
3. Gloria expects them to arrive at seven.
4. She bought gloves, a scarf, and two skirts.
5. I want my parents and my grandparents to know first.
6. Will you write her about your victory?
7. The new car has an automatic transmission and cruise control.
8. My mother injured her hand this morning.
9. For graduation my sister got a new laptop and a camera.
10. Tell Bill and them to wait for the decision.

▶ **Exercise 2**   **Using Direct Objects.**   Fill in the blanks in the sentences below with appropriate direct objects. Use both nouns and pronouns.

EXAMPLE: I reached _____New Haven_____ the next day.

1. After two hours I closed the _____.
2. Ask _____ about the second-half comeback.
3. I want _____ and _____ to represent us.
4. Will you remind _____ about the junior high dance?
5. In the bakery, buy some _____, _____, and _____.
6. I saw _____ at the movies yesterday.
7. On the weekend she wrote _____.
8. Do you have _____ for the football game?
9. We will welcome Ben and _____ to our class.
10. Next week Father will build a _____ and a _____.

19.5 **Direct Objects** (The Direct Object, Compound Direct Objects) • Practice 2

▶ **Exercise 1**   **Recognizing Direct Objects.**   Each of the following sentences contains a direct object. Underline each direct object.

EXAMPLE: She quickly opened the <u>letter</u>.

1. My aunt approached the door cautiously.
2. Sally gave our puppy to the Wilsons.
3. The patients take their medicine three times a day.
4. My mother sent the clothing to the Red Cross.
5. At night she often eats frozen dinners.
6. We received oranges from Florida.
7. I want them here now.
8. He winds his gold watch each morning.
9. After lunch she gave an account of the accident.
10. They did not serve any dessert after dinner.
11. Marlene picked six hollyhocks for her new vase.
12. Liz put the new saddle on the horse.
13. Bob examined the underside of the fern leaves.
14. The giant Ferris wheel carried fifty passengers.
15. The new student plays the cornet very well.

▶ **Exercise 2**   **Recognizing Compound Direct Objects.**   Each of the following sentences contains a compound direct object. Underline only the nouns or pronouns that make up each compound direct object.

EXAMPLE: Don't forget the <u>carrots</u> or the <u>spinach</u>.

1. At the market buy some lettuce, carrots, squash, and tomatoes.
2. After class Mr. Simpson complimented Ned and him on their project.
3. Did they buy a sedan or a minivan?
4. I shocked Mary and Bob with my story.
5. I saw him and her at the movies.
6. The train passed New York, Philadelphia, and Baltimore while I slept.
7. Linda and Alan planted marigolds and petunias in their garden.
8. The poet Sylvia Plath wrote many poems and one novel.
9. She has always loved ships and the sea.
10. Sara bought a new blouse and a yellow skirt and blue shoes.
11. For your sandwich, you can use tuna and lettuce.
12. Does Dan play the flute or the clarinet?
13. At the farm, we saw foals, calves, and lambs.
14. Robert dislikes fish and liver.
15. Butterflies, bees, and insects visited the roses, the irises, and the lilies.

19.5 Direct Objects (Direct Object, Adverb, or Object of a Preposition) • Practice 1

Direct Object, Adverb, or Object of a Preposition   A direct object is never an adverb or the noun or pronoun at the end of a prepositional phrase.

COMPARING DIRECT OBJECTS, ADVERBS, AND OBJECTS OF PREPOSITIONS
DO My sister cheered the team . (Cheered *what?* team) ADV My sister cheered wildly. (Cheered *what?* no direct object) PREP   OBJ OF PREP My sister cheered from the sideline. (Cheered *what?* no direct object)

▶ **Exercise 1**   **Distinguishing Between Direct Objects, Adverbs, and Objects of Prepositions.**   Label the underlined word in each sentence below. Use *DO* for a direct object, *ADV* for an adverb, and *OP* for an object of a preposition.

EXAMPLE: We agreed willingly to the change. _____ADV_____

1. I really need a new thesaurus. _____
2. At sunset we finally stopped at an old motel. _____
3. For years now my brother has played chess. _____
4. Leaving the space shuttle, the astronaut smiled happily. _____
5. My parents changed their decision without warning. _____
6. The defendant walked wearily into the courtroom. _____
7. I built these oak cabinets without any help. _____
8. Much to my surprise, the book ended strangely. _____
9. Are you still interested in the unknown ? _____
10. Last spring she planted tomatoes in her yard. _____

▶ **Exercise 2**   **Using Direct Objects, Adverbs, and Objects of Prepositions in Sentences.**   Fill in each blank with the kind of word indicated in the parentheses.

EXAMPLE: (direct object) I often enjoy _____hockey games_____ .

1. (adverb) When Uncle Ted arrived, we smiled _____.
2. (direct object) You can buy _____ in any drugstore.
3. (obj. of prep.) The photo you want is in the _____.
4. (direct object) If you go to the post office, I need some _____.
5. (adverb) Speak _____ during your interview.
6. (direct object) Who wrote _____?
7. (obj. of prep.) Wait for us under the _____.
8. (adverb) Bess reacted _____ to the suggestion.
9. (direct object) I put the _____ into the file cabinet.
10. (obj. of prep.) We enjoyed the performer on the _____.

19.5 Direct Objects (Direct Object, Adverb, or Object of a Preposition) • Practice 2

▶ **Exercise 1** Distinguishing Between Direct Objects, Adverbs, and Objects of Prepositions. In each of the following sentences, underline the direct objects and circle any adverbs or prepositional phrases. Not every sentence has all three.

EXAMPLE: The dragon roared (loudly) (in the night) .

1. Fred drove the old truck into our driveway.
2. She opened the letter slowly and cautiously.
3. My mother attended the parade in the park.
4. The lion chased the frightened animals through the field.
5. He practiced a new stunt for the competition.
6. Doreen immediately bought a copy of the program.
7. Camille and Troy asked a question about the alligator exhibit.
8. Sadly, Esperanza wrote a letter about the tragic incident.
9. On their trip to Hawaii, the Martins learned the meaning of the word *aloha.*
10. Dirk gets an allowance for his lunches and clothes.
11. Molly frantically hit the brakes.
12. Thoughtfully, George sent several boxes of boysenberries to Marie.
13. Megan took her brother to the bowling alley regularly for six months.
14. The showy flowers of the cactus attracted insects.
15. Mabel carefully followed the recipe in her cookbook.
16. Dean told a fascinating story about peacocks.
17. Kevin sent Allen to the store for pasta.
18. The delicate snowflakes fell gracefully and gently to the ground.
19. Henry proudly showed a picture of his family to Gabriella.
20. Generously, Brian gave a new catcher's mitt to Chuck.

▶ **Exercise 2** Writing Sentences with Direct Objects, Adverbs, and Objects of Prepositions. Write a sentence that contains the kind of word indicated in parentheses. Then underline that word.

EXAMPLE: (direct object)
Paul caught a big fish today.

1. (direct object) _____
2. (adverb) _____
3. (object of preposition) _____
4. (direct object) _____
5. (adverb) _____
6. (object of preposition) _____
7. (direct object) _____
8. (adverb) _____
9. (object of preposition) _____
10. (direct object) _____

19.5 Direct Objects (in Questions) • Practice 1

Direct Objects in Questions   A direct object in a sentence in normal word order is found after the verb. In a question the direct object is sometimes near the beginning of the sentence, before the verb.

Questions	Normal Word Order
DO What will she do now?	DO She will do what now.
DO Whom do they want ?	DO They do want whom.
DO Which road should we take?	DO We should take which road.

▶ **Exercise 1**   **Finding Direct Objects in Questions.**   Circle the direct object in each question below. Note that in three of the sentences, the direct object follows the verb.

EXAMPLE: Which (tool) do you need?

1. Whom did they call in Portland?
2. Which photograph did they lose?
3. When will the plumber fix the leaking sink?
4. What excuse can she possibly offer?
5. Which role in *Romeo and Juliet* does he want?
6. When will Sandy send the invitations to her party?
7. Whom does the principal expect?
8. How many CD's do you have?
9. Where will you bake the cookies for our get-together?
10. Which recipe will you use?

▶ **Exercise 2**   **Using Direct Objects in Sentences.**   Some of the sentences below are questions; others are not. Fill in an appropriate direct object in each blank space.

EXAMPLE: Which _____train_____ will you take to Boston?

1. For the car wash, I will make a _____ .
2. _____ did they invite to speak?
3. Which _____ by John Steinbeck do you want?
4. When will you prepare the _____ ?
5. We expect _____ to arrive at the airport tonight.
6. How many _____ do you need?
7. From the top of the hill I can see _____ .
8. _____ did the dean call?
9. Where will you buy the _____ ?
10. I think I can understand your _____ .

19.5 Direct Objects (in Questions) • Practice 2

▶ **Exercise 1** **Finding Direct Objects in Questions.** Underline the direct object in each of the following sentences.

EXAMPLE: <u>What</u> were you thinking?

1. Which photograph did she take?
2. Whom does he expect this evening?
3. What did you do with the package?
4. Where will you spend your vacation?
5. Which books have they read?
6. How many videos did you buy?
7. Which suggestions have they considered so far?
8. What have you heard about the astronauts?
9. When will the judges announce the awards?
10. Which color have they chosen for the new curtains?
11. Which dessert do you prefer?
12. Whom did you see at the video store?
13. What did you give Sarah for her graduation?
14. Where does Melissa keep her games?
15. Which puppy destroyed the pillow?
16. How many CD's did you play today?
17. Which pizza did Alfonse order for us?
18. When will the store have the books in stock?
19. How can you have forgotten that wonderful trip?
20. What message did you write in the letter?

▶ **Writing Application** **Writing Sentences with Direct Objects.** Write an original sentence for each of the following patterns. You may add additional words or details as long as you keep the assigned pattern.

EXAMPLE: subject + verb + direct object + direct object
<u>Becky collected both records and marbles.</u>

1. subject + verb + direct object

   _____

2. subject + verb + direct object + prepositional phrase

   _____

3. direct object + helping verb + subject + verb

   _____

4. subject + verb + direct object + conjunction + direct object

   _____

5. subject + verb + direct object + adverb + prepositional phrase

   _____

19.5 Indirect Objects (The Indirect Object, Compound Indirect Objects) • Practice 1

The Indirect Object   An indirect object is a noun or pronoun that comes after an action verb and before a direct object. It names the person or thing that something is given to or done for.

INDIRECT OBJECTS
IO   DO
I gave [her] the [pass] . (Gave the pass to whom? her)
IO   DO
She told [Sal] the [story] . (told the story to whom ? Sal)

Compound Indirect Objects   A compound indirect object is two or more nouns or pronouns that come after an action verb and before a direct object. It names the persons or things that something is given to or done for.

COMPOUND INDIRECT OBJECTS
IO   IO   DO
I gave [Bill] and [her] the [passes] . (gave the passes to whom ? Bill, her)
IO   IO   DO
She told [Sal] and [Mike] the [story] . (told the story to whom ? Sal, Mike)

▷ **Exercise 1**   **Recognizing Indirect Objects.**   Each sentence below contains a single indirect object or a compound indirect object. Circle each indirect object below.

EXAMPLE: I brought (Bill) and (him) tickets.

1. Please take Uncle John his medicine.
2. I will give Jason and Jeffrey their instructions.
3. Did you send Grandfather a postcard?
4. Beverly will show the customer the new model.
5. Can you teach us the game?
6. The police told my parents and me the entire story.
7. For Christmas, order Grandpa a new bathrobe.
8. I will sell the developers just a part of the land.
9. In the race you pass Josie the baton.
10. The coach handed Marie and Louise their awards.

▷ **Exercise 2**   **Recognizing Direct and Indirect Objects.**   In the sentences below underline the direct objects and circle the indirect objects.

EXAMPLE: Bring (me) the cookbook.

1. From his college my brother sent me a sweatshirt.
2. Pass your aunt the bowl of gravy.
3. We are making our parents a surprise anniversary party.
4. Did you bring your sister a new watch?
5. I will give the detective the information he wants.

19.5 Indirect Objects (The Indirect Object, Compound Indirect Objects) • Practice 2

▶ **Exercise 1** **Recognizing Indirect Objects.**   Each sentence contains a direct object and an indirect object. Underline each indirect object.

EXAMPLE: Finally, she told <u>him</u> the news.

 1. The coach gave him a special award.

 2. We sent her a bouquet of flowers.

 3. After dinner they told us the good news.

 4. Have you shown them the new puppy?

 5. Lucille lent her brother her umbrella.

 6. I later wrote my brother an explanation for my behavior.

 7. Pass your sister the vegetables.

 8. Vasco taught me several Portuguese words.

 9. I will order you some breakfast now.

10. Did you really sell him your collection of old records?

11. Clara told them an unbelievable story about a cowboy.

12. The principal awarded Mr. Franklin an engraved plaque.

13. The children fed the birds small pieces of the stale bread.

14. Uncle Steve bought his niece a treat at the ice-cream store.

15. Jared handed his teacher the unfinished homework.

▶ **Exercise 2**   **Recognizing Compound Indirect Objects.**   Each sentence contains a compound indirect object. Underline nouns or pronouns that make up each one.

EXAMPLE: Will he tell <u>Jay</u> and <u>Cathy</u> the truth?

 1. Give him and her an equal amount.

 2. Have you told Sally or Beth that story?

 3. We gave the birds and the fish new homes.

 4. Mother told the doctor and nurse our symptoms.

 5. Did you get Marie and Steve their consent slips?

 6. I gave the stairs and the porch a new coat of paint.

 7. Have you told Mother and him the wonderful news?

 8. Please read Bob and them the directions to the store.

 9. In the morning I will give Joyce and her father our decision.

10. Take Uncle Bill and Aunt Lila a cold drink.

11. Barbara sang Stuart and me a beautiful, sad song.

12. Would you show Carl and him the photograph?

13. The gardener told Sheila and James the bad news about the petunias.

14. Laura gave her brother and her sister a new board game.

15. Celeste made her mother and her father a solemn promise.

19.5 Indirect Objects (Indirect Object or Object of a Preposition?) • Practice 1

Indirect Object or Object of a Preposition?   Do not confuse an indirect object with the object of a preposition. An indirect object never follows the preposition *to* or *for* in a sentence.

INDIRECT OBJECT OR PREPOSITIONAL PHRASE?

            IO   DO
We brought Mother a beautiful plant .

                        DO   PREP PHRASE
We brought a beautiful plant to Mother.

         IO   DO
I prepared them a quick snack .

                 DO   PREP PHRASE
I prepared a quick snack for them.

▶ **Exercise 1**   **Distinguishing Between Indirect Objects and Objects of Prepositions.**   In each blank, write whether the underlined word is an *indirect object* or an *object of a preposition*.

EXAMPLE: Sally gave the note to <u>Bruce</u>.   *object of a preposition.*

1. I ordered <u>her</u> another pair of sunglasses. _____
2. The principal read <u>us</u> the new regulations. _____
3. Have you given the old lamps to the <u>volunteers</u> ? _____
4. I have saved the clippings for <u>her</u>. _____
5. Show your <u>father</u> that strange message. _____
6. In the national park the guide gave a detailed map to <u>him</u>. _____
7. Have you told <u>Donna</u> your startling story? _____
8. She can buy the <u>attendant</u> a present next time. _____
9. The student told an obvious lie to the <u>dean</u>. _____
10. The senior handed the <u>undergraduate</u> the banner. _____

▶ **Exercise 2**   **Writing Sentences with Indirect Objects and Objects of Prepositions.**   Rewrite each sentence above. Change each indirect object into a prepositional phrase. Change each prepositional phrase into an indirect object.

EXAMPLE: Sally gave <u>Bruce</u> the note.

1. _____
2. _____
3. _____
4. _____
5. _____
6. _____
7. _____
8. _____
9. _____
10. _____

19.5 # Indirect Objects (Indirect Object or Object of a Preposition?) • Practice 2

▶ **Exercise 1** **Distinguishing Between Indirect Objects and Objects of Prepositions.** In each of the following sentences, underline the indirect objects and circle the objects of a preposition.

EXAMPLE: Strawberries gave <u>him</u> a rash.

1. Sheepishly, she told her father the story.
2. Raphael gave a bone to the collie.
3. Did you tell him the price?
4. Surprisingly enough, she gave her aunt the bracelet.
5. My mother brought her car to the repair shop.
6. I definitely will hold him to his promise.
7. In anger he gave him the money.
8. I did offer her a choice.
9. Please buy a new radio for them.
10. Have you shown your mother the test paper?
11. Ryan allowed him one last chance.
12. Margaret handed Oliver the gift.
13. Did you show the directions to them?
14. Has the governor granted the prisoner a pardon?
15. Have they given the ball to the other team yet?
16. The quarterback threw Jerry the ball.
17. I'd like to play you a little song.
18. Tony showed his mom his new snowboard.
19. Shannon wrote a letter to Teresa.
20. Tom showed Becky his secret hiding place.

▶ **Writing Application** **Writing Sentences with Indirect Objects.** Follow the directions to write five sentences.

EXAMPLE: Write a sentence with three indirect objects.
          Mary Beth told Cindy, Craig, and Joel her secret.

1. Write a sentence that fits this pattern: Subject + Verb + Indirect Object + Direct Object.

   _____

2. Using the same subject, verb, and direct object as in the first item, change the sentence to Subject + Verb + Direct Object + Prepositional Phrase.

   _____

3. Write a sentence with a compound indirect object connected by *and*.

   _____

4. Write a sentence with a compound indirect object connected by *or*.

   _____

5. Rewrite the sentence in the example, changing the compound indirect object to a prepositional phrase.

   _____

19.5 Subject Complements (Predicate Nouns and Pronouns, Predicate Adjectives) • Practice 1

Predicate Nouns and Pronouns   A subject complement is a noun, pronoun, or adjective that follows a linking verb and tells something about the subject. A predicate noun or predicate pronoun follows a linking verb and renames or identifies the subject of the sentence.

PREDICATE NOUNS AND PRONOUNS
PN
Columbus is a city in Ohio. (*City* renames *Columbus*.)
PPN
Our representative will be you. (*You* renames *representative*.)

Predicate Adjectives   A predicate adjective follows a linking verb and describes the subject of the sentence.

PREDICATE ADJECTIVES
PA
This coffee cake is delicious. (*Delicious* describes *coffee cake*.)

▶ **Exercise 1**   **Recognizing Predicate Nouns and Predicate Pronouns.**   In each sentence below underline the predicate noun or predicate pronoun.

EXAMPLE: Melanie should be our captain.

1. Football is my favorite sport in the fall.
2. The brightest student has never been she.
3. New Hampshire has always been a scenic state.
4. Through hard work she became a huge success.
5. John Q. Adams remained a political force all his life.
6. In my new mystery novel, the butler is the murderer.
7. Ronald Reagan became president in 1981.
8. Our old Mercury was a car with an unusually smooth ride.
9. It is she whom our class chose.
10. Mark's idea is an option to consider.

▶ **Exercise 2**   **Recognizing Predicate Adjectives.**   In each sentence below underline the predicate adjective.

EXAMPLE: I feel sad about her failure.

1. Churchill's speech was inspiring to the people of London.
2. After the conference they seemed angry at everyone.
3. These curved roads are dangerous after a snow.
4. This old milk tastes sour in my coffee.
5. Barbara is unusually tall for her age.
6. Many of the buildings in this complex are new.
7. The express train seems late tonight.
8. The President appeared nervous in his first debate.
9. Until it was washed, this sweater felt roomy.
10. Your lettering on the poster is very colorful.

19.5 Subject Complements (Predicate Nouns and Pronouns, Predicate Adjectives) • **Practice 2**

▶ **Exercise 1** **Recognizing Predicate Nouns and Pronouns.** In each of the following sentences, underline the predicate noun or predicate pronoun.

EXAMPLE: That yellow shrub is a <u>forsythia</u>.

1. The capital of New Jersey is Trenton.
2. Peter Taylor is a notable short-story writer.
3. At this time Sheila appears to be the front-runner.
4. According to legend Prometheus was a Titan.
5. That young woman may someday become a fine doctor.
6. Many years ago Simla was the capital of British India.
7. Carlos and Juan have remained buddies for years.
8. The last person in line is she.
9. My favorite sport has always been basketball.
10. That camera was an excellent choice.
11. The koala is a small bearlike animal of Australia.
12. Helen is Antoinette's first cousin.
13. Darla has become the best soccer player on the team.
14. Katie seems the leader of the group.
15. Raymond was always a very funny guy.

▶ **Exercise 2** **Recognizing Predicate Adjectives.** In each of the following sentences, underline the predicate adjective.

EXAMPLE: The sky is <u>murky</u>.

1. The scent of the flowers is very sweet.
2. Many of the houses are quite old.
3. I felt sad about his misfortune.
4. At night this road becomes particularly dangerous.
5. The smoke from the fire remained heavy.
6. This chemical smells stronger than any other.
7. The view from the mountaintop was breathtaking.
8. The old windmill in Aruba is very attractive.
9. The carton seems too heavy to carry.
10. He has always been honest about his shortcomings.
11. That palm tree is unusually tall.
12. Those dance steps look extremely difficult.
13. The morning dew on the grass was quite beautiful.
14. Edward's editorial seems too harsh.
15. The butterfly is amazingly colorful.

19.5 Subject Complements (Compound Subject Complements) • Practice 1

Compound Subject Complements   Subject complements can be compound. A compound subject complement consists of two or more predicate nouns, pronouns, or adjectives.

COMPOUND SUBJECT COMPLEMENTS

<u>   </u> PN   PN
 My two favorite <u>subjects</u> <u><u>are</u></u> math and English .
                      PPN   PPN
 The <u>speakers</u> at graduation <u><u>will be</u></u> she and I .
             PA   PA
 His <u>voice</u> tonight <u><u>seems</u></u> deep and impressive .

▷ **Exercise 1**   **Recognizing Compound Subject Complements.**   Underline the compound subject complement in each sentence. If it consists of predicate nouns, label it *PN*. If it consists of predicate pronouns, label it *PPN*. If it consists of predicate adjectives, label it *PA*.

EXAMPLE: His small room is <u>dark</u> and <u>unpleasant</u>. ___*PA*___

1. The two members of my committee are Les and Sheila. _____
2. I think the winning teams will be they and we. _____
3. The top-rated cars were a sedan and an SUV. _____
4. Until the end, her dance seemed graceful and well executed. _____
5. Unfortunately, it is she and I who resisted. _____
6. This rare stamp must be old and valuable. _____
7. From the box your present is either a camera or a clock radio. _____
8. The strange flower was yellow and orange. _____
9. The finalist must be either he or she. _____
10. Is this telescope Japanese or German? _____

▷ **Exercise 2**   **Using Compound Subject Complements in Sentences.**   Fill in the blanks in each sentence with appropriate subject complements. The words in the parentheses will tell you which type to use.

EXAMPLE: (pred. adj.) Her hair is ___*auburn*___ and ___*silky*___ .

1. (pred. noun) My favorite actors are _____ and _____ .
2. (pred. adj.) In the morning the sea was _____ and _____ .
3. (pred. pron.) In the race the winners should be _____ and _____ .
4. (pred. noun) She was elected _____ and _____ .
5. (pred. adj.) This new camera seems _____ and _____ .
6. (pred. pron.) It is _____ and _____ who will go.
7. (pred. noun) The two books I remember best are _____ and _____ .
8. (pred. adj.) Are you _____ or _____ now?
9. (pred. pron.) The best artists in the class are _____ and _____ .
10. (pred. noun) The two desserts that we will serve at the party are _____ and _____ .

19.5 Subject Complements (Compound Subject Complements) • Practice 2

▶ **Exercise 1** **Recognizing Compound Subject Complements.** In the following sentences, underline each part of each compound subject complement. If a compound subject complement is made up of predicate adjectives, draw arrows pointing from each adjective to the subject.

EXAMPLE: The icing was <u>rich</u> and <u>sweet</u>.

1. Vacations in state parks can be interesting and inexpensive.

2. My favorite poets are Emily Dickinson and Langston Hughes.

3. The old bridge seems frail and dangerous.

4. The organizers of the crafts fair were Sonia and I.

5. That imported cheese tastes moldy and much too strong.

6. This fish is either flounder or sole.

7. Are the sails strong and seaworthy?

8. Their hands became raw and frostbitten in the icy wind.

9. The soup is neither too hot nor too cold.

10. The flame turned first orange, then blue.

▶ **Writing Application** **Writing Sentences with Subject Complements.** Use the following subjects and verbs to write sentences of your own. Include in each sentence the type of subject complement given in parentheses.

EXAMPLE: poem was (compound predicate adjectives)
     The poem was short but moving.

1. feet feel (predicate adjective)

   _____

2. Bob and Stan will be (predicate noun)

   _____

3. captains are (compound predicate pronouns)

   _____

4. dog is (compound predicate adjectives)

   _____

5. roast beef looks (predicate adjective)

   _____

Prepositional Phrases • Practice 1

Prepositional Phrases That Act as Adjectives A phrase is a group of words, without a subject and verb, that functions in a sentence as a single part of speech. An adjective phrase is a prepositional phrase that modifies a noun or pronoun.

ADJECTIVE PHRASES
The car *with the blue top* is my father's (*Which* car?)
I rented the room *in the attic.* (*Which* room?)

Prepositional Phrases That Act as Adverbs An adverb phrase is a prepositional phrase that modifies a verb, adjective, or adverb by pointing out where, when, in what manner, or to what extent.

ADVERB PHRASES
At dawn we drove *across the state.* (Drove *when?* Drove *where?*)
They are pleased *at my victory.* (Pleased *in what manner?*)

Exercise 1 **Identifying Adjective Phrases.** Underline each adjective phrase in the sentences below and circle the word it modifies.

EXAMPLE: I bought a (lamp) with a red shade.

1. I ordered a pancake with maple syrup.
2. A book without any illustration may be very interesting.
3. This is the new road to the state park.
4. The sound of the rain on the roof is very loud.
5. Mimi just read a book about Winston Churchill.
6. The winter coat in the closet no longer fits.
7. An investigator uncovered a file of important papers.
8. Strawberries with cream is grandmother's favorite.
9. When did the car in the driveway arrive?
10. I just lost my list of errands.

Exercise 2 **Identifying Adverb Phrases.** Underline each adverb phrase and circle the word it modifies.

EXAMPLE: In the breadbox you (will find) three rolls.

1. The heavy snow stopped in the late morning.
2. The teacher was disturbed at Bob's attitude.
3. Without their help we could never have finished the job.
4. The entire trial was completed in two weeks.
5. My parents left for their vacation a week later.
6. At two the post office reopened for business.
7. Foolishly, the fullback charged into Southside's huge line.
8. In a year a new bridge was built.
9. Yes, I certainly am ready for a good lunch.
10. Our basketball team practiced late into the night.

20.1 **Prepositional Phrases • Practice 2**

▶ **Exercise 1** **Identifying Adjective Phrases.** Each of the following sentences contains at least one prepositional phrase used as an adjective. Underline each adjective phrase and draw an arrow pointing from it to the word it modifies.

EXAMPLE: The room in the back is very damp.

1. Mr. Suarez bought a new car with a sun roof.

2. The book about Eleanor Roosevelt is inspiring.

3. Mary is the supervisor of all the nurses.

4. The house near the top of the hill has been sold.

5. The tree in the corner of the yard is a weeping cherry.

6. This is the way to the shopping mall.

7. The autographed picture of Reggie Jackson is one of my treasures.

8. The carton of eggs at the bottom of the bag has been crushed.

9. The captain of the precinct gave a talk about gun control.

10. The front steps of many houses in Baltimore are white marble.

▶ **Exercise 2** **Identifying Adverb Phrases.** Each sentence contains at least one prepositional phrase used as an adverb. Underline each adverb phrase and draw an arrow pointing from it to the word it modifies.

EXAMPLE: With increasing excitement she read the last chapter.

1. Our scout troop hiked through the forest.

2. At the traffic light, the road curves to the left.

3. They arrived early in the day.

4. Susan is upset about her science grades.

5. At the zoo many kinds of animals live in harmony.

20.1 Participles in Phrases (Participles, Verb or Participle?) • Practice 1

Participles   A participle is a form of a verb that acts as an adjective. There are two kinds of participles: present participles and past participles.

Present Participles	Past Participles
A *smiling* pupil received an award.	I can repair the *broken* watch.
Jogging, he reached a park.	*Finished*, we left for home.

Verb or Participle?   Verb phrases and participles are sometimes confused. When a participle comes after a helping verb it is part of a verb phrase. A participle used as an adjective stands by itself and modifies a noun or pronoun.

Verb Phrases	Participles
A child *was crying*.	I heard a *crying* child.
Bill *has been elected*.	Bill is our *elected* captain.

Exercise 1   **Identifying Present and Past Participles.**   Underline the participle in each sentence below. If it is a present participle, write *present*; if it is a past participle, write *past*.

EXAMPLE: The waiting bus suddenly left. _____*present*_____

1. Can you find a new reading exercise? _____
2. Mrs. Jones is a paid volunteer. _____
3. Laughing, the boys raced across the court. _____
4. We all agree that this is a growing problem. _____
5. Who is our chosen representative? _____

Exercise 2   **Distinguishing Between Verbs and Participles.**   Identify each of the underlined words as either a *verb* or *participle*. If the word is a participle, circle the word it modifies.

EXAMPLE: Yes, this is a growing (problem). _____*participle*_____

1. My uncle has been taken to the hospital. _____
2. The director decided to join the planning board. _____
3. Digging, she found a large metal trunk. _____
4. The scrubbed child looked strangely pale. _____
5. We are going to the concert this weekend. _____
6. The reference book was opened to the final chapter. _____
7. She made a highly praised speech. _____
8. Lewis was carefully pouring oil into the saucepan. _____
9. Bob, a good athlete, has been training daily. _____
10. Have you completed the assignment yet? _____

20.1 Participles in Phrases (Participles, Verb or Participle?) • Practice 2

Exercise 1 **Identifying Present and Past Participles.** Underline the participle in each sentence. Then write whether the participle is *past* or *present*.

EXAMPLE: The cracked vase cannot be repaired. _____past_____

1. A raging snowstorm struck the city. _____
2. Disturbed, she consulted her doctor about the symptoms. _____
3. The police shed a glaring light on the robber. _____
4. Singing, she stepped from the shower. _____
5. The frozen pipe burst. _____
6. Have you repaired the broken lamp? _____
7. I have used reading glasses for some time now. _____
8. The story of the haunted house was very popular. _____
9. Did you find the finished copies of the term paper? _____
10. Laughing, she bowed several times to the audience. _____
11. The trusting child held out her hand. _____
12. Donna dropped the freshly laundered shirts in the dirt. _____
13. My newly purchased silk shirt faded in the sunlight. _____
14. The wandering minstrel stopped at the inn. _____
15. The shivering dog could not find its way home. _____

Exercise 2 **Distinguishing Between Verbs and Participles.** Identify each underlined word as a *verb* or a *participle*. If the word is a participle, circle the word it modifies.

EXAMPLE: They found the written (test) easy to do. _____participle_____

1. The doctor is talking to a patient. _____
2. She has a growing understanding of the problem. _____
3. A broken window was part of the evidence. _____
4. Brian has finally chosen a topic for his report. _____
5. Do you have a thick marking pen? _____
6. We drove past a deserted railroad terminal. _____
7. In exchange she is asking for another radio. _____
8. I bought three pounds of ripened cheese. _____
9. She is always playing Mozart on her violin. _____
10. The prisoner was brought before the judge. _____
11. After oversleeping, I missed my appointment. _____
12. In her diary, I read about her forgotten dreams. _____
13. The frogs had been jumping from place to place. _____
14. What is the name of that brightly shining star? _____
15. Cindy could not stop smiling on that day. _____

20.1 Participles in Phrases (Participial Phrases)
• Practice 1

Participial Phrases A participial phrase is a present or past participle that is modified by an adverb or adverb phrase or that has a complement. The entire phrase acts as an adjective in a sentence.

Participial Phrases
Dancing smoothly, Margie easily won the contest.
Carl, *chosen by his class*, will go to the fair.
Mary, *finishing her paper*, would not come to the phone.

▶ **Exercise 1** **Recognizing Participial Phrases.** Underline each participial phrase in the sentences below and circle the noun or pronoun it modifies.

EXAMPLE: Driving carefully, (we) reached the school.

1. The company, paid by mail, failed to deliver the item.
2. Given any excuse, Tommy will tell a joke.
3. The reader, troubled by the article, wrote to the paper.
4. Shouting wildly, the team attached the goalpost.
5. Collecting stamps for years, Grandfather sold his collection.
6. His money, earned at part-time jobs, helped pay for the trip.
7. Involved in the book, Paul did not hear the bell.
8. Sketching in the background, the artist quickly finished.
9. The horses, standing in a row, kept inching forward.
10. Proceeding slowly, the governor shook everyone's hand.

▶ **Exercise 2** **Using Participles in Sentences.** Use the following participial phrases in original sentences. Make certain the phrase stands right in front or right after the noun it modifies.

EXAMPLE: given a job
          Given a job, Ted always does his best.

1. elected president _____
2. driving cautiously _____
3. asking a question _____
4. involved in the movie _____
5. assisted by a student _____
6. training daily _____
7. broken in half _____
8. urged to explain _____
9. playing her clarinet _____
10. camped in the mountains _____

20.1 Participles in Phrases (Participial Phrases)
• Practice 2

▶ **Exercise 1** **Recognizing Participial Phrases.**   Each of the following sentences contains a participial phrase. Underline each participial phrase and draw an arrow pointing from it to the word it modifies.

EXAMPLE: The frontier, spreading out endlessly to the west, excited the pioneers.

1. The plant, growing slowly, finally bloomed in June.

2. Chosen by the principal, Marie represented our school.

3. My father, walking the dog, met an old friend.

4. Laughing loudly, she ran from the room.

5. The coin, found in a cellar, proved to be valuable.

6. Telling her strange story, she began to giggle.

7. The detective, watching the suspect, discovered a clue.

8. Scolded by his father, he left the house and took a walk.

9. The students, listening carefully, followed the instructions perfectly.

10. The clipper, sailing majestically, reached the harbor in two hours.

▶ **Writing Application**   **Writing Sentences with Participial Phrases.**   Write an original sentence using each of the following participial phrases.

EXAMPLE: hitting a home run
              Hitting a home run, Chris tied the score.

1. speaking slowly

   _____

2. reminded twice

   _____

3. opening the door

   _____

4. moving very slowly

   _____

5. followed by a puppy

   _____

20.1 Appositives in Phrases • Practice 1

Appositives   An appositive is a noun or pronoun placed next to another noun or pronoun to identify, rename, or explain it.

APPOSITIVES
Ron Burns, *a dentist*, was elected to the City Council
Ellen wants this pin, *a cameo*.

Appositive Phrases   An appositive phrase is an appositive with modifiers. It stands next to a noun or pronoun and adds information or details. Appositives and appositive phrases can also be compound.

APPOSITIVE PHRASES
This rug, *an imported Chinese masterpiece*, is very expensive.
I admire my cousin Sue, *a highly talented artist*.

▶ **Exercise 1**   **Identifying Appositives and Appositive Phrases.**   Underline each appositive or appositive phrase and circle the word it renames.

EXAMPLE: I spoke to (Mr. Hartmann), the principal.

1. His favorite team, the Boston Celtics, always seems to win.
2. Sally's essay, a paper on the environment, needs some more work.
3. Your recipe, a favorite of your uncle's, is too rich.
4. I carefully examined the used car, a Plymouth.
5. She reported on the Gilbert Islands, a group of atolls in the Pacific.
6. Mozart, a musical genius, only lived to be thirty-six.
7. We all praised the letter, a magnificent piece of work.
8. Grace Willis, a graphic artist, will lecture to our class.
9. *Citizen Kane*, an early film by Orson Welles, has become a legend.
10. Marie chose her graduation presents, a pearl necklace and a gold watch.

▶ **Exercise 2**   **Using Appositives and Appositive Phrases in Sentences.**   Add an appositive or an appositive phrase in the space provided in each sentence.

EXAMPLE: I spoke to Dr. Brown, _____*a famous surgeon.*_____

1. I think I know Keith, _____
2. This novel, _____, is well written.
3. She will order her favorite dessert, _____.
4. Washington, D.C., _____, has many hotels.
5. My father, _____, has always been helpful.

20.1 Appositives in Phrases • Practice 2

▷ **Exercise 1** **Identifying Appositives and Appositive Phrases.** In the following sentences, underline each appositive or appositive phrase and draw an arrow pointing from it to the noun or pronoun it renames.

EXAMPLE: Gwendolyn Brooks, an American poet, grew up on Chicago's South Side.

1. Our math teacher, Mrs. Cruz, helped us solve a puzzle.

2. Two O. Henry stories, "The Gift of the Magi" and "The Last Leaf," are my personal favorites.

3. Two low-calorie vegetables, kale and bean sprouts, are highly recommended.

4. George Patton, a general in World War II, was the subject of a prize-winning film.

5. The book *The Matarese Circle* pits an American spy against a Russian.

▷ **Writing Application** **Writing Sentences With Appositives.** Use the following words or phrases as appositives in your own sentences.

EXAMPLE: a real mistake
_____ *His choice, a real mistake, was greeted with laughter.* _____

1. a fine teacher
_____

2. the captain
_____

3. a good driver
_____

4. my oldest friend
_____

5. a fascinating book
_____

6. my favorite team
_____

7. a restaurant in town
_____

8. a beautiful song
_____

9. a luscious dessert
_____

10. a town landmark
_____

20.1 # Gerunds in Phrases • Practice 1

Gerunds   A gerund is a form of verb that acts as a noun. Gerunds can be used as subjects, direct objects, predicate nouns, and objects of prepositions.

GERUNDS
Swimming is my favorite activity. (*Swimming* is the subject.)
I always enjoy *swimming*. (*Swimming* is the direct object.)

Gerund Phrases   A *gerund phrase* is a gerund with modifiers or a complement, all acting together as a noun.

GERUND PHRASES
Swimming every day is a regular activity. (Gerund phrase used as subject.)
I enjoy *swimming fast*. (Gerund phrase used as direct object.)

▶ **Exercise 1**   **Recognizing Gerunds and Gerund Phrases.**   Underline the gerund or gerund phrase in each sentence. In the space provided tell how it is used.

EXAMPLE: The counselor cautioned us against smoking. ___*obj. of prep.*___

1. Working hard is often its own reward. _____

2. My mother always enjoys driving. _____

3. I know people who are obsessed with eating all the time. _____

4. Groping in the dark is not my idea of fun. _____

5. It seems that his favorite activity is sleeping. _____

6. I don't believe in choosing sides. _____

7. Practicing lacrosse is all Willie does. _____

8. My father's job is managing the New York office. _____

9. Young people used to dream about making movies. _____

10. Yes, I began cleaning my room this morning. _____

▶ **Exercise 2**   **Using Gerunds and Gerund Phrases in Sentences.**   Write original sentences that use the gerunds or gerund phrases below.

EXAMPLE: growing tall
       Growing tall is his major goal.

1. driving to school _____

2. making excuses _____

3. laughing _____

4. baking chocolate chip cookies _____

5. cheating _____

20.1 Gerunds in Phrases • Practice 2

▷ **Exercise 1** **Identifying Gerunds.** Each of the following sentences contains one gerund. Underline the gerund in each sentence. Then write whether it is used as a *subject*, *direct object*, *predicate noun*, or *object of a preposition*.

EXAMPLE: <u>Dancing</u> is her favorite pastime. _____*subject*_____

1. Walking is excellent exercise. _____
2. My little sister observes my birthday by phoning. _____
3. This plant needs pruning. _____
4. Love is caring, and I always try to show I care. _____
5. Speeding led to the loss of her driver's license. _____
6. Our goal has always been winning. _____
7. Don't you ever get tired of studying? _____
8. Exercising is one way to burn up calories. _____
9. After several months Frank's grandmother stopped writing. _____
10. The team finished practicing at five o'clock. _____

▷ **Exercise 2** **Identifying Gerund Phrases.** Underline each gerund phrase. Then write whether the gerund phrase is used as a *subject*, *direct object*, *predicate noun*, or *object of a preposition*.

EXAMPLE: His favorite pastime was <u>writing limericks</u>. _____*predicate noun*_____

1. Drinking large amounts of water can help clear the kidneys. _____
2. His favorite hobby is raising guppies. _____
3. A loud knocking interrupted their dinner. _____
4. Nothing can be gained by choosing sides. _____
5. He enjoys composing all sorts of music. _____
6. The secretary kept perfect records by writing the dates of each event. _____
7. Insulating older homes helps conserve energy. _____
8. Tourists at the Acropolis are warned against taking stones for souvenirs. _____
9. Traveling by air is the fastest way to get there. _____
10. My plans for vacation include redecorating my room. _____

▷ **Writing Application** **Writing Sentences With Gerund Phrases.** Use each of the gerund phrases in an original sentence according to the instructions in parentheses.

EXAMPLE: singing in the shower (as a subject)
_____*Singing in the shower was her vocal exercise.*_____

1. driving too fast (as the object of a preposition)

_____

2. exercising in the morning (as a subject)

_____

3. collecting stamps and coins (as a direct object)

_____

4. cleaning her room thoroughly (as the object of a preposition)

_____

5. raising animals (as a subject)

_____

20.1 Infinitives in Phrases • Practice 1

Three Uses of Infinitives   An infinitive is the form of a verb that comes after the word *to* and acts as a noun, adjective, or adverb.

INFINITIVES
I want *to succeed*. (Used as a noun, the direct object)
The man *to see* is Dr. Chu. (Used as an adjective)
She is happy *to go*. (Used as an adverb)

Infinitive Phrases   An infinitive phrase is an infinitive with modifiers or a complement, all working as a single part of speech.

INFINITIVE PHRASES
I want *to succeed in high school*. (Used as a noun, the direct object)
The man *to see today* is Dr. Chu. (Used as an adjective)
She is happy *to go with us*. (Used as an adverb)

▷ **Exercise 1**   **Recognizing Infinitives and Infinitive Phrases.**   Underline the infinitive or infinitive phrase in each sentence. In the space provided, tell whether it is used as a noun, adjective, or adverb.

EXAMPLE: To win is not that important. _____noun_____

1. Louise decided to go tomorrow. _____
2. Her desire to act is very strong. _____
3. This new novel is easy to read. _____
4. To reach the high school is not that simple. _____
5. We expect to drive to Baltimore. _____
6. They are too lazy to walk to school. _____
7. The place to visit is the Library of Congress. _____
8. Her idea of breakfast is to have a cup of coffee. _____
9. To reach that number is not possible on this phone. _____
10. He had no choice except to go. _____

▷ **Exercise 2**   **Using Infinitives and Infinitive Phrases in Sentences.**   Write original sentences that use the infinitive or infinitive phrases below.

EXAMPLE: to wait for friends
_____*I have to wait for friends.*_____

1. to buy a backpack _____
2. to talk endlessly _____
3. to practice _____
4. to listen carefully _____
5. to open a window _____

20.1 Infinitives in Phrases • Practice 2

▶ **Exercise 1** **Identifying Infinitives.** Underline the infinitive in each of the following sentences.

EXAMPLE: They were always eager to answer.

1. She wants to go.
2. Impossible to miss, the monument is right on the lake.
3. The recipe to try is on the package itself.
4. To listen is not easy with that uproar.
5. He wanted nothing except to sleep.
6. The librarian was happy to help.
7. His greatest wish, to fly, was never fulfilled.
8. This is the best reference book to consult.
9. Susan's dream is to dance.
10. To whistle is difficult for some people.

▶ **Exercise 2** **Identifying Infinitive Phrases.** Underline each infinitive phrase.

EXAMPLE: To reach the peak was not possible in the blizzard.

1. To graduate a year early is my goal.
2. The teacher to ask for a reference is Miss Stevens.
3. I find it difficult to talk with strangers.
4. Her ambition is to direct a musical at school.
5. This is an offer to take very seriously.
6. To get home during the storm was quite difficult.
7. Our plan was to reach southern Maine by noon.
8. She was told to reorganize her composition.
9. The person to ask about that is James.
10. They want to wait another week before acting.

▶ **Writing Application** **Writing Sentences with Infinitive Phrases.** Write an original sentence using each of the following infinitive phrases according to the directions in parentheses.

EXAMPLE: to please Uncle Pete (as an adverb)
　　　　　　It was difficult to please Uncle Pete.

1. to succeed in English (as a subject at the beginning of the sentence)

   _____

2. to go into business (as a direct object with the verb *want*)

   _____

3. to reach the station (as an adverb after the adjective *easy*)

   _____

4. to become a lawyer (as a predicate noun after the verb *is*)

   _____

5. to ask for advice (as an adjective after the noun *teacher*)

   _____

Adjective Clauses (Recognizing Adjective Clauses)
• Practice 1

Recognizing Adjective Clauses A clause is a group of words with its own subject and verb. An independent clause has a subject and a verb and can stand by itself as a complete sentence. A subordinate clause has a subject and a verb but cannot stand by itself in a sentence. It is only part of a sentence. An *adjective clause* is a subordinate clause that modifies a noun or pronoun. Adjective clauses answer the questions *What kind?* or *Which one?* Most adjective clauses begin with one of the relative pronouns: *that, which, who, whom,* and *whose.* They can also begin with such words as *when, since,* or *where.*

ADJECTIVE CLAUSES
This is the statue *that he wrote about.*
The girl *whom we chose* is on the honor role.
In the days *since the accident occurred* the family has remained indoors.

▶ **Exercise 1** **Identifying Adjective Clauses.** Underline the adjective clause in each sentence, and circle the word it modifies.

EXAMPLE: The (ring) that you ordered is not available.

1. This is a day that we will all remember.

2. A painting which everyone dislikes was removed from the hall.

3. He is a man who someday may be our governor.

4. The Korean War, which dragged on for three long years, finally ended in 1953.

5. There was a time when I drove to the country each summer.

6. Fritz Kreisler, the famous violinist who was a child prodigy, also studied medicine and art.

7. The girl whose wallet I found has been absent for a week.

8. Cracow, which is also spelled Krakow, is a city in Poland.

9. Have you met the candidate whom he wants to nominate?

10. We have had three responses in the time since we placed the advertisement.

▶ **Exercise 2** **Writing Sentences With Adjective Clauses.** Add an adjective clause in each sentence below.

EXAMPLE: The book _____that I need now_____ was taken from the library.

1. This is the house _____ .

2. The teacher whom _____ just resigned.

3. Do you know the girl _____ ?

4. The report _____ is not accurate.

5. Here is a musician _____ .

6. The president _____ is George Washington.

7. A teacher whose _____ was Mrs. Gordon.

8. I know a doctor _____ .

9. This is the book _____ .

10. She remembers the store _____ .

20.2 # Adjective Clauses (Recognizing Adjective Clauses)
• Practice 2

▷ **Exercise 1** **Identifying Adjective Clauses.** Each of the following sentences contains an adjective clause. Underline each adjective clause and circle the word each clause modifies.

EXAMPLE: I like science fiction (books) that are believable.

1. The tailor who shortened my skirt is very reasonable.
2. This museum, which is described in our travel guide, was built in 1876.
3. The man whose dictionary I borrowed is a retired teacher.
4. Have you found a show that you would like to see?
5. In the month since he had the accident, his condition has improved greatly.
6. Have you visited the plaza where the statue was dedicated?
7. The painter whom she most admires is Georgia O'Keeffe.
8. The book that you wanted is no longer in print.
9. A play that I particularly liked was *All My Sons*.
10. That package, which just arrived, is for you.
11. Lavender, which is Kay's favorite color, is used throughout Kay's home.
12. The leash that I bought yesterday is too short for my dog.
13. Diane, whose laughter you can hear right now, is a very happy person.
14. The leather bag that fell into the river was holding my cell phone.
15. Would you like to help me with this jigsaw puzzle, which Wendy started?
16. One juror, who wishes to avoid publicity, changed everyone else's minds.
17. What punishment would fit the crime that this person committed?
18. The quizzical look that you see on your dog's face is very interesting.
19. Her pulse, which was very faint, could be heard only with special instruments.
20. The product that brings the store the most money is this cheap toy.

▷ **Exercise 2** **Writing Sentences With Adjective Clauses.** Add an adjective clause to complete each of the following sentences.

EXAMPLE: This is the room that has been completely redecorated.

1. Have you read the book _____
2. I am expecting my cousin _____
3. From the cliffs you can see a view _____
4. Donald bought a new software program _____
5. Susan pushed the stroller _____
6. We walked through the rose garden _____
7. Dustin went to the antique car show _____
8. I finally bought the jacket _____
9. Bruce ordered a copy of the movie _____
10. This is Adelle _____

Adjective Clauses (Combining Sentences with Adjective Clauses) • Practice 1

Combining Sentences with Adjective Clauses   Two sentences sometimes can be combined into one by changing one of them into an adjective clause. Such a combination is particularly useful when the information in both sentences is closely related.

COMBINING SENTENCES
Dr. Samuel Mudd set the broken leg of Lincoln's assassin. He was later sentenced to life imprisonment for this act. Dr. Samuel Mudd, *who set the broken leg of Lincoln's assassin*, was later sentenced to life imprisonment for this act.

▶ **Exercise 1**   **Combining Sentences With Adjective Clauses.**   Each item below contains two sentences. Change one of them into an adjective clause and combine it with the other sentence. You may change some words.

EXAMPLE: Enrico Caruso is considered the greatest operatic tenor of all time. He made his New York debut in 1903.

 Enrico Caruso, who made his New York debut in 1903, is considered the

 greatest operatic tenor of all time.

1. Bill Bradley was a United States Senator from New Jersey. He once had been an outstanding basketball player with the New York Knicks.

 _____

 _____

2. Casablanca is a port city in Morocco. President Roosevelt and Prime Minister Winston Churchill met there in 1943.

 _____

 _____

3. Castor oil is pressed from the castor bean. It is used for brake fluid and paints and as a general lubricant.

 _____

 _____

▶ **Exercise 2**   **Combining More Sentences With Adjective Clauses.**   Follow the directions in Exercise 1.

1. The Organization of American States (OAS) helps promote economic progress in the Americas. It was organized in 1948.

 _____

 _____

2. Soho is a district in West London in Great Britain. It is noted for its Italian and French restaurants.

 _____

 _____

20.2 Adjective Clauses (Combining Sentences with Adjective Clauses) • Practice 2

▶ **Exercise 1** **Using Adjective Clauses to Combine Sentences.**   Change the second sentence in each of the following groups into an adjective clause. Then make the adjective clause part of the first sentence. You will need to add a comma before and after each of these adjective clauses.

EXAMPLE: Phillis Wheatley was an early American poet. She was born in Africa.
_____ *Phillis Wheatley, who was born in Africa, was an early American poet.* _____

1. John Steinbeck wrote The Grapes of Wrath and The Pearl. He won the Nobel Prize in 1962.
_____

2. Albany has changed greatly through the years. It boasts the lavish Empire State Plaza.
_____

3. This hotel room will be more expensive. It has a view of the mountains.
_____

4. Katharine Hepburn won an Academy Award for her performance in The Lion in Winter. Her film career spanned fifty years.
_____

5. My mother recently bought a small economy car. She had always preferred large sedans.
_____

6. The earthquake caused severe damage to the area. It struck at 5:03 in the morning.
_____

7. The quality of this lace is very fine. It was made in Belgium.
_____

8. Maddy and Louise finally agreed. They had argued for at least two hours.
_____

9. This pumpkin will surely win the prize. It weighs almost eight hundred pounds.
_____

10. The marionettes were used to tell a touching story. They are operated by strings.
_____

▶ **Writing Application** **Writing Sentences With Adjective Clauses.**   Write five sentences containing adjective clauses, as specified. Underline each adjective clause and circle the word it modifies.

EXAMPLE: Write a sentence with a clause that begins with *whom.*
Thomas (Jefferson) , whom we know mainly as a statesman, was also a talented architect.

1. Write a sentence with a clause that begins with *who.*
_____

2. Write a sentence with a clause that begins with *that.*
_____

3. Write a sentence with a clause that begins with *which.*
_____

4. Write a sentence with a clause that begins with *whose.*
_____

5. Write a sentence with a clause that begins with *whom.*
_____

20.2 # Adverb Clauses (Recognizing Adverb Clauses)
• Practice 1

Recognizing Adverb Clauses   An adverb clause is a subordinate clause that modifies a verb, an adjective, or an adverb. Adverb clauses begin with subordinate conjunctions such as *as, although, since, when, if,* and *because.* Adverb clauses tell when, where, how, why, or to what extent.

Adverb Clauses
Chuck cannot go *since he has not finished his chores.*
Because she has been ill, Lisa takes a nap every day.
This trick is easier *when you practice it for a while.*
The book ends better *than I expected.*

▶ **Exercise 1**   **Identifying Adverb Clauses.**   Underline the adverb clause in each sentence. Circle the verb, adjective, or adverb it modifies.

EXAMPLE: I (came) because I was asked.

1. If the roads are sanded, we will leave immediately.

2. I am often tired after I work a six-day week.

3. His new idea sounds as if it might actually work.

4. My haircut and shampoo took longer than I had imagined.

5. Whenever I visit a museum, I greatly enjoy the exhibits.

6. Her apartment will be brighter when she repaints it.

7. Wait where I can signal you from the window.

8. Because he lied in court, his sentence was longer.

9. My brother was upset when I phoned from the station.

10. While you wait, the artist will complete your portrait.

▶ **Exercise 2**   **Writing Sentences With Adverb Clauses.**   Add an adverb clause in each sentence below.

EXAMPLE: _____*When I get your message*_____ , I will leave.

1. I will not make any plans _____.

2. _____ , Bill has been unable to work.

3. Your job will be easier _____.

4. Mom will pick up your photos _____.

5. My class lasted longer _____.

6. I will finish my homework early _____.

7. _____ , your room will look neater.

8. _____ , the teacher will consider changing your grade.

9. As soon as my aunt phoned from Los Angeles, _____.

10. I was much happier _____.

Name _____ Date _____

20.2 Adverb Clauses (Recognizing Adverb Clauses)
• Practice 2

▶ **Exercise 1**   **Identifying Adverb Clauses.**   Each of the following sentences contains an adverb clause. Underline each adverb clause and circle the verb, adjective, or adverb each clause modifies.

EXAMPLE: Before Pearl Buck married, her name (was) Pearl Sydenstricker.

1. Before we left on vacation, we took the dogs to the kennel.
2. Although you have explained your reasons, I must vote according to my own beliefs.
3. The plant will thrive as long as you do not overwater it.
4. The baby is sleepier than I have ever seen her.
5. If you can make the trip, you will enjoy the scenery.
6. Barbara reads more rapidly than anyone in our class.
7. I finished dinner at seven so that I could watch the movie.
8. My best friend is much wiser than most of us ever realized.
9. She acted as if she didn't expect to win the scholarship.
10. While I generally respect your ideas, I cannot agree with your present plan.
11. Whenever we go to the shore, I remember Emilia and her shell collection.
12. Let's stay outside until the sun goes down.
13. Unless you hear otherwise, just plan on meeting us at eleven o'clock.
14. I finished the project by myself because you failed to show up.
15. Since the two girls met, they have been close friends.
16. In order that everyone will get a chance to play, the time limit is ten minutes.
17. Carmen bought the red paint even though Axel didn't like the color.
18. After she finished her homework, Cameron played some basketball.
19. Wherever Mary went, her lambs followed.
20. When the moon comes over the mountain, look for me.

▶ **Exercise 2**   **Using Adverb Clauses in Sentences.**   Add an adverb clause to complete each of the following sentences.

EXAMPLE: He laughed when his best friend told a boring joke.

1. Ethel wanted that red coat _____
2. James tried out for soccer _____
3. Peggy danced _____
4. We'll play this game _____
5. The children looked for pretty shells _____
6. I am practicing two hours a day _____
7. Look at the bright side _____
8. Give me a smile _____
9. He will keep on driving _____
10. The detective followed the tall man _____

90 • Grammar Exercise Workbook   © Prentice-Hall, Inc.

20.2 Adverb Clauses (Elliptical Adverb Clauses)
• Practice 1

Elliptical Adverb Clauses In certain adverb clauses, words are left out. These clauses are said to be elliptical. In an elliptical adverb clause, the verb or the subject and verb are understood rather than actually stated.

| ELLIPTICAL ADVERB CLAUSES | |
Elliptical	Completely Written Out
Mark is older *than Bill*.	Mark is older *than Bill (is old)*.
My parents gave more to him *than to me*.	My parents gave more to him *than (they gave) to me*.
My sister is as tall *as I*.	My sister is as tall *as I (am tall)*.

▶ **Exercise 1** **Recognizing Elliptical Clauses.** Underline each elliptical clause in the sentences below. In the space provided write out what is missing from the clause.

EXAMPLE: My roast is better <u>than his</u>. ____*roast is*____

1. His explanation is just as likely as yours. _____

2. Lucy can run faster than Bill. _____

3. I think I understand him better than she. _____

4. Are they as lonely as I? _____

5. Our neighbors are much richer than we. _____

6. I know Barbara better than her. _____

7. The other team members were as angry as I. _____

8. Hank is always much later than Fred. _____

9. The guest spoke more to her than to me. _____

10. Do you think you are happier than she? _____

▶ **Exercise 2** **Writing Sentences Using Elliptical Clauses.** Use the elliptical clauses below in original sentences.

EXAMPLE: as humorous as I
_____*My friends say that Bobby is as humorous as I.*_____

1. than my father _____

2. as friendly as she _____

3. than they _____

4. as my friends _____

5. than she and I _____

6. hungrier than anyone else _____

7. than to me _____

8. more than she _____

9. as restless as he _____

10. than the principal _____

20.2 Adverb Clauses (Elliptical Adverb Clauses)
• Practice 2

▶ **Exercise 1** **Recognizing Elliptical Adverb Clauses.** Each of the following sentences contains an elliptical adverb clause. In the first column below the sentences, write the elliptical clause. In the second write out the full adverb clause, adding the understood words.

EXAMPLE: She is stronger than I.

Elliptical Clause	Full Clause
than I	than I am

1. Our sports car is faster than his.
2. This book is just as interesting as that one.
3. Mrs. Wilson is as pleasant as Miss Grogan.
4. Jennifer gave more to him than to her.
5. We are more willing to serve than they.
6. Sally has more talent than Esther.
7. This bracelet is much more appropriate than that one.
8. I would like to get a haircut as attractive as yours.
9. The small orchid costs as much as the larger one.
10. I like living here better than there.

Elliptical Clause   **Full Clause**

1. _____   _____
2. _____   _____
3. _____   _____
4. _____   _____
5. _____   _____
6. _____   _____
7. _____   _____
8. _____   _____
9. _____   _____
10. _____   _____

▶ **Writing Application** **Writing Sentences with Adverb Clauses.** Combine each of the following pairs of sentences into a single sentence by making one of them an adverb clause.

EXAMPLE: Joe stayed. The others went home.   _____after the others went home._____

1. She left the house early. She did not want to disturb anyone.

_____

2. You went into the kitchen. Did you notice anything new?

_____

3. Margie was very tired. She could not enjoy most of the game.

_____

4. Yeats first studied art. He soon realized that his real talents lay in writing poetry.

_____

5. We have finished all our homework. We want to go ice skating this afternoon.

_____

20.2 Classifying Sentences by Structure (Simple and Compound Sentences) • Practice 1

The Simple Sentence A simple sentence consists of a single independent clause. It must contain a subject and verb. Some simple sentences contain various compounds—a compound subject or a compound verb or both.

SIMPLE SENTENCES
This book is unusually interesting.
My brother and sister will arrive tomorrow.
He opened the package and found a new camera.

The Compound Sentence A compound sentence consists of two or more independent clauses. The independent clauses in a compound sentence are joined by a comma and one of the coordinating conjunctions: *and, but, nor, for, or, so, yet.* The two independent clauses can also be joined with a semicolon (;).

COMPOUND SENTENCES
This book is unusually interesting, and I will finish it tonight.
My brother will arrive tomorrow, but my sister will not come until Sunday.
He opened the package; it contained a new camera.

▶ **Exercise 1** **Examining Simple Sentences.** Each sentence below is a simple sentence. Underline all the subjects once and all the verbs twice.

EXAMPLE: Both bridges are under water and will not open.

1. The trains and the buses recently changed their schedules.

2. We reached the second traffic light and turned left.

3. Have you found the map to Albany yet?

4. Bill and Sue opened their gifts and examined them carefully.

5. Almost every afternoon my grandfather takes a nap.

▶ **Exercise 2** **Examining Compound Sentences.** Each sentence below is a compound sentence. Underline each subject once and each verb twice.

EXAMPLE: The bridge is down; all of the roads have been closed.

1. The situation is confusing, but I hope to have more news soon.

2. I hope to do better this year, and I am going to study regularly.

3. Movies are just great, but I still enjoy a good book often.

4. I have twenty compact disks; my brother has many more.

5. Tom and Steve will meet us at the game, or they will phone their regrets.

20.2 # Classifying Sentences by Structure (Simple and Compound Sentences) • Practice 2

▷ **Exercise 1**   **Recognizing Simple Sentences.**   In each of the following simple sentences, underline the subject once and the verb twice. Some of the subjects and verbs may be compound.

EXAMPLE: Many streets and schools are given the names of famous people.

1. He swam to the canoe and paddled the rest of the way to the shore.
2. Waiting near the bridge, we finally spotted the caravan of trucks.
3. Jennie passed French but failed algebra.
4. My mother, my father, and my sister all attended the play.
5. Both the bus and the taxi had engine trouble and arrived late.
6. Rubbing her elbow and wincing in pain, Ellen walked away from the accident.
7. Rodney is not only ambitious but hard-working as well.
8. The ambulance raced down the street and headed toward the hospital.
9. Caught with the evidence, Karen confessed.
10. Though just an amateur, Wilma trains like a professional.
11. Sylvia could not hide her admiration for Mr. Williams.
12. Hank played with the band in the afternoon and marched in a parade that night.
13. Corn, wheat, and rye are grown on the plains of America.
14. I agree with John and Charles and plan to support them in the debate.
15. Mike and Suzie began their adventure with a hike to the waterfall.

▷ **Exercise 2**   **Recognizing Compound Sentences.**   In each of the following compound sentences, underline the subject once and the verb twice in each independent clause.

EXAMPLE: Bolivia has no seacoast; Paraguay is also landlocked.

1. Our first stop was the port of Hamilton in Bermuda; our second stop was at Nassau in the Bahamas.
2. Several tiles fell off the space shuttle during liftoff, but the craft nonetheless landed safely.
3. Susan baked the bread, and Ron prepared the salad.
4. Your argument is weak, for you have no proof to support your ideas.
5. Many islands dot the coast of Yugoslavia, yet few of them have inhabitants.
6. Colleen's ancestors came from Ireland; Bobby's family came from France.
7. Stephen studied long hours, but he never did enjoy that subject.
8. Angela has a cocker spaniel, and Agnes has a poodle.
9. You deserve this piano, for you have practiced daily for two years.
10. The sky was full of threatening dark clouds, yet it never rained.
11. Sharon will go to Kate's house, or Kate will come to hers.
12. We shopped for weeks for camping gear, for we were planning a long trip.
13. Rhoda and Jean were close friends; they did everything together.
14. Emma planted the seeds, but her plants did not grow.
15. Bill and Frank bought the supplies, and then they began building the wall.

20.2 Classifying Sentences by Structure
(Complex and Compound-Complex Sentences) • Practice 1

The Complex Sentence   A complex sentence consists of one independent clause and one or more subordinate clauses. The subordinate clause can be an adjective or adverb clause.

> **COMPLEX SENTENCES**
> INDEPENDENT CLAUSE   SUBORDINATE CLAUSE
> *This is the expensive camera* (that he wants to buy).
> SUBORDINATE CLAUSE   INDEPENDENT CLAUSE
> (If I visit the county fair,) *I will bring you something.*

The Compound-Complex Sentence   A compound-complex sentence consists of two or more independent clauses and one or more subordinate clauses.

> **COMPOUND-COMPLEX SENTENCES**
> SUBORDINATE CLAUSE   INDEPENDENT CLAUSE
> (If I play first-string,) *this concert will be an important milestone for me,*
> INDEPENDENT CLAUSE   SUBORDINATE CLAUSE
> but *I am also afraid* (that the challenge will be too great).

▶ **Exercise 1**   **Recognizing Complex and Compound-Complex Sentences.**   Label each sentence *complex* or *compound-complex*. Underline each independent clause and put parentheses around each subordinate clause.

EXAMPLE: The house (that you described) is too large. _____*complex*_____

1. As soon as I got the letter, I read the instructions, and I knew that I wanted to go. _____

2. This is the book that Margo wants for her birthday. _____

3. I will help you plan the picnic, which, unfortunately, I will not be able to attend. _____

4. I know the way to the state capital, but I may get lost as we get close since I really have been there only once. _____

5. The company that contacted me by phone happens to have a bad reputation. _____

▶ **Exercise 2**   **More Work With Complex and Compound-Complex Sentences.**   Follow the directions for Exercise 1.

1. Although I studied my notes carefully, I still did poorly on the test. _____

2. I can reach my father on the phone, or I will go to his office if I have enough time. _____

3. Is this the tie that Father really wants? _____

4. When I get to London, I will buy you a present, but I can't really promise since I may be very busy. _____

5. I like to play my CD player, or I listen to my radio, whenever I have the time. _____

20.2 Classifying Sentences by Structure
(Complex and Compound-Complex Sentences) • Practice 2

▶ **Exercise 1** **Recognizing Complex Sentences.** The following are complex sentences. In each clause underline the subjects once and the verbs twice.

EXAMPLE: The player who scores the most points wins.

1. I will leave after you are safely indoors.
2. Although he is a marvelous science student, he is weak in mathematics.
3. The noise that shattered the window was a sonic boom.
4. You may sit here if you like.
5. The museum that we wanted to visit is not open today.

▶ **Exercise 2** **Recognizing Compound-Complex Sentences.** The following are compound-complex sentences. In each clause underline the subjects once and the verbs twice. Then put parentheses around each subordinate clause that you find.

EXAMPLE: The person (who knows it best) is not here, but we can try it anyway.

1. The mountain areas are barren, but the valleys are fertile since they are irrigated daily.
2. The musicians who appeared for the audition were generally excellent, but a few were real amateurs.
3. Since the blizzard ended, the schools have remained closed, but shops in town have reopened.
4. Our school band seems ready for the concert, and the chorus will again be in top shape because its leading tenor has returned after a long illness.
5. Although the two-hundred-year-old house has been declared a landmark, its plumbing is nearly in ruins, and few people have shown any interest in buying it.

▶ **Exercise 3** **Identifying the Structure of Sentences.** Identify the structure of each of the following sentences as either *simple, compound, complex,* or *compound-complex.*

EXAMPLE: Without thinking, we asked again. _____simple_____

1. If this offense is reported, he will receive a severe fine. _____
2. The apples, peaches, and pears are in the refrigerator. _____
3. Father will fly home from Dallas tomorrow, or he will phone the family. _____
4. Antoinette carefully described the people that she had seen. _____
5. The room is dark in the morning, but sunlight floods it in the afternoon. _____
6. Gilberto left suddenly in the middle of the school committee meeting and did not reappear until more than two hours later. _____
7. She gave him a battered copy of *Bartlett's Familiar Quotations*, and he used it until his fiancée gave him a new dictionary of quotations. _____
8. The book is very long; it does, nevertheless, have many interesting passages. _____
9. Marco Polo was born on the walled island of Korcula in the Adriatic. _____
10. She described the method that she had used to save her brother's life. _____

21.1 The Four Functions of Sentences • Practice 1

Identifying the Four Functions of Sentences   Sentences are classified according to what they do. There are four types: *declarative, interrogative, imperative,* and *exclamatory.*

THE FOUR FUNCTIONS OF SENTENCES		
Type	**Use**	**Example**
Declarative	States an idea and ends with a period	Glen Cove has a population of 24, 000.
Interrogative	Asks a question and ends with a question mark.	What do you expect to learn?
Imperative	Gives an order or a direction; ends with a period or an exclamation mark.	Turn now to the chapter on space exploration. Close the door!
Exclamatory	Conveys a strong emotion and ends with an exclamation mark.	What a total disaster!

▷ **Exercise 1**   **Recognizing the Four Functions of Sentences.**   Identify the type of each sentence below. Use *D* for declarative, *Int.* for interrogative, *Imp.* for imperative, and *Exc.* for exclamatory.

EXAMPLE: Who is this strange person? ____*Int.*____

1. Please correct your misspelled words now. _____

2. Ginseng is an herb used for medicinal purposes. _____

3. What a terrible accident! _____

4. Which artist do you admire the most? _____

5. Mary Pickford starred in *My Best Girl.* _____

6. How many videotapes do you have in your collection? _____

7. Drive to the first traffic light and turn right. _____

8. How happy we all are today! _____

9. In Greek mythology Orpheus wrote beautiful music. _____

10. Stop that shouting at once! _____

▷ **Exercise 2**   **Writing Different Types of Sentences.**   Write the types of sentences described below.

1. Write a declarative sentence about a famous person.

   _____

2. Write a question concerning school work.

   _____

3. Write an exclamation about a pleasant event.

   _____

4. Write an imperative sentence giving an order or direction.

   _____

5. Write a question concerning the future.

   _____

21.1 The Four Functions of Sentences • Practice 2

▶ **Exercise 1**   **Identifying the Use of Sentences.**   Read each of the following sentences and identify its use as *declarative*, *interrogative*, *imperative*, or *exclamatory*. After each answer, write the appropriate punctuation mark for that sentence.

EXAMPLE: What a mistake that was _____*exclamatory*___!___

1. Have you visited the dentist yet this year _____

2. Choose the hat with the best fit _____

3. Between 1629 and 1640, almost 60, 000 people emigrated from England _____

4. She worked very hard as governor _____

5. Stand absolutely still now, please _____

6. What are the other ingredients needed for the molasses cookies _____

7. I agree with the editorial in this newspaper _____

8. What an excellent magazine this is _____

9. How much do they want for it now _____

10. Give two reasons supporting your opening statement _____

▶ **Writing Application**   **Writing Sentences With Different Uses.**   Write a sentence according to the directions given for each of the following items.

EXAMPLE: Write an imperative sentence that ends with an exclamation mark.
_____*Do it now!*_____

1. Write an imperative sentence that begins with a verb.

   _____

2. Write a question beginning with *Which*.

   _____

3. Write a declarative sentence about your favorite hobby.

   _____

4. Write an exclamatory sentence showing your surprise at something.

   _____

5. Write a question beginning with a verb.

   _____

6. Write an imperative sentence that begins with someone's name.

   _____

7. Write a declarative sentence about a fact from history.

   _____

8. Write an exclamatory sentence beginning with *How*.

   _____

9. Write a question beginning with *When*.

   _____

10. Write a declarative sentence about music you enjoy.

   _____

21.2 Expanding Short Sentences (Adding Details, Sentence Combining) • Practice 1

Adding Details   Improve short sentences by adding details to the subjects, verbs, or complements.

Short Sentences	Details Added
Ellen's story won first prize.	Ellen's story, *a spooky thriller*, won first prize. (in subject)
She described both the characters and the setting.	She described the characters and the setting *vividly and realistically*. (in predicate)
I especially liked the ending.	I especially liked the *dramatic* ending. (in object)

Sentence Combining
Combine two or more short simple sentences to make a longer simple sentence, a compound sentence, a complex sentence, or a compound-complex sentence.

Short, Choppy Sentences	Combined Sentences
Ed took a shower. He fixed himself a snack.	After his shower, Ed fixed himself a snack.
He was hot. He was hungry.	Ed took a shower and then fixed himself a snack.
	Because he was hot and hungry, Ed took a shower and then fixed himself a snack.

▶ **Exercise 1**   **Expanding Sentences.**   Add details to the sentences below.

EXAMPLE: We ordered a pizza.
_____*We ordered a medium pizza with pepperoni and extra cheese.*_____

1. A teacher can inspire students.

   _____

2. Have you eaten at that restaurant?

   _____

3. The car still runs well.

   _____

4. The child looked cute.

   _____

▶ **Exercise 2**   **Sentence Combining.**   Combine the sentences in each group below into a single sentence.

EXAMPLE: Autumn days are shorter. They are cooler too. Trees stop making chlorophyll.
_____*Because autumn days are shorter and cooler, trees stop making chlorophyll.*_____

1. Monique just moved here from France. She is the new student in homeroom.

   _____

   _____

2. The model looks difficult. It is not. Follow the diagrams.

   _____

   _____

21.2 Expanding Short Sentences (Adding Details, Sentence Combining) • Practice 2

▷ **Exercise 1** **Adding Your Own Details.** Rewrite the following sentences to make each one more informative and descriptive. Add at least two different details to each.

EXAMPLE: I drank the water.
Hot and thirsty, I drank the cold water shooting out of the drinking fountain.

1. Mary walked the dog.

   _____

2. A herd of cattle grazed.

   _____

3. The waves broke violently.

   _____

4. A rainbow appeared.

   _____

5. His uncle spoke on television.

   _____

▷ **Exercise 2** **Combining Short, Choppy Sentences.** Read each of the following groups of short, choppy sentences and then combine two or more of the sentences in each group. In any group that contains three sentences, you may decide to leave one sentence unchanged.

1. The show closed. Many of the cast members auditioned for daytime soap operas.

   _____

2. The city began to enforce the law against double-parking more strictly. Too many drivers had been ignoring the law.

   _____

3. The sun rose beyond the water. It cast a pink glow on the lighthouse.

   _____

4. I enjoy seeing all the animals at the zoo. The gorillas are my favorites.

   _____

5. Our school's choral group is one of the finest in the country. It requires special auditions for admission.

   _____

6. The supermarket was so crowded. People stood in checkout lines stretching back into the aisles.

   _____

7. The streets of that city can be quiet and calm. They can be noisy and full of life. It depends on the time of day.

   _____

8. A burglar entered the house through the window. He escaped with the jewelry. The jewelry was worth thousands of dollars.

   _____

9. Hockey is a fast-moving game. Players skate by with great speed. Hockey pucks can travel at eighty miles per hour.

   _____

10. Alexander was a remarkable animal. He could understand words and sign language. He could also invent his own games and tricks.

   _____

21.3 Simplifying Long, Confusing Sentences
(Shortening Long Compound Sentences, Shortening Long Complex Sentences) • Practice 1

Shortening Long Compound Sentences Recognize compound sentences that ramble, and separate them into two or more shorter sentences.

Rambling Compound Sentence	Revision
Joe has several computer games, and Paul has several different ones, so they trade from time to time, and neither gets bored with his own.	Joe has several computer games, and Paul has several different ones. They trade from time to time, so neither gets bored with his own.

Shortening Long Complex Sentences Recognize complex sentences that are too complicated, and separate them into shorter sentences.

Complicated Complex Sentence	Revision
The first transcontinental auto trip, which was made in 1903 when two men drove from San Francisco to New York City, was a remarkable feat because roads were poor and gasoline was hard to find.	The first transcontinental auto trip was made in 1903 when two men drove from San Francisco to New York City. It was a remarkable feat because roads were poor and gasoline was hard to find.

▶ **Exercise 1** Shortening Long Compound Sentences. Divide each long compound sentence into two or more shorter sentences.

EXAMPLE: Few people are indifferent to cats, for most either love them or hate them, and they make no secret of their feelings.

Few people are indifferent to cats. Most either love them or hate them and make no secret of their feelings.

1. The Nile overflowed every spring and deposited a layer of rich soil, and as a result the soil along the banks of the river never wore out.

   _____

   _____

2. Young Ben Franklin helped his father make candles and soap, but he found the work boring, and he eagerly accepted his brother's offer to teach him printing.

   _____

   _____

▶ **Exercise 2** Shortening Complicated Complex Sentences. Divide each long complex sentence into two or more shorter sentences.

1. Although the Bisons were far behind at the half, their fans, who rarely became discouraged, continued to hope for a miracle, which occurred in the third period when the Bisons scored three quick touchdowns and held on to win.

   _____

   _____

2. The action of the movie takes place on the *Twentieth Century Limited*, a fast train which used to travel between New York and Chicago but which has been discontinued.

   _____

   _____

21.3 Simplifying Long, Confusing Sentences
(Shortening Long Compound Sentences, Shortening Long Complex Sentences) • Practice 2

▶ **Exercise 1** **Shortening Long Compound Sentences.** Rewrite each compound sentence by breaking it up into shorter sentences.

EXAMPLE: The batter slugged a line drive to left field and easily made it to first base, and then the ball was thrown to the infield, and he slid into second head first, and the shortstop missed the tag, so the runner was safe with a double.

The batter slugged a line drive to left field and easily made it to first base. Then the ball was thrown to the infield, and he slid into second, head first. The shortstop missed the tag, so the runner was safe with a double.

1. The myths of ancient Greece have inspired writers for centuries, and writers have studied the personalities of many Greek characters, and they have followed many of the plots of Greek stories.

   _____

   _____

2. A dog can be both an ally and a burden to its master, and it can often be a source of protection and love, but it can also be both an expense and a continuous responsibility.

   _____

   _____

3. To wire the driftwood as a lamp, you must drill a hole through it, and then you must mount it on a stand, and next you must pull electrical wire through the wood and attach a light socket to the top.

   _____

   _____

▶ **Exercise 2** **Shortening Complicated Complex Sentences.** Break up the complex sentences into shorter sentences by changing the order of ideas and adding or eliminating words.

EXAMPLE: New York is a fast-paced city that can never bore the people who visit it because it contains fascinating museums and historical sights, which tourists can explore, as well as many restaurants, concerts, and plays, which they can enjoy.

New York is a fast-paced city that can never bore the people who visit it. It contains fascinating museums and historical sights, which tourists can explore, as well as many restaurants, concerts, and plays, which they can enjoy.

1. Although Joe had not been fishing in a number of years, he surprised himself by catching a very large swordfish, which, when it was measured, set a local record, which was mentioned in the newspapers.

   _____

   _____

2. Some of today's television stars seem to worry more about contracts than they do about providing entertainment, which, as a result, leaves the audience wondering which star will disappear next from their favorite shows.

   _____

   _____

3. My last trip to Africa included my first safari, which was very exciting and which began at sunrise and lasted until the late afternoon when we all sat together and recounted the adventures that we had enjoyed in the bush country.

   _____

   _____

   _____

21.3 Using a Variety of Sentences (Using Different Sentence Openers and Structures) • Practice 1

Using Different Sentence Openers Begin your sentences with different openers: subjects, single-word modifiers, phrases, and clauses.

WAYS TO BEGIN SENTENCES
Subject: The *cast* and *crew* had worked very hard.
Modifier: *Finally,* the big night had arrived.
Phrase: *Behind the curtain,* the actors took their places.
Clause: *As soon as the curtain rose,* the audience applauded.

Using Different Sentence Structures Use a variety of sentence structures—simple, compound, complex, and possibly compound-complex—in your writing.

Monotonous Simple Sentences	Revised with Variety
The stands were packed for the big game. The teams took the field. The fans roared. Our team had better pitching. They had better hitters. The ninth inning ended. The score was tied. The game went into extra innings.	The stands were packed for the big game. When the teams took the field, the fans roared. Our team had better pitching, but they had better hitters. When the ninth inning ended, the score was tied, so the game went into extra innings.

Exercise 1 **Using Different Sentence Openers.** Rewrite each sentence to make it begin with a one-word modifier, a phrase, or a clause.

EXAMPLE: I will help you as soon as I finish my homework.
_____As soon as I finish my homework, I will help you._____

1. The threat of forest fires has increased because of the long drought.

   _____

2. Gerry acts quite irresponsibly sometimes.

   _____

3. Hugh entered the contest even though his chances of winning were slim.

   _____

4. A pot of geraniums sat on either side of the front steps.

   _____

Exercise 2 **Using a Variety of Sentence Structures.** Rewrite the passage below using a variety of sentence structures to make it more interesting.

Our camping trip had its share of problems from the start. Dad had reserved a site early. There were no lakeside places left. The site we did get was next to the recreation room. The sound of arcade games could be heard day and night. It didn't seem likely that we would have the peace and quiet we wanted.

_____

_____

_____

_____

_____

_____

_____

21.3 Using a Variety of Sentences (Using Different Sentence Openers and Structures) • Practice 2

▶ **Exercise 1** **Using Different Sentence Openers.** Each of the following sentences can be rewritten with a different opener. Look for a modifier, phrase, or clause that can be placed at the beginning of the sentence.

EXAMPLE: The robins used twigs, string, and newspaper to build their nest.
To build their nest, the robins used twigs, string, and newspaper.

1. We ventured out in the boat when the bay became calm.

_____

2. We can usually count on Maxwell's help in the evenings.

_____

3. The planes soared in formation high above the clouds.

_____

4. One must practice diligently to become proficient on a musical instrument.

_____

5. The board of trustees made painful cuts in services and personnel, although they avoided bankruptcy.

_____

6. The audience stood from the band's first note to its last.

_____

7. The sound of the collision naturally brought people running from their homes.

_____

8. I met with Dr. Chung at exactly 2:30 P.M.

_____

9. Mr. McCauley played basketball while holding one hand behind his back.

_____

10. The truck convoy lost twenty minutes waiting for a slow-moving freight train to pass.

_____

▶ **Exercise 2** **Revising Sentence Openers.** The passage contains a series of sentences that all begin the same way. Find different openers for *most* of the sentences. Then rewrite the passage to produce a smoother, more interesting style.

(1) A sharp knock at the door startled everyone in the room. (2) All heads instantly turned toward the door. (3) They then looked upward to the room where George Washington slept. (4) No one spoke as the knock sounded again and again. (5) Margaret rose at last and walked unsteadily toward the door to face the enemy. (6) A captain of the British Army stood motionless, his face hidden in the darkness of the night, when the door swung open. (7) A small cluster of redcoats stood behind him. (8) The captain strode past Margaret without a word and swept into the room. (9) Four other soldiers followed him. (10) They began to search the house at their officer's command.

_____

_____

_____

_____

_____

21.4 Avoiding Fragments (Recognizing Fragments)
• Practice 1

Recognizing Fragments   A fragment is a group of words that does not express a complete thought. It is only part of a sentence. Any group of words that cannot stand alone is a fragment.

Fragments	Complete Sentences
at the football game	We met at the football game.
should have arrived there	My family should have arrived there.
a woman in a yellow dress	A woman in a yellow dress asked to see you.
when I received the letter	When I received the letter, I answered immediately.

▶ **Exercise 1**   **Recognizing Fragments.**   Label each fragment *F* and each sentence *S*.

EXAMPLE: Since you expect an answer now.   ___*F*___

1. Would be able to go tomorrow. _____
2. If I can remember the directions to her house. _____
3. We can leave at once. _____
4. At the end of the first half. _____
5. A group of boys charging down the path. _____
6. When we spoke to them on the phone yesterday. _____
7. The arrangements have been made in advance. _____
8. In spite of all their objections. _____
9. Have not charged full price for this album. _____
10. Birds sing. _____

▶ **Exercise 2**   **Recognizing More Fragments.**   Follow the directions in Exercise 1.

1. On the morning of the big game. _____
2. Leave now. _____
3. A bus racing toward the intersection. _____
4. Although he invited me to the party. _____
5. Must be out of the apartment by this time tomorrow. _____
6. I know the way to the downtown shopping area. _____
7. The book with the World War II pictures. _____
8. After trying to convince them all morning. _____
9. Gum chewing is not allowed. _____
10. At another time, perhaps in another era. _____

21.4 Avoiding Fragments (Recognizing Fragments)
• Practice 2

▷ **Exercise 1** **Recognizing Sentence Fragments.** Each of the following groups of words is either a sentence or a fragment. For each group write *F* if it is a fragment and *S* if it is a complete sentence.

EXAMPLE: Near the end of the story. ____*F*____

1. On top of the hill. _____
2. A policeman standing on the corner. _____
3. The money stolen from the largest bank in town. _____
4. This road leads to the state assembly building. _____
5. The person waiting for us at the bus stop. _____
6. When Aunt Millie stepped from the plane. _____
7. Near the ledge by the window in the living room. _____
8. Please sit down. _____
9. Because she waited too long to call for help. _____
10. The robber rattled by the noises in the attic. _____
11. Time flies. _____
12. Should report to the manager's office. _____
13. Although I always try to be on time. _____
14. Between you and me. _____
15. Don't worry. _____
16. A man identifying himself as a CIA agent. _____
17. Since my last visit to Chile and Peru. _____
18. Only a part of the sentence. _____
19. They're equal. _____
20. Two or three miles down the highway at the traffic light. _____

▷ **Exercise 2** **Recognizing Sentence Fragments.** Each of the following groups of words is either a sentence or a fragment. For each group write *F* if it is a fragment and *S* if it is a complete sentence.

EXAMPLE: For more than two hours in the rain. ____*F*____

1. Darlene was angry, but nobody knew why. _____
2. Got a scratch on her ankle. _____
3. To her advantage, Isabel. _____
4. Apologizing for nothing and acting proud, Jerry. _____
5. Was a difficult adjustment for her. _____
6. She was accustomed to getting her own way. _____
7. Be still. _____
8. Offered a believable alibi. _____
9. The agile and talented acrobat. _____
10. Ballet was more than just an activity for her. _____

21.4 # Avoiding Fragments (Phrase Fragments, Clause Fragments) • Practice 1

Phrase Fragments   There are four kinds of phrases—prepositional, participial, gerund, and infinitive. Phrases should not be capitalized and punctuated as if they were sentences.

PHRASE FRAGMENTS
near the old television
smiling to the crowd

Clause Fragments   Adjective and adverb clauses are not complete sentences although they have subjects and verbs. These subordinate clauses should not be capitalized as if they were sentences.

CLAUSE FRAGMENTS
if they want to do something foolish
that I wanted to buy

▶ **Exercise 1**   **Changing Phrase Fragments into Sentences.**   Use each of the phrase fragments below anywhere in a complete sentence. You must add a *subject* and a *verb*.

EXAMPLE: under the staircase
_____*Under the staircase I found my skates.*_____

1. in half an hour _____

2. between you and me _____

3. changing my clothes _____

4. to reach the station _____

5. smoking cigarettes _____

6. of another kind _____

7. growing different vegetables _____

8. with all her friends _____

9. to open my present _____

10. told to report to the principal _____

▶ **Exercise 2**   **Changing Clause Fragments into Sentences.**   Use each clause fragment below in a complete sentence. You must add a complete *independent clause* with another subject and verb.

EXAMPLE: that I need
_____*The file that I need is on a shelf.*_____

1. if I get his message _____

2. whom she asked _____

3. because I like them _____

4. which Bill wants _____

5. whose wallet I found _____

6. since you chose to go _____

7. until the new family moved in _____

8. who was in the room _____

9. that I found there _____

10. whenever I write _____

21.4 Avoiding Fragments (Phrase Fragments, Clause Fragments) • Practice 2

▶ **Exercise 1** **Changing Phrase Fragments into Sentences.** Use each of the following phrase fragments in a sentence. You may use the phrase at the beginning, at the end, or in any other position in the sentence.

EXAMPLE: in Chicago and St. Louis
    Major fairs have been held in Chicago and St. Louis.

1. near the broken window
    _____

2. chewing gum
    _____

3. lost for several hours
    _____

4. in the kitchen
    _____

5. chosen by the committee
    _____

6. to eat too fast
    _____

7. holding my grandmother's hand
    _____

8. in the morning after breakfast
    _____

9. crossing the street carefully
    _____

10. to read a newspaper
    _____

▶ **Exercise 2** **Changing Clause Fragments into Sentences.** Use each of the following clause fragments in a sentence.

EXAMPLE: if I ever see Paris
    If I ever see Paris, I will send you a postcard.

1. when the delivery man rang the bell
    _____

2. who reserved rooms in the new motel
    _____

3. that he wanted to use
    _____

4. which she had saved for over a year
    _____

5. that he intends to carry out
    _____

21.4 Avoiding Run-ons (Two Kinds of Run-ons)
• Practice 1

Two Kinds of Run-ons   A run-on is two or more complete sentences that are not properly joined or separated. One kind consists of two sentences that are not joined or separated by any punctuation at all. Another kind consists of two sentences punctuated only with a comma.

Run-ons With No Punctuation	Run-ons With Only a Comma
A trip to a state park seemed like a good idea everyone agreed to go next Sunday.	The aroma from the oven was overwhelming, I opened the stove door and saw a large tray of chocolate-chip cookies.

▶ **Exercise 1**   **Recognizing Run-ons.**   Some of the sentences are complete sentences; others are run-ons. Write *S* if the item is a complete sentence and *RO* if the item is a run-on.

EXAMPLE: I inflated the bike tire, it wouldn't hold the air. ___*RO*___

1. Jakob Grimm and his brother Wilhelm collected German folk tales, these were later published and became famous as *Grimm's Fairy Tales.* _____

2. People in this area like to talk about the great flood water that covered the entire downtown shopping center and many other parts of the town. _____

3. She opens her mail every day; she pays her bills every week. _____

4. Jute is a tropical plant grown primarily for its fiber, it is used to make burlap, twine, and backing yarns for rugs. _____

5. Juneau is the capital of Alaska it has an airport, an ice-free harbor, and a seaplane base. _____

▶ **Exercise 2**   **More Work with Run-ons.**   Follow the same directions as above.

1. Paso Robles in southern California is a resort city that features hot springs. _____

2. Rhinoceroses have thick skin and feature one or two nasal horns, there are both black and white types. _____

3. Rhubarb is a plant whose leaf blades are poisonous it also has fleshy leaf-stalks that are used to make delicious pies and sauces. _____

4. The Rhine, an 820-mile river in Europe, is used by freighters to transport coal, iron, and grain. _____

5. Sir Walter Scott was a famous British writer and poet, among his famous works are *Ivanhoe, Kenilworth,* and *The Bride of Lammermoor.* _____

21.4 Avoiding Run-ons (Two Kinds of Run-ons)
• Practice 2

▶ **Exercise 1** **Recognizing Run-ons.** Write *S* for complete sentences and *RO* for run-ons.

EXAMPLE: Her horse fell, she landed in a ditch. ___*RO*___

1. A comedy of manners usually deals with the behavior of people these witty plays are often about middle- and upper-class men and women. _____

2. The Johnstown Flood was brought about by the collapse of the Conemaugh Reservoir in Pennsylvania, it occurred during a period of very heavy rainfall. _____

3. In an attempt to correct the leak, he actually caused much more damage. _____

4. Beethoven's Seventh Symphony has often been called the *Dance Symphony*, the composer himself conducted the first performance of it in Vienna in 1813. _____

5. A highlight of a trip through the coastal region of Norway is a cruise through the fjords. _____

6. He had read all of Jack London's books the first one was *Call of the Wild*. _____

7. Smoking is now prohibited on airline flights, it is banned in all sections. _____

8. Irrigation was first begun in the United States by the Mormons sometime before the Civil War. _____

9. The storm flooded major highways, motorists were warned to stay at home. _____

10. In 1700 the Natchez Indians lived between the Yazoo and Pearl rivers on the east side of the Mississippi. _____

▶ **Exercise 2** **Recognizing Run-ons.** Write *S* for complete sentences and *RO* for run-ons.

EXAMPLE: Janice and Marsha shared the biggest bedroom in the house, the two sisters could never agree on a color to paint the walls. ___*RO*___

1. The diamond is one of the hardest substances in nature, fine cutting and polishing releases its brilliance. _____

2. Four thousand years ago, the people of Babylonia were the first to make New Year's resolutions, and the custom continues to this day. _____

3. It wasn't until the Renaissance that civilized people ate with utensils; until then, people used their hands to put the food into their mouths. _____

4. When eating, Roman peasants would use all five fingers, but those of the upper class used only three fingers, keeping the ring finger and the pinkie clean. _____

5. The word *fork* comes from a Latin word that refers to a farmer's pitchfork, the earliest forks had only two tines. _____

6. The spoon has been in use for at least twenty thousand years, it was especially useful for eating liquids like soup or porridge. _____

7. The small napkins that we use today would not have been big enough in the old days, for people who ate with their hands needed napkins the size of towels. _____

8. The word *bowl* comes from the Anglo-Saxon word *bolla*, this word simply means "round." _____

9. Today we use a saucer to hold a cup, but long ago it was a special dish for holding sauces to flavor meats. _____

10. The word *plate* comes from an Old French word, *plat*, which means "flat," we also see this word root in our word *platter*. _____

21.4

Avoiding Run-ons (Three Ways to Correct Run-ons)
• Practice 1

Three Ways to Correct Run-ons   There are three ways to correct a run-on—using an end mark, using a comma and a coordinating conjunction, or using a semicolon.

<table>
<tr><th colspan="2">THREE WAYS TO CORRECT A RUN-ON</th></tr>
<tr><td>Run-on</td><td>Leonard Bernstein is a famous American conductor you probably know him best as the composer of West Side Story.</td></tr>
<tr><td>Method</td><td>Corrected Run-on</td></tr>
<tr><td>End mark—period (.)</td><td>Leonard Bernstein is a famous American conductor. You probably know him best as the composer of West Side Story.</td></tr>
<tr><td>A comma and a coordinating conj. (, but)</td><td>Leonard Bernstein is a famous American conductor, but you probably know him best as the composer of West Side Story.</td></tr>
<tr><td>A semicolon (;)</td><td>Leonard Bernstein is a famous American conductor; you probably know him best as the composer of West Side Story.</td></tr>
</table>

▷ **Exercise 1**   **Correcting Run-ons.**   Each sentence below is a run-on. On a separate sheet of paper, rewrite each run-on using one of the three methods of correction shown above. Vary your methods.

1. Howard Pyle writes stories of adventure and chivalry, he is the author of *The Merry Adventures of Robin Hood of Great Renown*.

2. Nebraska was admitted to the union in 1867 as the 37th state today it is an important agricultural state in which corn, wheat, and sorghum are grown.

3. Our hockey team ended the season with a heartbreaking loss, the players cleaned out their lockers quickly and left for home.

4. Thomas Masaryk was the chief founder of Czechoslovakia he was also its first president.

5. We must have a complete physical examination each year before practicing any sport in fact the coach won't allow anyone on the field without a medical clearance.

▷ **Exercise 2**   **Correcting More Run-ons.**   Follow the directions in Exercise 1.

1. The city of Paterson, New Jersey, was founded by Alexander Hamilton in 1791, soon it was a center of the textile industry with both cotton-spinning mills and silk manufacturing.

2. My family has not decided what to do about moving, we may either rent an apartment in town or try to buy another house.

3. The shamrock is a plant with leaves of three leaflets for some time it has been the emblem of Ireland.

4. Shallots are used by many chefs in cooking they are similar to the onion but not quite as strong in flavor.

5. Gilbert Stuart was the most famous American painter of his day, he is best known for his three portraits of George Washington.

21.4 Avoiding Run-ons (Three Ways to Correct Run-ons)
• Practice 2

▶ **Exercise 1** **Correcting Run-ons.** Rewrite each of the following run-ons, using any of the three methods described in this section. Use each method at least three times.

EXAMPLE: They were in a hurry, the crowd was enormous.
They were in a hurry, but the crowd was enormous.

1. The first rocket launching was unsuccessful the second fulfilled all our expectations.
   _____
   _____

2. Tell the truth, it is easier than lying.
   _____
   _____

3. My father watches football, basketball, and baseball on TV my mother prefers to watch comedies, concerts, and documentaries.
   _____
   _____

4. I think the book itself was poor, the film version was a disaster.
   _____
   _____

5. The Marquis de Lafayette reached New York on August 16, 1824, he had been invited by President Monroe.
   _____
   _____

6. I hope to visit Denmark and Sweden this summer, however, I will have to see how expensive it will be.
   _____
   _____

7. The plants in our garden are not doing well they seem dry and lifeless.
   _____
   _____

8. Lotteries go back to pre-Revolutionary times, even then they were used to raise money for schools, roads, and bridges.
   _____
   _____

9. My brothers and I always crave dessert all my parents ever have is black coffee.
   _____
   _____

10. The first English settlers brought a primary loom to this country, a better Dutch loom with a fly shuttle soon replaced the English loom.
    _____
    _____

21.4 Avoiding Misplaced Modifiers (Recognizing Misplaced Modifiers) • Practice 1

Recognizing Misplaced Modifiers   When modifiers, phrases and clauses that act as adjectives or adverbs, are placed too far from the words they modify, confusion can result. A modifier should be placed as close as possible to the word it modifies. A modifier that is placed incorrectly is called a misplaced modifier.

MISPLACED MODIFIERS	CORRECTED
I often eat fish in a restaurant *with french fries.*	In a restaurant, I often eat fish *with french fries.*
While waiting at the station, her ticket was lost.	*While waiting at the station,* she lost her ticket.

▷ **Exercise 1**   **Recognizing Misplaced Modifiers.**   Some of the sentences below are correct; others contain misplaced modifiers. If the sentence is correct, write *C*. If the sentence contains a misplaced modifier, write *MM*.

EXAMPLE: Having phoned my parents, the bus began to pull out. ____*MM*____

1. After staying out late, the house was hard to find. _____
2. The statue was destroyed in the storm erected in 1869. _____
3. Changing into my jeans, I began to work in the garden. _____
4. Flying near the airport, the cars looked like small beetles. _____
5. The dinner prepared by a chef was allowed to spoil. _____
6. Skating on the frozen canal, I felt my ankles begin to swell. _____
7. Racing to the gate, I greeted my Uncle Bill. _____
8. The speaker was late who was chosen to go first. _____
9. To get this free offer, a phone call must be made. _____
10. To get a refund, you must send in a coupon. _____

▷ **Exercise 2**   **Recognizing More Misplaced Modifiers.**   Follow the directions in Exercise 1.

1. Bill counted the days waiting for Christmas. _____
2. The room is too expensive with a view of the lake. _____
3. Opening the envelope, Joan found her lost identification card. _____
4. Walking through the lobby, grandfather's beard almost touched the floor. _____
5. The graphic is missing that was designed by the famous artist. _____
6. The wall around the city needs to be repaired. _____
7. Examining his shoe, Bob saw a hole on the bottom. _____
8. To prepare the stew, the potatoes should be cut in cubes. _____
9. Thinking very hard, Edward finally found the answer. _____
10. To clean brass, you should use a soft cloth. _____

21.4 Avoiding Misplaced Modifiers (Recognizing Misplaced Modifiers) • Practice 2

▷ **Exercise 1**   **Recognizing Misplaced Modifiers.**   Some of the following sentences are correct, but most of them contain misplaced modifiers. If the sentence is correct, write *C*. If the sentence contains a misplaced modifier, write *MM*.

EXAMPLE: Writing a letter, his signature is almost always illegible. _____*MM*_____

1. Crossing the bridge, a tollbooth was hit by the car. _____
2. I always prefer a room in a motel with a window. _____
3. Choosing his words carefully, the school principal began to speak. _____
4. Having had our dinner, the boat continued the journey. _____
5. Having received a medal, my dream was fulfilled. _____
6. She gave the letter to Mr. Gross with the envelope. _____
7. Driven to the station early, we decided to have lunch. _____
8. I chose that hat for my mother with the flower. _____
9. Reaching the end of the road, the farm came into view. _____
10. Frightened by the noise, my screams were heard down the hall. _____
11. Strolling along the country road, an acorn fell on my head. _____
12. Dancing till after midnight, the band finally stopped playing. _____
13. Coming to the end of the book, I realized that I had just read a masterpiece. _____
14. Pitch me over home plate the ball. _____
15. Throwing a line into the lake, the fish seemed to jump right on the hook. _____

▷ **Exercise 2**   **Recognizing Misplaced Modifiers.**   Some of the following sentences are correct, but most of them contain misplaced modifiers. If the sentence is correct, write *C*. If the sentence contains a misplaced modifier, write *MM*.

EXAMPLE: Knocking on the front door, the dogs began to bark. _____*MM*_____

1. Arriving with bonbons and other gifts, the visitors were most welcome. _____
2. Having lost my gloves, my hands were very cold. _____
3. Breathless with anticipation, the evening went very well. _____
4. I presented the iguana to my cousin in the cage. _____
5. Greeting the crowd gathered below, the queen smiled slightly. _____
6. Wishing to thank you for a wonderful time, please accept this little gift. _____
7. Failing to go off, I missed the appointment because of my alarm. _____
8. After feeding the ducks, the geese came over to get some bread. _____
9. Earnestly wishing to succeed, Marie studied every night. _____
10. Stopped at the door by the guard, my invitation had been left at home. _____
11. Janelle gave the mystery to her friend with the last page missing. _____
12. Arlene got into the blue car wearing her new leather boots. _____
13. Following a tourist tradition, the coins were thrown into the fountain. _____
14. Dudley arranged the flowers in the yellow vase and the ferns. _____
15. Singing loudly and out of key, the microphone was turned off. _____

21.4 Avoiding Misplaced Modifiers (Correcting Misplaced Modifiers) • Practice 1

Correcting Misplaced Modifiers   Three kinds of modifiers are commonly misplaced—prepositional phrases, participial phrases, and adjective clauses. Misplaced modifiers are corrected by placing the modifier as close as possible to the word it modifies.

MISPLACED MODIFIER	CORRECTED
The art critic found a painting in an abandoned warehouse *that had been missing for fifty years.*	The art critic found a painting *that had been missing for fifty years* in an abandoned warehouse.

▶ **Exercise 1**   **Correcting Misplaced Modifiers.**   Each sentence below contains a misplaced modifier. Rewrite the sentence by moving the modifier close to the word it modifies. You may change words if necessary.

EXAMPLE: Rushing toward the accident victim, his body was covered with a blanket.
_____ *Rushing toward the accident victim, I covered his body with a blanket.* _____

1. Smiling at the rock singer, his autograph was given to me.

   _____

2. A movie began the film festival that won an Academy Award.

   _____

3. Reaching the box office, the concert tickets were sold out.

   _____

4. To begin a research project, the card catalog should be checked first.

   _____

5. The batter hit a home run who had been in a terrible slump.

   _____

▶ **Exercise 2**   **Correcting More Misplaced Modifiers.**   Follow the directions in Exercise 1.

1. My mother usually makes spaghetti from her own recipe with meatballs.

   _____

2. Climbing the stairs slowly, the fifth floor was finally reached.

   _____

3. I looked in the textbook for the meaning of the word in the glossary.

   _____

4. The fare to the city is too expensive that he wants to visit.

   _____

5. Running downstairs in his pajamas, his embarrassment wouldn't let him open the door.

   _____

21.4 Avoiding Misplaced Modifiers (Correcting Misplaced Modifiers) • Practice 2

▶ **Exercise 1**   **Correcting Misplaced Modifiers.**   Rewrite each of the following sentences, eliminating the misplaced modifier.

EXAMPLE: Swimming leisurely, his worries were left behind.
_____*Swimming leisurely, he left his worries behind.*_____

1. The book was not available that he wanted.
   _____

2. Entering the movie, my best friend was seen in the last row.
   _____

3. We are sending you a package of seeds by parcel post with planting instructions.
   _____

4. The man was really very stingy that many people admired.
   _____

5. Eating lunch rapidly, my trip was soon continued.
   _____

6. Mother bought strawberries at the supermarket that tasted delicious.
   _____

7. Swimming as fast as possible, the drowning girl was reached.
   _____

8. The train is unusually late that I always take into the city.
   _____

9. Diapered and fed, the crying of the baby stopped.
   _____

10. I welcomed my old friend as soon as he arrived with great affection.
    _____

▶ **Writing Application**   **Correcting Misplaced Modifiers in a Composition.**   Three of the sentences in the following composition contain misplaced modifiers. Rewrite the entire paragraph and correct these errors.

EXAMPLE: Herodotus is best remembered for his works about history by many people.
_____*By many people Herodotus is best remembered for his works about history.*_____

   (1) Except for his writings, little is known of Herodotus' life. (2) Born about 490 B.C., several years of his early adulthood were spent by him in travel. (3) He must have been filled by the lands he visited—Egypt, Mesopotamia, Palestine, southern Russia—with awe. (4) At Thurii in southern Italy, he wrote his famous *History*, where he had retired. (5) Reading Herodotus' accounts, one almost envies the life of the man who is called the Father of History.

_____
_____
_____
_____
_____
_____

21.4 Double Negatives • Practice 1

The Mistaken Use of Double Negatives Do not write sentences with double negatives.

AVOIDING DOUBLE NEGATIVES	
Double Negative	**Corrected Sentence**
I ca*n't* *never* remember his name.	I can *never* remember his name
	I ca*n't* ever remember his name.
They have*n't* given me *none*.	They have given me *none*.
	They have*n't* given me any.
We *never* saw *no* lions.	We *never* saw any lions.
	We saw *no* lions.

▷ **Exercise 1** **Avoiding Double Negatives in Sentences.** Underline the word in parentheses that completes each sentence correctly.

EXAMPLE: I haven't (never, ever) been to Japan.

1. Our group (will, won't) never be able to finish on time.

2. He didn't say (nothing, anything) about his future plans.

3. I (do, don't) want to see anything on television this evening.

4. Nobody had heard (nothing, anything) about the speech.

5. My sister doesn't (ever, never) get up early on weekends.

6. The chairman hasn't appointed (no one, anyone) to head the committee.

7. He (should, shouldn't) never have expected everyone to assist him.

8. She hasn't (ever, never) explained why she is studying this area.

9. We (could, couldn't) see nothing from where we sat.

10. She won't lend me (none, any) of her books.

▷ **Exercise 2** **Correcting Sentences With Double Negatives.** Rewrite each sentence below in two different ways.

EXAMPLE: I haven't never been to Cape Cod.
  I have never been to Cape Cod.
  I haven't ever been to Cape Cod.

1. Don't do nothing until you receive further instructions.

  _____

  _____

2. There isn't no one on our team who plays as well as James.

  _____

  _____

3. William can't find none of the original drafts of his story.

  _____

  _____

4. They couldn't determine no cause for such an action.

  _____

  _____

5. They won't allow no one in until 7:45 P.M.

  _____

  _____

21.4 Double Negatives • Practice 2

▷ **Exercise 1** **Correcting Double Negatives.** The following sentences contain double negatives. Rewrite each sentence in *two* ways.

EXAMPLE: We didn't tell Frank nothing about the surprise.
>*We didn't tell Frank anything about the surprise.*
>*We told Frank nothing about the surprise.*

1. Jennifer didn't see nobody she knew at the conference.

   _____

   _____

2. Michael couldn't find nothing about his topic in the encyclopedia.

   _____

   _____

3. Franklin never suggests nothing really original.

   _____

   _____

4. I haven't never eaten octopus.

   _____

   _____

5. Don't say nothing about the contest to Don.

   _____

   _____

▷ **Writing Application** **Writing Negative Sentences.** Use each of the following words in a negative sentence.

EXAMPLE: nobody
>*When I called her house, nobody answered.*

1. wasn't
2. never
3. not
4. didn't
5. none

6. can't
7. nowhere
8. nothing
9. wouldn't
10. no

1. _____
2. _____
3. _____
4. _____
5. _____
6. _____
7. _____
8. _____
9. _____
10. _____

21.4 # Common Usage Problems • **Practice 1**

Usage Problems   Note the following words and expressions that cause usage problems. Some usage problems occur because two or more words have similar spellings or meanings. Other usage problems occur because the word or words are inappropriate and should be eliminated.

USAGE PROBLEMS	
Words with Similar Spellings or Meanings	
accept and *except*	*farther* and *further*
advice and *advise*	*in* and *into*
affect and *effect*	*than* and *then*
all ready and *already*	*that, which,* and *who*
among and *between*	*their, there,* and *they're*
beside and *besides*	*to, too,* and *two*
Words or Expressions to Avoid	
at (after *where*)	*due to the fact that*
because (after *the reason*)	*kind of, sort of*
different than	*this here* (omit *here*)
like (before a subject and a verb)	*that there* (omit *there*)

▶ **Exercise 1**   **Recognizing Correct Usage.**   Underline the form in parentheses that correctly completes each sentence.

EXAMPLE: The lawyer gave his client some (<u>advice</u>, advise).

1. Terry has (all ready, already) signed us up for swimming lessons.
2. This story is quite (different from, different than) your last one.
3. We will discuss this issue (further, farther) at another time.
4. Alan is the candidate (which, whom) I supported for class president.
5. Everyone (accept, except) John agrees with the decision.
6. (Their, They're) all waiting for a bus.
7. Valerie goes to the movies more often (than, then) I do.
8. (Due to the fact that, Because) our plane was delayed, we were late.
9. Divide these souvenirs (among, between) the three children.
10. What (affect, effect) does diet have on a person's health?

▶ **Exercise 2**   **More Practice Recognizing Correct Usage.**   Underline the form in parentheses that correctly completes each sentence.

EXAMPLE: Henry decided to (<u>accept</u>, except) the invitation to the party.

1. I am looking for it, but I don't know exactly where (it's at, it is).
2. Jennifer was (too, to) tired to watch the late movie.
3. First I read several sources, and (then, than) I planned my report.
4. (This here, This) coat is on sale.
5. The reason I am happy (is that, is because) I won the contest.
6. (Their, There) comments were very funny.
7. I moved the desk (in, into) the corner of the room.
8. The results were (sort of, rather) startling.
9. It rained during the afternoon just (like, as) you predicted.
10. Will anyone (beside, besides) Eileen help with the decorations?

21.4 # Common Usage Problems • Practice 2

▶ **Exercise 1**   Avoiding Usage Problems.   Correctly complete each of the following sentences by underlining the correct form from the choices in parentheses.

EXAMPLE: (Among, Between) the six of them, we should be able to find someone with a sense of humor.

1. Evelyn gave me some good (advice, advise).
2. The huge sandwich was divided (between, among) Kit, Mary, and Stan.
3. The team members were (all ready, already) for the game.
4. (Accept, Except) for Steven no one had any difficulty finding the restaurant.
5. Hot weather (affects, effects) people in different ways.
6. This place is (all ready, already) beginning to look more attractive.
7. The senator asked several experts to (advice, advise) her on the subject of energy.
8. Joan's words had a strange (affect, effect) on him: He fainted.
9. The conversation (among, between) the two sounded like a comedy routine.
10. It is always difficult to (accept, except) one's own limitations.

▶ **Exercise 2**   Avoiding Usage Problems.   Correctly complete each of the following sentences by underlining the correct form from the choices in parentheses.

1. The hayride was canceled (due to the fact that, because) rain was predicted.
2. I don't know where my algebra book could (be, be at).
3. The reason we came is (because, that) your letter alarmed us.
4. (Due to the fact that, Since) Janet has studied Italian, she will give the waiter our order.
5. (Beside, Besides) us, who will help decorate the gym?
6. Chris didn't want his new room to be any different (from, than) his old one.
7. Do you know where bait can be (found, found at)?
8. His reason for resigning was (because, that) his family needed him.
9. The girls moved the picnic table so that they could eat (beside, besides) the lake.
10. This version of the story is different (from, than) yours.

▶ **Exercise 3**   Avoiding Usage Problems.   Correctly complete each of the following sentences by underlining the correct form from the choices in parentheses.

1. Kathleen walked (in, into) the room and announced the name of the winner.
2. His progress in his studies was greater (than, then) his friends imagined.
3. It seems (like, that) you were expecting us all along.
4. Wynn looked (kind of, rather) green after eating all those peppers.
5. (In, Into) the closet Kelly found the missing keys.
6. Nathan has a good speaking voice, but he sings (as, like) a frog.
7. First I dropped the turkey, and (than, then) I spilled the gravy.
8. Andy wrote every day, just (like, as) she had promised.
9. It looks (sort of, rather) silly for you to leave after just arriving.
10. As you climb (farther, further) up the mountain, the trees become sparse.

22.1 The Principal Parts of Verbs (Regular Verbs)
• Practice 1

Regular Verbs   Every verb has four principal parts: the present, the present participle, the past, and the past participle. Regular verbs form the past and past participle by adding *-ed* or *-d* to the present form.

PRINCIPAL PARTS OF REGULAR VERBS			
Present	Present Participle	Past	Past Participle
look	(am) looking	looked	(have) looked
inform	(am) informing	informed	(have) informed
move	(am) moving	moved	(have) moved
use	(am) using	used	(have) used

In sentences the four principal parts are used alone or with helping verbs.

SENTENCES USING THE PRINCIPAL PARTS OF *CALL*
Present: I *call* my aunt every week.
Present Participle: I *am calling* Dr. Johnson this morning.
Past: She *called* to invite me to a party.
Past Participle: He *has called* three different stores.

▶ **Exercise 1**   **Identifying the Principal Parts of Regular Verbs.**   Underline the verb or verb phrase in each sentence. Then identify the principal part used to form the verb.

EXAMPLE: We <u>watched</u> the tennis match. _____*past*_____

1. I write a column for the school newspaper. _____
2. Gary waited half an hour for the bus. _____
3. Karen is visiting her relatives in Iowa. _____
4. Are you listening to the explanation? _____
5. The speaker had paused for a moment. _____
6. They were wearing their basketball uniforms. _____
7. Mr. Kelly coached the football team last season. _____
8. Amy had remembered to pack a flashlight. _____
9. We are planning a number of surprises. _____
10. These musicians usually play some contemporary music. _____

▶ **Exercise 2**   **Using Principal Parts of Regular Verbs.**   Write the form of the verb in parentheses that correctly completes the sentence.

EXAMPLE: We are (begin) the project tomorrow. _____*beginning*_____

1. Kevin has (live) in Kentucky all his life. _____
2. The players were (discuss) their strategies. _____
3. I still (exercise) every day. _____
4. We have (agree) to meet at 7 P.M. _____
5. Before he spoke, the entertainer (smile) at the audience. _____
6. Frank had already (perform) his act before I arrived. _____
7. He is (attempt) to run a four-minute mile. _____
8. Yesterday Jennifer (promise) she would join our group. _____
9. Kenneth is (practice) a new song on his clarinet. _____
10. I am (suggest) that you make several changes. _____

22.1 The Principal Parts of Verbs (Regular Verbs)
• Practice 2

▶ **Exercise 1** **Recognizing the Principal Parts of Regular Verbs.**   Underline the verb or verb phrase in each of the following sentences. Then identify the principal part used to form the verb.

EXAMPLE: Frank <u>was serving</u> dinner when he heard the news.   *present participle*

1. I practice my music every day. _____
2. Antonio rubbed his hiking boots carefully with saddle soap. _____
3. Celia has wanted to meet my twin cousins for a long time. _____
4. The twins are competing against each other in the debate next week. _____
5. Henry mailed the letter without a stamp and without a ZIP code. _____
6. Were you laughing at the actress's joke or at her costume? _____
7. Because of the thunderstorm, we postponed our trip to the beach. _____
8. Lawrence had already changed his mind twice before breakfast. _____
9. Those dogwood trees in the park always blossom in the spring. _____
10. What is she placing over the door? _____
11. Does he really mean it? _____
12. Will has been coming to this park for years. _____
13. Glenda should have written sooner. _____
14. Where have you been keeping yourself? _____
15. How many times have you seen her there? _____

▶ **Exercise 2**   **Using the Principal Parts of Regular Verbs.**   For each of the following sentences, write the correct form of the word given in parentheses.

EXAMPLE: The caterpillar has ____*changed*____ into a moth. (change)

1. Meredith is _____ weights to increase her strength. (lift)
2. Edgar had already _____ his tie six times before the interview began. (straighten)
3. The baby tipped over the cup and _____ the milk on his feet. (spill)
4. I am happy that they still _____ me every summer. (visit)
5. Alexandra is _____ a special table for her work room. (design)
6. Car chases in movies have always _____ me. (frighten)
7. Had you _____ your newspaper when the bus arrived? (finish)
8. His grandmother _____ her own exotic desserts for years. (create)
9. Who is _____ at the back door? (knock)
10. He has _____ the character in his story on his Uncle Robert. (base)
11. The substitute teacher should be _____ any minute now. (arrive)
12. Her application has been _____ already. (reject)
13. Do you think Gary's contract will be _____? (renew)
14. Despite their similar appearances, Sandra and Andrea are not _____. (relate)
15. The suitcases have always been _____ in the hall closet. (store)

22.1 The Principal Parts of Verbs (Irregular Verbs)
• Practice 1

Irregular Verbs An irregular verb does not form the past and past participle by adding *-ed* or *-d* to the present form. Irregular forms must be memorized.

PRINCIPAL PARTS OF SOME IRREGULAR VERBS			
Present	**Present Participle**	**Past**	**Past Participle**
be	(am) being	was	(have) been
bring	(am) bringing	brought	(have(brought
burst	(am) bursting	burst	(have) burst
choose	(am) choosing	chose	(have) chosen
cost	(am) costing	cost	(have) cost
drink	(am) drinking	drank	(have) drunk
fly	(am) flying	flew	(have) flown
grow	(am) growing	grew	(have) grown
pay	(am) paying	paid	(have) paid
rise	(am) rising	rose	(have) risen
swear	(am) swearing	swore	(have) sworn
swim	(am) swimming	swam	(have) swum
teach	(am) teaching	taught	(have) taught
throw	(am) throwing	threw	(have) thrown
write	(am) writing	wrote	(have) written

▶ **Exercise 1** **Supplying the Principal Parts of Irregular Verbs.** Fill in the missing principal parts in the exercise below.

EXAMPLE:

drive _____ *driving* _____ *drove* _____ *driven* _____

1. _____ _____ swore _____
2. pay _____ _____ _____
3. _____ being _____ _____
4. _____ _____ _____ cost
5. write _____ _____ _____
6. _____ bringing _____ _____
7. _____ _____ _____ risen
8. _____ _____ chose _____
9. burst _____ _____ _____
10. _____ _____ threw _____

▶ **Exercise 2** **Using the Principal Parts of Irregular Verbs.** Fill in the blanks with the correct verb form from the choices shown in parentheses.

EXAMPLE: Angela _____*threw*_____ the ball to first base. (threw, throwed)

1. Edward had never _____ so far before. (swam, swum)

2. My grandmother _____ me how to bake bread. (taught, teached)

3. Last summer I _____ to California. (flied, flew)

4. We have _____ all the juice in the refrigerator. (drank, drunk)

5. I have already _____ two inches this year. (grown, grew)

22.1 The Principal Parts of Verbs (Irregular Verbs)
• Practice 2

▶ **Exercise 1** **Completing the Principal Parts of Irregular Verbs.** Write the missing principal parts for the following irregular verbs.

	Present	Present Participle	Past	Past Participle
1.	_____	_____	froze	_____
2.	run	_____	_____	_____
3.	_____	_____	_____	lain
4.	swing	_____	_____	_____
5.	_____	_____	set	_____
6.	_____	holding	_____	_____
7.	_____	_____	_____	taught
8.	_____	paying	_____	_____
9.	bring	_____	_____	_____
10.	_____	_____	laid	_____

▶ **Exercise 2** **Using the Past of Irregular Verbs.** For each of the following sentences, choose the correct verb from the choices in parentheses and write it in the blank.

EXAMPLE: We ___*froze*___ the vegetables. (freezed, froze)

1. The camping trip was fun, but my sister _____ a bad cold. (catched, caught)
2. The pitcher _____ the ball to third base. (threw, throwed)
3. This bicycle _____ much more than my last one. (costed, cost)
4. After dinner Earl _____ down for a rest. (lay, lied)
5. Maggie's father _____ their house himself. (built, builded)
6. Ron _____ that he would never go near the highway again. (swore, sweared)
7. Jessie _____ the balloons up for Seth's party. (blowed, blew)
8. The bear quickly _____ her paw into the beehive. (put, putted)
9. The baseball _____ the new bay windows of the shoe store. (broke, breaked)
10. Last winter we _____ down to Orlando to visit my grandmother. (flied, flew)

▶ **Exercise 3** **Using the Past Participle of Irregular Verbs.** For each of the following sentences, choose the correct verb from the choices in parentheses and write it in the blank.

EXAMPLE: Angel Clare should not have ___*spoken*___ to Tess that way. (spoke, spoken)

1. Has the sun _____ yet? (rose, risen)
2. Gary has _____ these designs for our parade float. (drawn, drew)
3. I had _____ home to meet you, but you never came. (ran, run)
4. Colleen and Marcie have _____ all the plums. (ate, eaten)
5. The bell had already _____ when the new teacher arrived. (rung, rang)
6. I have _____ to study, not to waste time. (came, come)
7. Don must have _____ four inches in the last year. (grown, grew)
8. Joyce had _____ a bathing suit to the picnic. (wore, worn)
9. The sandbar had already _____ out of sight by the time we arrived. (sunk, sank)
10. I was pleased that you had _____ that album. (chose, chosen)

22.2 # The Six Tenses of Verbs • **Practice 1**

The Basic Forms of the Six Tenses Tenses are verb forms that indicate time of action or state of being. Each of the six tenses has a basic form. All basic forms are derived from three principal parts: the present, the past, and the past participle.

Tense	Basic Form of *Take*	Principal Part Used
Present	I take	Present
Past	I took	Past
Future	I will take	Present
Present Perfect	I have taken	Past Participle
Past Perfect	I had taken	Past Participle
Future Perfect	I will have taken	Past Participle

Conjugating the Basic Forms of Verbs A conjugation is a list of the singular and plural forms of a verb in a particular tense. A short conjugation shows the forms of a verb used with one personal pronoun. Note that the verb forms used with *he* are also used with *she* and *it*, and the verb forms used with *we* are also used with *you* and *they*.

BASIC FORMS OF *SEE*			
Tense	With *I*	With *he*	With *we*
Present	I see	he sees	we see
Past	I saw	he saw	we saw
Future	I will see	he will see	we will see
Present Perfect	I have seen	he has seen	we have seen
Past Perfect	I had seen	he had seen	we had seen
Future Perfect	I will have seen	he will have seen	we will have seen

▶ **Exercise 1** **Recognizing Basic Forms and Tenses.** Underline the verb or verb phrase in each sentence. Then write the tense of the verb on the line to the right.

EXAMPLE: We will have completed the training program by next fall. _____*future perfect*_____

1. She will attend a conference in Washington, D.C. _____

2. Barbara and Marie refused to sign the petition. _____

3. The dancers rehearse every day. _____

4. We had considered several alternative plans. _____

5. I have memorized two poems by Walt Whitman. _____

▶ **Exercise 2** **Conjugating Basic Forms.** Complete both of the short conjugations below. Use the pronouns shown in parentheses.

want (with *she*)	1. visit (with *he*)	2. say (with *they*)
she wants	_____	_____
she wanted	_____	_____
she will want	_____	_____
she has wanted	_____	_____
she had wanted	_____	_____
she will have wanted	_____	_____

22.2 The Six Tenses of Verbs • Practice 2

▷ **Exercise 1** **Identifying the Basic Forms of Verbs.** Underline the verb in each of the following sentences. Then identify the tense of the verb.

EXAMPLE: We have collected a ton of newspapers for recycling. _____present perfect_____

1. Gabriel will present his report first. _____
2. We lived in Idaho for ten years. _____
3. They had notified us of their arrival. _____
4. Elaine and June practice their figure skating for two hours every day. _____
5. Our dogs have bitten no one. _____
6. The family will have finished dinner by seven. _____
7. Linda and Alison arrived at school earlier than usual. _____
8. We have seen that movie twice. _____
9. I will stay here no longer. _____
10. The Lochtefeld family owns an art gallery on Nantucket. _____

▷ **Exercise 2** **Conjugating the Basic Forms of Verbs.** Conjugate each of the following verbs with the pronoun shown in parentheses. The first two verbs are regular; the third is irregular.

1. ask (with *I*)   2. move (with *you*)   3. begin (with *they*)

_____   _____   _____
_____   _____   _____
_____   _____   _____
_____   _____   _____
_____   _____   _____
_____   _____   _____

▷ **Exercise 3** **Supplying the Correct Tense.** Supply the basic form of the verb as directed in parentheses.

EXAMPLE: Helen Keller _____spoke_____ her first word when she was an infant. (speak—past)

1. We _____ the police officer for directions to the museum. (ask—past)
2. The Johnsons _____ three times in the past year. (move—present perfect)
3. They _____ everything they wanted to by the end of their vacation. (see—past perfect)
4. Lou always _____ his homework after dinner. (begin—present)
5. By the end of their tour, the group _____ in eleven cities. (perform—future perfect)
6. We _____ the Uffizi Gallery when we go to Florence this summer. (visit—future)
7. Sharon _____ to her counselor earlier in the day. (talk—past perfect)
8. He never _____ what he is told to do. (do—present)
9. We _____ very fond of our new neighbors. (grow—present perfect)
10. She _____ you a chance to play yesterday. (give—past)

The Progressive Forms of Verbs • Practice 1

Recognizing Progressive Forms   Each of the six tenses has a progressive form. The six progressive forms of a verb make use of one principal part: the present participle.

THE PROGRESSIVE FORMS OF *WRITE*		
Tense	**Progressive Form**	**Principal Part Used**
Present	I am writing	
Past	I was writing	
Future	I will have been writing	Present Participle
Present Perfect	I have been writing	
Past Perfect	I had been writing	
Future Perfect	I will have been writing	

Conjugating the Progressive Forms of Verbs   To conjugate the progressive forms of a verb, add the present participle of a verb to a conjugation of the basic forms of *be*. Below are progressive forms of the verb *try* used with two different pronouns.

THE PROGRESSIVE FORMS OF *TRY*		
Tense	**With *I***	**With *she***
Present	I am trying	she is trying
Past	I was trying	she was trying
Future	I will be trying	she will be trying
Present Perfect	I have been trying	she has been trying
Past Perfect	I had been trying	she had been trying
Future Perfect	I will have been trying	she will have been trying

▶ **Exercise 1**   **Recognizing Progressive Forms and Tenses.**   Each sentence below contains a verb in its progressive form. Underline the verb phrase in each sentence. Then write the form of that verb phrase on the line at the right.

EXAMPLE: She had been studying all afternoon.   *past perfect   progressive*

1. The workers will be repairing the building. _____

2. The architect is explaining his plans. _____

3. Susan will have been working for two hours by 9 A.M. _____

4. They were discussing important political issues. _____

5. Diane has been telling us a folk tale. _____

▶ **Exercise 2**   **Conjugating Progressive Forms.**   Complete a short conjugation of the progressive forms of each verb below. Use the pronouns shown in parentheses.

buy (with *you*)   1. study (with *I*)   2. watch (with *he*)

you are buying   _____   _____

you were buying   _____   _____

you will be buying   _____   _____

you have been buying   _____   _____

you had been buying   _____   _____

you will have been buying   _____   _____

22.2 The Progressive Forms of Verbs • Practice 2

▷ **Exercise 1** **Identifying the Tense of Progressive Forms of Verbs.** Identify the tense of each of the following verbs.

EXAMPLE: was thinking _____past_____

1. will be going _____
2. have been seeing _____
3. am helping _____
4. will have been hiking _____
5. was carrying _____
6. had been visiting _____
7. am leaving _____
8. will be making _____
9. was playing _____
10. had been practicing _____

11. have been buying _____
12. will have been trying _____
13. was teaching _____
14. am writing _____
15. had been catching _____
16. will be singing _____
17. have been putting _____
18. was sitting _____
19. will have been waiting _____
20. am collecting _____

▷ **Exercise 2** **Conjugating the Progressive Forms of Verbs.** Conjugate the progressive forms of each of the following verbs with the pronoun shown in parentheses.

1. move (with *I*)

_____
_____
_____
_____
_____

2. freeze (with *she*)

_____
_____
_____
_____
_____

▷ **Exercise 3** **Supplying the Correct Tense.** Supply the progressive form of the verb as directed in parentheses.

EXAMPLE: He _____is going_____ to Alabama to visit his relatives. (go—present progressive)

1. I _____ to you when you telephoned me. (write—past progressive)
2. Clarissa _____ music at a special camp this summer. (study—future progressive)
3. Reggie _____ a heavy course load this year. (carry—present perfect progressive)
4. Despite her height, Kate _____ to make the basketball team. (hope—present progressive)
5. I was very relieved because I _____ a much lower grade. (expect—past perfect progressive)
6. The rain _____ all of our plans. (ruin—present progressive)
7. He _____ for two hours by noon. (swim—future perfect progressive)
8. Nick _____ second thoughts about the concert. (have—present perfect progressive)
9. The last ferry _____ soon. (leave—future progressive)
10. We _____ the dancer carefully all evening. (watch—past perfect progressive)

22.2 Active and Passive Voice (Two Voices, Forming the Tenses of Passive Verbs) • Practice 1

Two Voices Most verbs have two voices—the active and the passive. A verb is active when its subject performs the action. A verb is passive when its subject does not perform the action.

TWO VOICES	
Active Voice	**Passive Voice**
Kenneth *completed* the job.	The job *was completed* by Kenneth.
Ann *interviewed* the artist.	The artist *was interviewed* by Ann.

Forming the Tenses of Passive Verbs A passive verb is made from a form of *be* plus a past participle.

THE PASSIVE FORMS OF THE VERB *SAVE*	
Tense	**Passive Form**
Present	it is saved
Past	it was saved
Future	it will be saved
Present Perfect	it has been saved
Past Perfect	it had been saved
Future Perfect	it will have been saved

▶ **Exercise 1** **Distinguishing Between Active and Passive Voice.** On the line at the right identify the verb in each sentence as active or passive.

EXAMPLE: These flowers were grown by my neighbor. ___*passive*___

1. Peter built this model airplane. _____
2. The blue ceramic bowl was purchased by Arlene. _____
3. The chaotic scene was described by an eyewitness. _____
4. The decorator removed the painting from the wall. _____
5. A well-informed guide led us through the museum. _____
6. This event will be remembered for a long time. _____
7. Harvey took pictures of the graduation ceremony. _____
8. An amusing anecdote was told to me by my nephew. _____
9. The new student was introduced to the class. _____
10. Francis faced the crowd of people. _____

▶ **Exercise 2** **Conjugating Verbs in the Passive Voice.** Complete a short conjugation of the verbs below in the passive voice. Use the pronouns indicated in parentheses.

find (with *it*)
it is found

it was found

it will be found

it has been found

it had been found

it will have been found

1. ask (with *he*)
_____

_____

_____

_____

_____

_____

2. change (with *it*)
_____

_____

_____

_____

_____

_____

22.2 # Active and Passive Voice (Two Voices, Forming the Tenses of Passive Verbs) • Practice 2

▶ **Exercise 1** **Distinguishing Between Active and Passive Voice.** Underline the verb or verb phrase in each of the following sentences. Then identify the voice of the verb or verb phrase as either *active* or *passive*.

EXAMPLE: Those flowers were sent without a card. _____*passive*_____

1. Ted was hurt by Julie's reaction to his song. _____
2. The play was pronounced a great success by the producer and the critics. _____
3. Unfortunately, nobody believed him. _____
4. That sapling was bent by last December's unexpected ice storm. _____
5. Hot, tired, and out of breath, Kim finally reached the top of the Statue of Liberty. _____
6. The desk clerk directed us to the hotel dining room. _____
7. The note was left in this bottle more than fifty years ago. _____
8. Simon jumped the fence into the lilac bush. _____
9. After a long wait, Jill was admitted to the club. _____
10. Sam befriended me on my first day here, more than five years ago. _____
11. We were enchanted by the sea. _____
12. Marion forgave Richard long ago for his foolishness. _____
13. The snow covered the rooftops. _____
14. Most of the requirements were fulfilled by Denise. _____
15. A quick glance was sent my way by Tracy. _____
16. Grandma left her fortune to charity. _____
17. Michael framed each and every one of those photographs. _____
18. She was erasing her errors. _____
19. Clara was given a special gift by her aunt. _____
20. June had ripped the wrapping paper from the package. _____

▶ **Exercise 2** **Conjugating Verbs in the Passive Voice.** Conjugate the following two verbs in the passive voice. In each conjugation include the pronouns indicated in parentheses.

1. do (with *it*)

_____
_____
_____
_____
_____
_____

2. scold (with *he*)

_____
_____
_____
_____
_____
_____

22.2 Active and Passive Voice (Using Active and Passive Voice) • Practice 1

Using Active and Passive Voices   Use the active voice whenever possible. Use the passive voice to emphasize the receiver of an action or to point out the receiver whenever the performer is unknown, unimportant, or not named in the sentence.

USES OF ACTIVE AND PASSIVE VOICES
The touchdown *was scored* by Martin. (Wordy and weak passive; better as active voice: Martin *scored* the touchdown.)
Mayor Johnson *was honored* by his colleagues. (Correct passive; emphasizes Mayor Johnson, the receiver of the action.)
We *were told* to leave the building at once. (Correct passive; the performer is not named in the sentence.)

▶ **Exercise 1**   **Using Verbs in the Active Voice.**   Rewrite each sentence below, changing the verb from passive voice to active voice. Make any necessary word changes.

EXAMPLE: New computers were recently purchased by our school.
        Our school recently purchased new computers.

1. The awards were presented by the principal.

   _____

2. During the first act, a solo was performed by Gloria.

   _____

3. Our trip to Tucson, Arizona, was planned by Russell and John.

   _____

4. A hole in one was shot by Louis on his first try.

   _____

5. An important speech was made by the president.

   _____

6. A number of pictures have been drawn by me since my arrival.

   _____

7. A bright red cap was worn by Harriet.

   _____

8. A large CD collection is shared by the members of my family.

   _____

9. I have been asked by Mr. Peterson to prepare a short speech.

   _____

10. You will be trained by an experienced craftsman.

   _____

▶ **Exercise 2**   **Avoiding Unnecessary Uses of the Passive Tense.**   Rewrite the sentences in the following paragraph. Change passive verbs to active ones to improve the paragraph. Use a separate sheet of paper.

EXAMPLE: The Jamestown settlers were helped by Native Americans.
        Native Americans helped the Jamestown settlers.

    (1) The colony of Jamestown was settled by the English in 1607. (2) One hundred and four men and boys had been sent by a group of merchants in England. (3) The settlers had been instructed by their sponsors to look for gold and other valuables. (4) They were also told by the merchants to find a route to Asia. (5) A difficult beginning was experienced by these early settlers, but eventually they prospered.

22.2 Active and Passive Voice (Using Active and Passive Voice) • Practice 2

▶ **Exercise 1** **Using the Active Voice.** Rewrite each of the following sentences, changing the verb from the passive voice to the active voice and making whatever other changes are necessary.

EXAMPLE: This old watch was found by me in my grandmother's bureau.
I found this old watch in my grandmother's bureau.

1. All the hamburgers were eaten by us in less than five minutes.
   _____

2. Television is hardly ever watched by Randy and Caroline.
   _____

3. The story was blurted out by the twins to everyone in the room.
   _____

4. A decision was suddenly reached by the President.
   _____

5. A home run was hit by Andy in his first time at bat.
   _____

6. Sequined tank suits were worn by the members of the precision swim team.
   _____

7. Many books have been read by me since I got a library card.
   _____

8. The javelin was hurled forcefully into the air by Don.
   _____

9. A remarkable opportunity was missed by you yesterday.
   _____

10. Four languages are spoken by him fluently.
    _____

▶ **Writing Application** **Correcting Unnecessary Use of the Passive Voice.** Most of the underlined verbs in the following paragraph are in the passive voice. Rewrite the paragraph, changing as many of the passive verbs into active ones as you think necessary to improve the paragraph. It is not necessary to change every passive verb. Use a separate sheet of paper.

EXAMPLE: Vehicles of many different sorts have been sent into space by the United States.
The United States has sent vehicles of many different sorts into space.

(1) After years of preparation and many delays, the first space shuttle was launched by the United States in 1981. (2) The shuttle had been designed by NASA engineers to make a number of voyages into outer space. (3) The very first voyage was made by the spacecraft *Columbia* on April 12, 1981. (4) The spaceship was manned by astronauts John Young and Robert Crippen. (5) These men had been carefully trained for many years by NASA to participate in the space shuttle program. (6) The *Columbia* was lifted into space from Cape Canaveral by several rockets that could be reused by the space program. (7) These rockets were later recovered by the Navy from the Atlantic Ocean. (8) The spacecraft with its human cargo orbited the earth for two days. (9) It was finally guided back to the earth and was landed on the ground at Bakersfield, California, by astronauts Young and Crippen. (10) The successful flight was heralded by millions of Americans as this country's return to outer space.

22.3 # Glossary of Troublesome Verbs • Practice 1

Troublesome Verbs   Study the principal parts of troublesome verbs. Learn to distinguish between the meanings of confusing pairs of verbs.

INFORMATION ABOUT TROUBLESOME VERBS
1 *Ain't:* Avoid using *ain't* in both writing and speaking.
2 *Burst:* The present, past, and past participle of *burst* are all *burst. Bust* and *busted* are incorrect.
3 *Did and Done: Did* is used alone as a main verb. *Done* requires a helping verb such as *have* or *has.*
4 *Dragged and Drug: Drag* is a regular verb. *Drug* is not one of its principal parts.
5 *Drowned and Drownded:* The past and past participle of *drown* is *drowned. Drownded* is incorrect.
6 *Gone and Went: Gone* is the past participle of the verb *go. Gone* requires a helping verb such as *have* or *has. Went* is the past of *go* and is never used with a helping verb.
7 *Have and Of:* Do not use *of* in place of the helping verb *have.*
8 *Lay and Lie: Lay* means "to put" or "to place." It is followed by a direct object. *Lie* means "to rest in a reclining position" or "to be situated." It is never followed by a direct object.
9 *Learn and Teach: Learn* means "to receive knowledge." *Teach* means "to give knowledge."
10 *Leave and Let: Leave* means "to allow to remain." *Let* means "to permit."

▶ **Exercise 1**   **Using Troublesome Verbs Correctly.**   Circle the verb in the parentheses that correctly completes each sentence.

EXAMPLE: We had (went, ⬭gone⬭) to the park with Karen.

1. We (ain't, aren't) ready to begin.

2. Have you (dragged, drug) this scarf through the mud?

3. The lifeguard saved the swimmer before she (drownded, drowned).

4. I could (of, have) listened to that music for hours.

5. Where have I (laid, lay) my briefcase?

6. When the balloon (busted, burst), I was startled.

7. I want Cindy to (learn, teach) me how to make a quilt.

8. The cost of living has (risen, raised) sharply.

9. (Let, Leave) me finish what I am doing.

10. Joseph (did, done) his homework before dinner.

▶ **Exercise 2**   **Using Troublesome Verbs in Sentences.**   Use each verb listed below in a sentence.

EXAMPLE: sneaked
            The burglars sneaked through the empty house.

1. drowned _____

2. done _____

3. dragged _____

4. lay _____

5. learn _____

22.3 Glossary of Troublesome Verbs • Practice 2

▶ **Exercise 1**   Avoiding Problems with Troublesome Verbs.   For each of the following sentences, write the correct verb from the choices in parentheses.

EXAMPLE: Amelia Earhart ____*did*____ what few other people dared to do. (did, done)

1. The child _____ his stuffed bear across the playground. (dragged, drug)
2. _____ you finished with your homework yet? (Ain't, Aren't)
3. The happy guests _____ into the dining room. (busted, burst)
4. The patriot said, "I _____ my best for my country." (done, did)
5. Her answer was _____ in catcalls. (drowned, drownded)
6. My bicycle is _____ and can't be fixed. (busted, broken)
7. You look like something the cat _____ in. (drug, dragged)
8. The workers _____ everything on our list. (done, have done)
9. It _____ right to drop pennies from tall buildings. (ain't, isn't)
10. The weak swimmer almost _____ in the brutal current. (drowned, drownded)

▶ **Exercise 2**   Avoiding Problems with Troublesome Verbs.   For each of the following sentences, write the correct verb from the choices in parentheses.

1. Ms. Barker should _____ given us more time to finish that job. (of, have)
2. When we left, we _____ a blanket over the antique chair to protect it. (lay, laid)
3. I wish you would _____ me how to water-ski. (learn, teach)
4. _____ your brother alone! (Let, Leave)
5. _____ him go! (Let, Leave)
6. My mother would have _____ to college if she had had the money. (went, gone)
7. Children, _____ still until I call you. (lie, lay)
8. I am going to _____ myself how to cook in a Chinese Wok. (teach, learn)
9. You should _____ seen your face when they called out your name. (of, have)
10. They _____ away without saying goodbye. (went, gone)

▶ **Exercise 3**   Avoiding Problems with Troublesome Verbs.   For each of the following sentences, write the correct verb from the choices in parentheses.

1. The beam isn't balanced; _____ your end a little bit. (rise, raise)
2. We _____ down to a delicious lobster dinner. (set, sat)
3. The space shot was the most spectacular thing I've ever _____. (saw, seen)
4. He pointed to the carrot and _____, "Let's feed the rabbit." (said, says)
5. Harriet and Shirley _____ back to the wings of the theater. (snuck, sneaked)
6. He was proud that I _____ how well he did. (seen, saw)
7. Then the witch smiled and _____, "Look, I'll take a bite of the apple myself." (says, said)
8. "_____ the bird cage in that corner, please." (Sit, Set)
9. Inflation occurs when prices _____. (raise, rise)
10. Allen _____ a look at his birthday presents. (snuck, sneaked)

23 Cases of Personal Pronouns (Three Cases)
• Practice 1

Three Cases   The relation between a pronoun's form and its use in a sentence is known as *case*. English has three cases: nominative, objective, and possessive.

	THE THREE CASES OF PERSONAL PRONOUNS	
Case	**Pronoun Forms**	**Uses in Sentences**
Nominative	I, we; you; he, she, it, they	Subject of a Verb
		Predicate Pronoun
Objective	me, us; you; him, her, it, them	Direct Object
		Indirect Object
		Object of a Preposition
Possessive	my, mine, our, ours; your, yours, his, her, hers, its, their, theirs	To Show Ownership

▶ **Exercise 1**   **Determining Case.**   On the lines at the right write the case of the underlined personal pronoun in each sentence below.

EXAMPLE: <u>They</u> urged Louise to accept the job. _____*nominative*_____

1. It was <u>I</u> who delivered the message. _____

2. The members of the club elected <u>him</u> president. _____

3. Is this jacket <u>yours</u>? _____

4. <u>She</u> redecorated the room. _____

5. Please show <u>us</u> the letter. _____

6. A woman with a large hat sat in front of <u>me</u>. _____

7. The person in charge is <u>he</u>. _____

8. <u>Their</u> home is in Indiana. _____

9. <u>Mine</u> is the umbrella with the blue handle. _____

10. The orchestra played a song for <u>them</u>. _____

▶ **Exercise 2**   **Identifying Case and Use.**   Write the case of each underlined pronoun. Then write its use.

EXAMPLE: <u>He</u> met the new instructor. _____*nominative*_____ _____*subject of a verb*_____

1. The blue sedan is <u>ours</u>. _____ _____

2. <u>They</u> made an important announcement. _____ _____

3. Madeline showed <u>me</u> the photograph. _____ _____

4. Neil recognized <u>them</u> immediately. _____ _____

5. <u>His</u> ideas are quite original. _____ _____

6. The first speaker will be <u>she</u>. _____ _____

7. Sandra sat down beside <u>me</u>. _____ _____

8. Donna lent Jane <u>her</u> suitcase. _____ _____

9. Rachel and <u>I</u> played tennis yesterday. _____ _____

10. Patrick sent Bill and <u>me</u> tickets to the show. _____ _____

23 Cases of Personal Pronouns (Three Cases)
• Practice 2

▶ **Exercise 1**   **Identifying Case.**   Write the case of the personal pronouns that are underlined in the following sentences.

EXAMPLE: Melvin left the theater without us. _____objective_____

1. His photograph was awarded second prize. _____
2. Frances wrote me about the party for Vickie. _____
3. The first actors onstage will be he and I. _____
4. The collie caught the Frisbee and ran away with it. _____
5. Lauren and I haven't finished the kite yet. _____
6. As soon as the lights came on, Rennie saw them. _____
7. Uncle Norma forgave us for playing that band's music. _____
8. According to your count, how many people came to the second performance? _____
9. Unfortunately, he was the last person to leave the house. _____
10. Don't tell me any more bad news. _____
11. Their furniture needs refinishing. _____
12. Tina gave us plenty of time to prepare for the surprise. _____
13. Those letters belong to him and me. _____
14. That jar of buttons is mine. _____
15. Would you like an invitation to the dance? _____

▶ **Exercise 2**   **Identifying Pronoun Case and Use.**   Write the case of the underlined pronoun. Then write its use.

EXAMPLE: How many of you would like to enter a talent contest? _objective_   _object of a preposition_

1. She and I have worked out a plan. _____ _____
2. This is my book, and that one is yours. _____ _____
3. Their house is being repainted this weekend. _____ _____
4. Should we bring some form of identification? _____ _____
5. Did he give you permission to attend the play? _____ _____
6. Marla asked him a very personal question. _____ _____
7. The person at the counter is she. _____ _____
8. I heard him quite clearly. _____ _____
9. The mail carrier has an envelope for you. _____ _____
10. Please give him one of these pears. _____ _____
11. Does your dog bite? _____ _____
12. That is not my dog. _____ _____
13. What a show! Have you seen it yet? _____ _____
14. She doesn't know how important this is. _____ _____
15. I dropped off the dry cleaning for her. _____ _____

23 Cases of Personal Pronouns (The Nominative Case, The Objective Case) • Practice 1

The Nominative Case   Use a personal pronoun in the nominative case (1) as the subject of a verb or (2) as a predicate pronoun.

USES OF THE NOMINATIVE CASE	
Subject of a Verb	*They* are expecting a package.
	After school Ralph and *he* headed for home.
Predicate Pronoun	The chairperson will be *she*.

The Objective Case   Use a personal pronoun in the objective case as (1) a direct object, (2) an indirect object, or (3) the object of a preposition.

USES OF THE OBJECTIVE CASE	
Direct Object	I admire *him*.
	Deborah met Tom and *her* in the gym.
Indirect Object	The usher handed *them* a program.
Object of a Preposition	Alice sat beside *her*.
	Do not leave without Michael and *me*.

▶ **Exercise 1**   **Using Nominative Pronouns.**   Fill in each blank with a nominative pronoun. Then write how the pronoun is used in the sentence.

EXAMPLE: _____*You*_____ can accompany me to the museum. _____*subject of a verb*_____

1. Since this morning, _____ has been reading. _____

2. Henry and _____ took a walk together. _____

3. The most outstanding dancer in the class is _____ . _____

4. Carefully, _____ moved the priceless antique statue. _____

5. According to the plan, _____ will meet in Chicago. _____

6. The scientist who made the discovery is _____ . _____

7. It was _____ who answered the telephone. _____

8. The Robinsons and _____ vacationed in Colorado. _____

9. The losers will probably be John and _____ . _____

10. The film reviewers are Nancy and _____ . _____

▶ **Exercise 2**   **Using Objective Pronouns.**   Fill in each blank with an objective pronoun. Then write how the pronoun is used in the sentence.

EXAMPLE: A friend introduced _____*us*_____ . _____*direct object*_____

1. I have not seen _____ for a long time. _____

2. We enjoy having people around _____ . _____

3. The speaker's arguments convinced _____ . _____

4. Alexandra showed _____ her latest drawings. _____

5. The younger children sat in front of _____ . _____

6. The artist painted _____ a picture. _____

7. During the conference, we sat opposite _____ . _____

8. The hostess thanked _____ for the gift. _____

9. Daniel wrote _____ a note last week. _____

10. Carol is playing against _____ in the semifinals. _____

23 Cases of Personal Pronouns (The Nominative Case, The Objective Case) • Practice 2

▶ **Exercise 1**   **Using Pronouns in the Nominative Case.**   Complete each of the following sentences by writing a nominative pronoun. Then write how each pronoun is used in the sentence.

EXAMPLE: Without question ____*she*____ had to care for the pony herself. ____*subject*____

1. After losing the match, _____ boarded a bus and drove silently out of town. _____

2. Georgina and _____ both wanted something smaller. _____

3. The winner of the first prize for the best essay would obviously be _____. _____

4. Only _____ knows where practice is today. _____

5. _____ are sanding an old oak desk. _____

6. Doris always answered the telephone formally by saying, "It is _____." _____

7. When the airport came into view, _____ began to talk excitedly. _____

8. The first person in line to buy tickets to the concert was _____. _____

9. In addition to that old letter, _____ found two high-buttoned shoes. _____

10. Unfortunately, _____ can't possibly finish the job by tomorrow morning. _____

▶ **Exercise 2**   **Using Pronouns in the Objective Case.**   Complete each of the following sentences by writing an objective pronoun. Then write how each pronoun is used in the sentence.

EXAMPLE: His grandmother's stories gave ____*him*____ ideas that he later used in his writing. ____*indirect object*____

1. Rain or shine, Ellen always brought happiness with _____. _____

2. Henry visited _____ on his trip out West. _____

3. Please tell _____ your problems. _____

4. In the 1000-meter run, Jonathan timed _____ with a stopwatch. _____

5. Richard dedicated his book to _____. _____

6. The rainy weather gives _____ very little opportunity for swimming. _____

7. Caroline sent Max and _____ a message about the change in plans. _____

8. Beth ran behind _____ and hid the present. _____

9. Jerry should show _____ his prize lamb. _____

10. We left _____ at home with the baby. _____

23 Cases of Personal Pronouns (The Possessive Case) • Practice 1

The Possessive Case   Use the possessive case of personal pronouns before nouns to show possession. Use certain personal pronouns by themselves to indicate possession. Personal pronouns in the possessive case are never written with apostrophes.

USES OF THE POSSESSIVE CASE	
Before Nouns	*His* brother plays the clarinet. Can you come to *our* house?
By Themselves	*Mine* is the gray suitcase. Is that notebook *yours*?

▶ **Exercise 1**   **Using Possessive Pronouns.**   Circle the correct word from the choices in parentheses.

EXAMPLE: (Their's, (Theirs)) are the skis in the corner.

1. Is (your's, yours) the gray cap on the sofa?
2. The kitten was playing with (its, it's) favorite toy.
3. (Hers, Her's) was an exceptionally interesting childhood.
4. I always enjoy (you're, your) Sunday dinners.
5. Thomas brought (his, his') radio to the beach.
6. (It's, Its) too early to know for sure.
7. One of (me, my) favorite movies is on television tonight.
8. This store claims that (their's, theirs) are the lowest prices.
9. (They're, Their) first business venture was a great success.
10. The final decision is (your's, yours).

▶ **Exercise 2**   **Using the Three Cases of Personal Pronouns.**   Circle the correct word from the choices in parentheses.

EXAMPLE: The senator and ((he), him) spoke to the committee.

1. It must have been (them, they) who sent me this gift.
2. We expect Barbara and (he, him) to arrive shortly.
3. Grace and (me, I) explored the area.
4. No one listened to Donald and (me, I).
5. The composer of the song I am playing is (he, him).
6. (Their's, Theirs) is a productive collaboration.
7. Can the hotel accommodate them and (us, we)?
8. The Turners and (we, us) went to the theater.
9. The dog wagged (it's, its) tail as his master appeared.
10. The attorney asked Eugene and (me, I) some questions.

23 Cases of Personal Pronouns (The Possessive Case) • Practice 2

▷ **Exercise 1** **Using Pronouns in the Possessive Case.** For each of the following sentences, write the correct word from the choices in parentheses.

1. _____ exceptional voice brought Len to the conductor's attention. (His, His')

2. The chimpanzee and _____ master walk in the park each day. (it's, its)

3. I will never understand _____ joy in working on a stamp collection. (you, your)

4. The bicycles were _____. (theirs, their's)

5. _____ last letter to him was ten pages long. (My, Me)

6. You may use this room while _____ is being painted. (your's, yours)

7. The album was clearly _____. (hers, her's)

8. The bird was so friendly that _____ chirps ceased to irritate us. (its, it's)

9. George grabbed the pie and yelled, "_____ mine!" (Its, It's)

10. Fred now felt he could call the house of his host _____ own. (his', his)

▷ **Exercise 2** **Checking the Case of Personal Pronouns.** Identify each pronoun error and write the correct form. For sentences without any errors, write *correct*.

EXAMPLE: I sent invitations to Jeremy and he. ___*he, him*___

1. The lion in the center ring kept looking at her and me. _____

2. Donald gave no real reason for leaving his' suitcase in the station. _____

3. This room and it's furnishings were designed by my uncle's firm. _____

4. He will probably decide to sit between you and I at the concert. _____

5. The flowers wilting in the heat are theirs. _____

6. The person on the other end of the line was him. _____

7. Harry, Jessie, and me worked all afternoon. _____

8. We will never forget the way that you told that joke. _____

9. The students finally chosen were they and us. _____

10. These books used to be Regina's, but now they are your's. _____

▷ **Writing Application** **Using Pronouns Correctly.** Use each of the following pronouns in a sentence of your own according to the instructions in parentheses.

1. us and them (with a preposition)

_____

2. he and I (as predicate pronouns)

_____

3. its (to show possession)

_____

4. your (to show possession)

_____

5. her (as an indirect object)

_____

23 Cases of *Who* and *Whom* • Practice 1

Separate Uses in Sentences   *Who* is a pronoun in the nominative case. Like other nominative pronouns, *who* is used as the subject of a verb.

USING *WHO*	
The Subject of a Question	*Who* finished first?
The Subject of a Subordinate Clause	I met the woman *who* directs the recreation program here.

Whom is a pronoun in the objective case. Like other objective pronouns, *whom* is used (1) as the direct object of a verb or (2) as the object of a preposition.

USING *WHOM*	
The Direct Object of a Verb	*Whom* did she ask to return?
	It was William *whom* they interviewed.
The Object of a Preposition	To *whom* shall I address this note?
	Here is the artist about *whom* I was speaking.

▶ **Exercise 1**   **Using *Who* and *Whom*.**   Write *who* or *whom* in each blank below.

EXAMPLE: Ronald, after ____*whom*____ do I speak?

1. Beside _____ are you sitting?

2. Have you met the pilot _____ is flying the plane?

3. For _____ are we waiting?

4. The actor _____ the critics selected received an award.

5. Tell me the name of the congressman _____ you are describing.

6. You recommended _____ for the job?

7. _____ drew this cartoon?

8. Everyone _____ we polled agreed with us.

9. Alfred Hitchcock is the filmmaker _____ he most admires.

10. _____ has traveled through the most states?

▶ **Exercise 2**   **Choosing the Correct Form and Use of *Who* and *Whom*.**   Circle the correct form of the pronoun in parentheses. Then write the number that describes how the pronoun is used in the sentence: *1* (subject of a question); *2* (subject of a subordinate clause); *3* (direct object of a verb); *4* (object of a preposition).

EXAMPLE: She is the author ((who), whom) wrote this novel. ____*2*____

1. (Who, Whom) received the most votes? _____

2. (Who, Whom) have they nominated for secretary? _____

3. With (who, whom) are you having lunch? _____

4. Michael is the runner (who, whom) came in first. _____

5. (Who, Whom) besides you can't find his notebook? _____

6. John was the person (who, whom) they sent to California. _____

7. Mary is the one (who, whom) represents us on the student council. _____

8. (Who, Whom) in the first act has the most lines? _____

9. I photographed the man (who, whom) works with my father. _____

10. Alan is the person to (who, whom) he dedicated his first book. _____

23 Cases of *Who* and *Whom* • Practice 2

▷ **Exercise 1** Using *Who* and *Whom* in Questions. For each of the following sentences, write the correct pronoun from the choices given in parentheses.

EXAMPLE: _____*Whom*_____ did you ask to the party? (Who, Whom)

1. To _____ were you just speaking? (who, whom)

2. _____ among us has met a famous person? (Who, Whom)

3. This article was written by _____? (who, whom)

4. _____ were you helping in the cafeteria the other day? (Who, Whom)

5. Of the two, _____ is more capable? (who, whom)

6. _____ is your favorite singer? (Who, Whom)

7. _____ wouldn't know you, even in that disguise? (Who, Whom)

8. _____ did she leave with the children? (Who, Whom)

9. For _____ should I ask at the Governor's office? (who, whom)

10. _____ in this group could be at the theater by seven o'clock? (Who, Whom)

▷ **Exercise 2** Using *Who* and *Whom* in Subordinate Clauses. Underline the subordinate clause in each of the following sentences. Then indicate the way in which *who* or *whom* is being used in the subordinate clause.

EXAMPLE: What is the name of the person who is calling ? _____*subject*_____

1. My sister Emily, for whom I wrote this poem, is hiding in the maple tree. _____

2. I know the singer who performed at your party. _____

3. I can introduce you to Walter, whom you have been admiring from afar. _____

4. We were eager to meet the woman who will be our candidate. _____

5. Guess the name of the person who told me that. _____

6. Give it to the person in whom you place the most trust. _____

7. Guess what happened to the man whom we met in the lobby at intermission. _____

8. Gil is one person in whom I have absolute confidence. _____

9. Please don't invite the person who spilled the coffee last time. _____

10. I asked Jim to tell me the name of the person who wrote the limerick. _____

▷ **Writing Application** Writing Sentences with *Who* and *Whom*. Write five original sentences, each using *who* or *whom* according to the instructions given in parentheses.

1. who (as subject in a question)

_____

2. whom (as direct object in a question)

_____

3. who (as subject in a subordinate clause)

_____

4. whom (as direct object in a subordinate clause)

_____

5. whom (as direct object of a preposition in a subordinate clause)

_____

24.1 Agreement Between Subjects and Verbs
(The Number of Nouns, Pronouns, and Verbs) • Practice 1

The Number of Nouns and Pronouns   Nouns and pronouns have number. They are either singular, indicating one, or plural, indicating more than one.

NOUNS AND PRONOUNS		
Part of Speech	**Singular**	**Plural**
Nouns	mountain	mountains
	tax	taxes
	mouse	mice
Personal Pronouns	I, me, my, mine	we, us, our, ours
	you, your, yours	you, your, yours
	he, him, his, she, her, it, its	they, them, their, theirs
Indefinite Pronouns	anybody, each, nobody	both, few, many

The Number of Verbs   Verbs also have number. Subjects and verbs must agree in number. Third-person singular verb forms in the present tense change to show number. The third-person singular form adds an -s, or -es. Forms of the verb *be* also change to show number.

VERBS	
Singular	*First and Second Person*: (I, you) begin
	Third Person: (he, she, it) begins
Plural	*First, Second, and Third Person*: (we, you, they) begin

▶ **Exercise 1**   **Identifying the Number of Nouns and Pronouns.**   Label each of the following words as *singular* or *plural*.

EXAMPLE: cities _____*plural*_____

1. home _____
2. he _____
3. ranches _____
4. we _____
5. nobody _____
6. several _____
7. women _____
8. everyone _____
9. it _____
10. acres _____

11. railroads _____
12. I _____
13. she _____
14. desert _____
15. they _____
16. others _____
17. oxen _____
18. something _____
19. children _____
20. lunches _____

▶ **Exercise 2**   **Identifying the Number of Verbs.**   Underline the present tense verb in the parentheses that agrees with the subject in each sentence. Then label the verb as *singular* or *plural*.

EXAMPLE: He (teaches, teach) science. _____*singular*_____

1. They (enjoy, enjoys) singing. _____
2. A dog (bark, barks) loudly. _____
3. Our guests (arrives, arrive) shortly. _____
4. Plants (grow, grows) slowly. _____
5. I (am, are) happy on my birthday. _____

24.1 Agreement Between Subjects and Verbs
(The Number of Nouns, Pronouns, and Verbs) • Practice 2

▷ **Exercise 1** Recognizing the Number of Nouns and Pronouns. Label each of the following words *singular* or *plural*.

1. I _____
2. it _____
3. gas _____
4. we _____
5. they _____
6. others _____
7. bees _____
8. boxes _____
9. bird _____
10. mess _____

11. mouse _____
12. both _____
13. roses _____
14. each _____
15. those _____
16. houses _____
17. player _____
18. someone _____
19. women _____
20. friendship _____

▷ **Exercise 2** Recognizing the Number of Verbs. For each of the following items, underline the verb from the choices in parentheses that agrees in number with the pronoun. Then write whether the verb is *singular* or *plural*.

EXAMPLE: he (begin, <u>begins</u>) _____*singular*_____

1. we (knows, know) _____
2. they (was, were) _____
3. she (knows, know) _____
4. I (is, am) _____
5. he (were, was) _____
6. we (is, are) _____
7. they (have, has) _____
8. it (was, were) _____
9. she (have, has) _____
10. we (argues, argue) _____

▷ **Exercise 3** Recognizing the Number of Verbs. Underline the present tense verb in the parentheses that agrees with the subject in each sentence. Then label the verb as *singular* or *plural*.

EXAMPLE: He (enjoy, <u>enjoys</u>) riding a bicycle. _____*singular*_____

1. They (accept, accepts) your offer. _____
2. She (whirl, whirls) around on the stage. _____
3. We (bargain, bargains) with the salesperson. _____
4. It slowly (trickle, trickles) out of the spout. _____
5. They (build, builds) things out of blocks. _____
6. Before work, she (clear, clears) a space on her desk. _____
7. They (are flying, is flying) in formation. _____
8. He (is, are) a perfect house guest. _____
9. We (is accepting, are accepting) the terms of the offer. _____
10. He (plant, plants) his summer garden. _____

24.1 Agreement Between Subjects and Verbs
(Agreement with Singular and Plural Subjects) • Practice 1

Agreement With Singular and Plural Subjects A singular subject requires a singular verb. A plural subject requires a plural verb.

AGREEMENT BETWEEN SUBJECTS AND VERBS	
Singular	**Plural**
Our car usually starts easily.	The students play basketball on Thursdays.
Jean collects antique furniture.	According to the newspaper, leaders are meeting in Washington.

When a prepositional phrase comes between a subject and its verb, it does not affect subject-verb agreement.

A PREPOSITIONAL PHRASE SEPARATING A SUBJECT AND ITS VERB
That book of riddles amuses me.
The magazines on this shelf belong to me.

▶ **Exercise 1** **Recognizing Subject-Verb Agreement.** Underline the subject of each sentence once. Then select the verb in parentheses that agrees with this subject and underline it twice.

EXAMPLE: The customers on the long line (wait, waits) patiently.

1. A delivery of eggs (arrive, arrives) early each morning.
2. The cafeteria (open, opens) at noon.
3. The tree near the tulips (shade, shades) the porch.
4. That old train station (look, looks) very familiar.
5. My aunt usually (send, sends) me a picture postcard when she travels.
6. The invitations to the party (is, are) ready to send.
7. The children (walk, walks) to the meadow each day.
8. The people on the crowded street (rush, rushes) home.
9. Our weekly meetings (begin, begins) at 7:30 P.M.
10. The animals in the show (belong, belongs) to members of our club.

▶ **Exercise 2** **Selecting Verbs that Agree with Singular and Plural Subjects.** For each sentence, underline the verb in parentheses that agrees with the subject. Then label the sentence *S* if the subject is singular and *P* if the subject is plural.

EXAMPLE: The chairs in the auditorium (is, are) new. _____P_____

1. The members of the committee (speak, speaks) to us today. _____
2. The barn across from the stables (belong, belongs) to us. _____
3. Several men (assist, assists) us in the shop. _____
4. A cabinet filled with trophies (stand, stands) in the corner. _____
5. The tourists on the bus (admire, admires) the scenery. _____
6. The paintings along this wall (is, are) family portraits. _____
7. His idea really (interest, interests) me. _____
8. His plans to travel to Peru (sound, sounds) exciting. _____
9. The houses along the shore (is, are) vacant now. _____
10. The designer of all this clothing (live, lives) in Paris. _____

24.1 Agreement Between Subjects and Verbs
(Agreement with Singular and Plural Subjects) • Practice 2

▶ **Exercise 1**   **Making Verbs Agree with Singular and Plural Subjects.**   For each of the following sentences, underline the correct verb of the two shown in parentheses.

EXAMPLE: The books on the shelf (was, <u>were</u>) dog-eared.

1. The wind always (makes, make) the screen door rattle during the summer.
2. The keys to our house (is, are) on a ring just inside the garage.
3. The geese (migrates, migrate) north every year at this time.
4. My friends never (knows, know) what I will do next.
5. A famous painting of those trees and windmills (hangs, hang) in the art museum.
6. The parents of my best friend (has, have) invited me to the ballet.
7. The silence (was, were) deafening after the prosecution rested its case.
8. The secret of her many successes (lies, lie) in her diligence.
9. Red roses on a white wooden trellis (blooms, bloom) in my aunt's lovely garden.
10. The child with two sets of grandparents (enjoys, enjoy) the attention of many doting adults.
11. The owner of the three dogs (hesitate, hesitates) before ringing the doorbell.
12. The bees from the disturbed hive (buzz, buzzes) angrily around David's head.
13. The peasants from that village (grind, grinds) corn by hand.
14. The dogs in the neighbors' yard (growl, growls) at the baby.
15. The active two-year-old near the swings (cause, causes) the accident.

▶ **Exercise 2**   **Making Verbs Agree with Singular and Plural Subjects.**   For each sentence, underline the subject once, and underline the verb that agrees with the subject twice. Then label the sentence *S* if the subject is singular and *P* if the subject is plural.

EXAMPLE: The <u>train</u> (<u>waits</u>, wait) for only five minutes at this station. _____S_____

1. A clattering sound on the roof (startle, startles) Mr. Malloy. _____
2. Our victory over all the other teams (is, are) unexpected. _____
3. The newspapers (give, gives) more details than I care to read. _____
4. The girls' project (earn, earns) them a very good grade. _____
5. The ostrich at the zoo (miss, misses) its natural home. _____
6. Two painters (need, needs) two days to complete the job. _____
7. The astronomers at the observatory (discover, discovers) another galaxy. _____
8. For obvious reasons, the children (play, plays) inside today. _____
9. The parrots in that large cage (squawk, squawks) at strangers. _____
10. Magnets (attract, attracts) steel but not plastic. _____
11. The medals on the old soldier's uniform (were, was) quite impressive. _____
12. The mellow tones of the dance band (fill, fills) the air. _____
13. Two lizards on one warm rock (sun, suns) themselves. _____
14. One measure of this powder (make, makes) a gallon of juice. _____
15. The liquid in these bottles (come, comes) from that vat. _____

24.1 Agreement Between Subjects and Verbs
(Agreement with Compound Subjects) • Practice 1

Agreement with Compound Subjects Two or more singular subjects joined by *or* or *nor* require a singular verb. However, if one part of a compound subject joined by *or* or *nor* is singular and the other part is plural, the verb agrees with the closest subject.

COMPOUND SUBJECTS JOINED BY *OR* OR *NOR*	
Two Singular Subjects	Vivian or Mark writes the editorial.
	Neither Carl nor Eve remembers his name.
One Singular and One Plural Subject	Neither the coach nor the players are here.
	Neither the players nor the coach is here.

A compound subject joined by *and* requires a plural verb. The only exceptions are (1) when the parts of the subject are considered one thing or (2) when the subject is modified by *each* or *every*.

COMPOUND SUBJECTS JOINED BY *AND*
Spring and summer are my favorite seasons.
Macaroni and cheese is on the menu.
Each boy and girl receives a souvenir.

▷ **Exercise 1** **Using Compound Subjects Joined by *Or* or *Nor*.** Underline the verb in parentheses that agrees with the subject of each sentence.

EXAMPLE: Either Ann or Ted (<u>inspects</u>, inspect) the equipment.

1. Even though it is late, neither Evan nor Betty (is, are) here.
2. Either the students or their teacher (conduct, conducts) the debate.
3. Neither the lifeguard nor the swimmers (stay, stays) here all day.
4. A salad or two vegetables (comes, come) with your dinner.
5. Either the salespeople or the manager (demonstrate, demonstrates) the equipment.
6. Neither my parents nor Dianne (agrees, agree) with me.
7. Either the librarian or her assistant (is, are) available to help.
8. Neither the trainees nor their instructor (uses, use) shortcuts.
9. It is possible that the lawyer or his client (is, are) mistaken.
10. Neither the fruit juice nor the sandwiches (is, are) ready.

▷ **Exercise 2** **Using Compound Subjects Joined by *And*.** Underline the verb in parentheses that agrees with the subject of each sentence.

EXAMPLE: Marcia and her colleagues (gives, <u>give</u>) their report today.

1. Each volunteer and contributor (receives, receive) an invitation.
2. The governor and the senator (discusses, discuss) political issues.
3. Spaghetti and meatballs (was, were) served for lunch.
4. Both Carla and Brian (agrees, agree) that more planning is needed.
5. Every record and book (is, are) on sale today.
6. The costumes and props (belongs, belong) backstage.
7. The Hendersons and their niece (goes, go) skiing every winter.
8. Bacon and eggs (is, are) my favorite breakfast.
9. Mr. Gordon and his boss (has, have) offices on this floor.
10. Each flower and bush (is, are) carefully tended.

24.1 Agreement Between Subjects and Verbs
(Agreement with Compound Subjects) • Practice 2

▶ **Exercise 1** **Making Verbs Agree with Compound Subjects Joined by *Or* and *Nor*.** For each of the following sentences, write the correct verb from the choices in parentheses.

EXAMPLE: Neither the soup nor the salad ___*was*___ ready. (was, were)

1. Either Mary or John _____ going in my place. (is, are)

2. Neither Kate nor her parents _____ ever met anyone like Ace. (has, have)

3. Bread or fruit always _____ well with cheese. (goes, go)

4. Neither the nails nor the hammer _____ there. (was, were)

5. Either Joanna or Howard _____ the children to school each day. (takes, take)

▶ **Exercise 2** **Making Verbs Agree with Compound Subjects Joined by *And*.** For each of the following sentences, write the correct verb from the choices in parentheses.

EXAMPLE: Every knife and fork in the house ___*has*___ disappeared. (has, have)

1. Clocks and sundials _____ time. (measures, measure)

2. Cake and pie _____ Murray's favorite dessert. (is, are)

3. The gingham dog and the calico cat _____ not get along. (does, do)

4. The decorations and the centerpiece _____ beautiful. (was, were)

5. Every book and record in this library _____ signs of wear. (shows, show)

▶ **Exercise 3** **Recognizing Subjects and Verbs That Agree.** For each of the following sentences, write the correct verb from the choices in parentheses.

EXAMPLE: Either Elizabeth Blackwell or Amelia Earhart ___*is*___ the subject of her report. (is, are)

1. Marcy and Julio _____ directing the class play. (is, are)

2. Because of the wind, the doors in the deserted house next to the cemetery _____ open and shut all night long. (creaks, creak)

3. Either Vanessa or Robert _____ enough votes to win the election. (has, have)

4. To decorators, a combination of red and green _____ Christmas. (represents, represent)

5. Every cat and dog _____ adorned with a large ribbon. (was, were)

6. Neither the walls nor the floor of your room _____ very clean. (looks, look)

7. Spaghetti and meatballs _____ a popular dinner. (is, are)

8. Each television and radio in the store _____ tuned to a different station. (was, were)

9. Either my mother or my brothers _____ the fish we catch. (cleans, clean)

10. The mice in our attic _____ when we sleep. (scampers, scamper)

24.1 Special Problems with Subject-Verb Agreement • Practice 1

Agreement in Sentences with Unusual Word Order   When a subject follows a verb, they still must agree in number.

SENTENCES WITH INVERTED WORD ORDER
In this envelope <u>are</u> several newspaper <u>clippings</u>.
There <u>were</u> two <u>letters</u> on my desk.
Here <u>are</u> the <u>photographs</u> I took at the beach.
Where <u>are</u> the <u>tickets</u> to the concert?

Agreement with Indefinite Pronouns   An indefinite pronoun used as a subject must agree with its verb. Some indefinite subjects are always singular. Other indefinite pronouns are always plural. Still other indefinite pronouns can be either singular or plural depending on the number of the pronoun's antecedent.

INDEFINITE PRONOUNS						
Always Singular			**Always Plural**		**Singular or Plural**	
anyone	somebody	each	both	many	all	most
everybody	someone	no one	few	others	any	none
everything	something	one			more	some

▷ **Exercise 1**   Recognizing Subject-Verb Agreement in Sentences with Inverted Word Order.   Underline the subject in each sentence. Then circle the verb in parentheses that agrees with it.

EXAMPLE: Across from the park ((stand), stands) the <u>buses</u>.

1. Inside this box (is, are) important papers.

2. There (was, were) many paintings on the walls.

3. When (is, are) the next Giants game?

4. Along the winding roads (walk, walks) the traveler.

5. Around the corner (is, are) a new boutique.

6. Here (is, are) four samples I want you to examine.

7. (Is, Are) each of the senators on two committees?

8. (Is, Are) Mark Oliva the leading candidate for governor?

9. There (is, are) the elevator that goes to the top floor.

10. Here on the left (is, are) the horses they usually ride.

▷ **Exercise 2**   Making Indefinite Pronouns and Verbs Agree.   Underline the verb in parentheses that best completes each sentence.

EXAMPLE: No one (<u>expects</u>, expect) this warm weather to last.

1. Each of the problems (was, were) solved.

2. Few of the participants (remember, remembers) the incident.

3. All of his pets (demand, demands) a great deal of attention.

4. Everything stated in these reports (appears, appear) to be correct.

5. Both of the writers (agree, agrees) that we need to make changes.

24.1 Special Problems with Subject-Verb Agreement • Practice 2

▶ **Exercise 1** **Checking Agreement in Sentences with Inverted Word Order.** Underline the subject from each of the following sentences. Then write the correct verb from the choices in parentheses.

EXAMPLE: There _____are_____ the missing giraffes. (is, are)

1. Where in your desk _____ your green pens? (is, are)
2. High above other skyscrapers _____ the Empire State Building. (looms, loom)
3. Here _____ the letter I mentioned to you. (is, are)
4. Why _____ all three outfielders looking the wrong way? (is, are)
5. There _____ many possible reasons for their behavior. (is, are)
6. Crawling behind the sofa _____ two loudly giggling children. (was, were)
7. Here in this box _____ several toys from my childhood. (is, are)
8. How often _____ he manage to take a break from his responsibilities? (does, do)
9. How silently and softly _____ the rain. (falls, fall)
10. There _____ no excuses for such table manners. (is, are)

▶ **Exercise 2** **Checking Agreement with Indefinite Pronouns.** For each of the following sentences, write the correct verb from the choices in parentheses.

EXAMPLE: All of the trees in the garden _____were_____ swaying in the wind. (was, were)

1. Both of you _____ well enough to enter the essay contest. (writes, write)
2. Everyone _____ the day the emergency sprinklers flooded our classroom with six inches of water. (remembers, remember)
3. Most of the movie _____ shown at the wrong speed. (was, were)
4. Some of the students _____ to school. (drive, drives)
5. Few of those classroom television sets _____ properly. (works, work)
6. Most of the books we read _____ our knowledge of the world. (expands, expand)
7. _____ any of them play on the junior high field hockey team? (Does, Do)
8. Some of the bread _____ stale. (feels, feel)
9. Each of you _____ to receive the good citizenship award. (deserves, deserve)
10. All of the subjects in the paper _____ been researched thoroughly. (has, have)

▶ **Exercise 3** **Checking Special Problems in Agreement.** For each of the following sentences, write the correct verb from the choices in parentheses.

EXAMPLE: Here _____are_____ the rings you asked to see. (is, are)

1. Most of the students _____ to every session. (comes, come)
2. Some of the tourists _____ speak English. (doesn't, don't)
3. Over the roof and down the pillar _____ the ivy. (creeps, creep)
4. Each of the boys _____ with both oils and watercolors. (paints, paint)
5. Here _____ the missing report and the book. (is, are)

24.2 Agreement Between Pronouns and Antecedents • Practice 1

Making Personal Pronouns and Antecedents Agree   A personal pronoun must agree with its antecedent in person and number. Avoid shifts in person. Never use *you* to refer to the person you are writing about. Avoid shifts in number. Use a singular personal pronoun to refer to two or more singular antecedents joined by *or* or *nor*.

PRONOUN-ANTECEDENT AGREEMENT

William left his football here.

Either Rebecca or Judith will show her designs.

Bruce and Edward have passed their examinations.

Agreement Between Personal Pronouns and Indefinite Pronouns   Use a singular personal pronoun when the antecedent is a singular indefinite pronoun.

AGREEMENT WITH INDEFINITE PRONOUNS

Each of the actors supplies his or her own costume.

Take one of these forms and mail it back to me.

Neither of the automobiles is in its correct spot.

▶ **Exercise 1**   **Writing Personal Pronouns That Agree with Antecedents.**   Complete each sentence with an appropriate personal pronoun.

EXAMPLE: After the presentation, each student returned to _____*his or her*_____ seat.

1. Either Mary or Ellen will lend you _____ camera.
2. The doctor and his wife signed _____ names to the petition.
3. Neither Stephen or James remembered to bring _____ football.
4. The desk has a calendar and a pencil sharpener on _____.
5. The cat, awakened by the noise, opened _____ eyes.
6. My parents want me to write to _____ often while I am away.
7. Gabriel said _____ had never seen such an exciting movie.
8. The girls explored the area on _____ bicycles.
9. Margaret explained why _____ decided to study Latin.
10. Kenneth welcomed _____ cousins when they arrived.

▶ **Exercise 2**   **Choosing Personal Pronouns That Agree with Indefinite Pronouns.**   Underline the pronoun in parentheses that correctly completes each sentence below.

1. Everyone on the committee completed (his or her, their) research.
2. Both of the generals are in (his, their) uniforms.
3. See if either of the girls wants (her, their) lesson now.
4. Every camper brought (his or her, their) own gear.
5. Everything in the museum is in (its, their) proper place.

24.2 **Agreement Between Pronouns and Antecedents • Practice 2**

▶ **Exercise 1** **Making Pronouns and Antecedents Agree.** Rewrite each of the following sentences, filling in the blank with an appropriate pronoun.

EXAMPLE: The trees had dropped _____*their*_____ leaves all over the brick path.

1. Philip and Carla were proud of _____ new kitchen.
2. Each boy on the soccer team had _____ own special memories of the game.
3. The people in the park all seemed to have smiles on _____ faces.
4. Julie is going to Japan, a country _____ has always wanted to visit.
5. Paul would never forget _____ day at the fair.
6. The poodle, a new mother, was carefully guarding _____ litter.
7. Either Sarah or Susan will certainly remember to bring _____ book.
8. The three children were proudly wearing _____ new boots.
9. All travelers can benefit from planning _____ trips ahead of time.
10. Neither Ian nor Peter was sure about _____ answer on the test.

▶ **Exercise 2** **Avoiding Shifts in Person and Number.** Each of the following sentences contains a single error in pronoun-antecedent agreement. Rewrite each sentence correctly, underlining the pronoun that you have changed and its antecedent.

EXAMPLE: Bill wants to know where you can go to study art.
          <u>Bill</u> wants to know where <u>he</u> can go to study art.

1. Alex has put together a racing bike you couldn't buy in a store.

   _____

2. Neither Caroline nor Leah has decided whether they can come to the party.

   _____

3. All Brownie leaders should gather with her troops at 3:15.

   _____

4. Each bronco tried their luck at unseating the champion.

   _____

5. Jill is going to a clinic where you can get a flu immunization shot.

   _____

▶ **Exercise 3** **Making Personal Pronouns and Indefinite Pronouns Agree.** For each of the following sentences, choose the correct pronoun from the choices in parentheses and write it in the blank.

EXAMPLE: Each of the boys has _____*his*_____ money in hand. (his, their)

1. Neither of the parakeets has eaten _____ food. (its, their)
2. Not one of the apples had fallen from _____ branch. (its, their)
3. Give each of the girls a lab coat of _____ own. (her, their)
4. Several of the players were eating _____ lunches. (his, their)
5. Fortunately, each of the books was filed in _____ correct location. (its, their)

25.1 Regular Adjectives and Adverbs • Practice 1

Modifiers of One or Two Syllables   Adjectives and adverbs have three degrees of comparison: positive, comparative, and superlative. Use -er or more to form the comparative degree and -est and most to form the superlative degree. Use more and most with two-syllable modifiers that sound awkward with -er and -est and with most adverbs ending in -ly.

DEGREES OF COMPARISON—MODIFIERS OF ONE OR TWO SYLLABLES		
Positive	**Comparative**	**Superlative**
cold	colder	coldest
early	earlier	earliest
painful	more painful	most painful
quickly	more quickly	most quickly

Modifiers of Three or More Syllables   Use more and most to form the comparative and superlative degrees of modifiers of three or more syllables.

DEGREES OF COMPARISON—MODIFIERS OF THREE OR MORE SYLLABLES		
Positive	**Comparative**	**Superlative**
beautiful	more beautiful	most beautiful
carefully	more carefully	most carefully

▶ **Exercise 1**   **Recognizing The Three Degrees of Comparison.**   Identify the degree of comparison of each underlined modifier by writing *P* for positive, *C* for comparative, or *S* for superlative on the line.

EXAMPLE: Margaret is <u>older</u> than I am. _____C_____

1. Gregory is the <u>fastest</u> of all the runners here. _____
2. Louise felt <u>tired</u>. _____
3. These letters arrived <u>sooner</u> than I expected. _____
4. Donald is <u>more conscientious</u> about his work than he used to be. _____
5. I <u>slowly</u> removed the lid. _____
6. Then the <u>most unexpected</u> thing happened. _____
7. This jewel is <u>more precious</u> than that one. _____
8. The lecture hall is <u>larger</u> than the lounge. _____
9. I pedaled <u>furiously</u> up the hill. _____
10. He is the <u>most intelligent</u> person I know. _____

▶ **Exercise 2**   **Forming the Comparative and Superlative Degrees of Regular Modifiers.**   Fill in the chart below by writing the comparative and superlative degrees of each modifier. Whenever possible, use the -er and -est forms.

EXAMPLE: casual _____*more casual*_____ _____*most casual*_____

1. long _____ _____
2. fine _____ _____
3. foolish _____ _____
4. neat _____ _____
5. sympathetic _____ _____

25.1 Regular Adjectives and Adverbs • Practice 2

▶ **Exercise 1** Forming the Comparative and Superlative Degrees of One- and Two-Syllable Modifiers. Write the comparative and superlative degrees of the following modifiers. If the degrees can be formed in either way, write the -er and -est forms.

1. cloudy _____ _____
2. sunny _____ _____
3. hopeful _____ _____
4. rapid _____ _____
5. rudely _____ _____
6. just _____ _____
7. narrow _____ _____
8. strange _____ _____
9. lucky _____ _____
10. awkward _____ _____

▶ **Exercise 2** Forming the Comparative and Superlative Degrees of Modifiers with More than Two Syllables. Write the comparative and superlative degrees of the following modifiers. Use *more* and *most* and then *less* and *least* for each.

EXAMPLE: happily _____*more happily*_____ _____*most happily*_____ _____*less happily*_____ _____*least happily*_____

1. intelligent _____ _____
_____ _____
2. effective _____ _____
_____ _____
3. affectionate _____ _____
_____ _____
4. overburdened _____ _____
_____ _____
5. glittery _____ _____
_____ _____

▶ **Writing Application** Forming the Comparative and Superlative Degrees of Regular Modifiers. Write two sentences for each of the following modifiers. Write one sentence using the comparative degree of the modifier and one sentence using the superlative degree.

EXAMPLE: ambitious _____*Bernadette was always more ambitious than her sister Annemarie.*_____
_____*Maryellen, however, was the most ambitious one of all.*_____

1. kind _____
_____
2. lonely _____
_____
3. careful _____
_____
4. exciting _____
_____
5. handsome _____
_____

25.1 Irregular Adjectives and Adverbs • Practice 1

Irregular Modifiers   Learn the irregular comparative and superlative forms of adjectives and adverbs.

DEGREES OF COMPARISON—IRREGULAR MODIFIERS		
Positive	**Comparative**	**Superlative**
bad	worse	worst
badly	worse	worst
far (distance)	farther	farthest
far (extent)	further	furthest
good	better	best
many	more	most
much	more	most
well	better	best

▶ **Exercise 1**   **Using the Comparative and Superlative Forms of Irregular Modifiers.**   Fill in each blank with the correct form of the modifier in parentheses.

EXAMPLE: This is the ____*best*____ story I have ever written. (good)

1. I feel _____ today than I did yesterday. (bad)

2. Ellen spends _____ time practicing the piano than I do. (much)

3. Of all my friends, Joseph lives the _____ from my house. (far)

4. I did _____ on the exam than Julia. (well)

5. Justin is a _____ swimmer than his brother. (good)

6. That is the _____ colorful flower in the shop. (much)

7. I will not tolerate a _____ delay. (far)

8. The team played _____ today than they did last week. (badly)

9. This is the _____ news I have heard all day. (good)

10. Ted scored the _____ points of his career this season. (many)

▶ **Exercise 2**   **Using Irregular Modifiers in Sentences.**   Use each word listed below in a sentence. Follow the directions as to which degree of comparison to use.

EXAMPLE: good—comparative degree
_____*Tina draws better than I do.*_____

1. bad—comparative degree

   _____

2. far (distance)—superlative

   _____

3. badly—comparative

   _____

4. good—superlative

   _____

5. well—comparative

   _____

25.1 Irregular Adjectives and Adverbs • Practice 2

▷ **Exercise 1** **Using the Comparative and Superlative Degrees of Irregular Modifiers.** Fill in the blank with the form of the modifier requested in parentheses.

EXAMPLE: Joanna feels _____*better*_____ today. (well—comparative)

1. Milt did _____ on this test than on the previous one. (badly—comparative)

2. Jean can speak _____ languages than anyone else in our class. (many—comparative)

3. I always work _____ under pressure. (well—superlative)

4. Among all his qualities, Leonardo da Vinci is admired _____ for the versatility of his genius. (much—superlative)

5. Marilyn's _____ fears were realized when she forgot to study for her history examination. (bad—superlative)

6. One thousand miles is the _____ I have ever been from home. (far—superlative)

7. Your antique car will look _____ after you polish it. (good—comparative)

8. Who found the _____ items in the scavenger hunt? (many—superlative)

9. Jan enjoys reading poetry _____ than any other kind of writing. (much—comparative)

10. Michael's _____ character trait is his honesty. (good—superlative)

▷ **Writing Application** **Forming the Comparative and Superlative Degrees of Irregular Modifiers.** Write two sentences for each of the following modifiers, one using the comparative degree and one using the superlative degree.

EXAMPLE: much
  I like cider more than apple juice.
  However, the drink I like most is papaya juice.

1. far _____

_____

2. bad _____

_____

3. many _____

_____

4. well _____

_____

5. good _____

_____

25.1 Using Comparative and Superlative Degrees • Practice 1

Comparative and Superlative Degrees   Use the comparative degree to compare two people, places, or things. Use the superlative degree to compare three or more people, places, or things. Avoid double comparisons. Do not use both -er and more or both -est and most.

USING THE COMPARATIVE DEGREE

Alexander is two years *older* than his brother.
This novel has *fewer* pages than that one.
Catherine is *more interested* in sports than I am.

USING THE SUPERLATIVE DEGREE

Here is the *latest* edition of our newspaper.
Of all my friends, Joyce is the *most patient*.
I think New York is the *most exciting* city of all.

▶ **Exercise 1**   **Using the Comparative and Superlative Degrees.**   Underline the correct comparative or superlative form in each sentence.

EXAMPLE: The meeting was the (longer, longest) one we ever had.

1. The first exercise is the (simpler, simplest) of the two.
2. Helen is the (better, best) violinist in our school.
3. This antique is (older, oldest) than any other in my collection.
4. Justine has been waiting the (longer, longest) of all.
5. When I began dancing, I was much (clumsier, clumsiest) than Susan.
6. Lancaster is the (closer, closest) of the two locations.
7. John is the (wealthiest, wealthier) of his four brothers.
8. Theirs is the (larger, largest) of all the houses on this block.
9. It is (sunnier, sunniest) this week than it was last week.
10. It is obvious that Robert is the (taller, tallest) of the twins.

▶ **Exercise 2**   **Correcting Sentences with Incorrectly Formed Comparisons.**   On the line after each sentence write the comparative or superlative form that will correct the underlined errors.

EXAMPLE: She is the most popular of the two candidates. ___*more popular*___

1. Of the two hotels, this one is the most luxurious. _____
2. This is the most hardest job I have ever had. _____
3. Yours seems to be the best of the two ideas. _____
4. I am feeling more better now that I have had some rest. _____
5. Which of the three sisters is the more athletic? _____
6. We are hoping we can do more better in the next tournament. _____
7. Steven lives more farther from the school than I do. _____
8. I am not certain which of these four hills is the steeper. _____
9. Of all the jokes he told, the last one was the most funniest. _____
10. Conditions here are more worse than they were a year ago. _____

25.1 Using Comparative and Superlative Degrees • Practice 2

▶ **Exercise 1** **Correcting Errors in Degree.** Some of the following sentences contain errors in degree. Rewrite the incorrect sentences. Write *correct* if the sentence contains no errors.

1. Henrietta's watercolors were the most palest in the painting class.

   _____

2. Of the two jackets Betram bought yesterday, I like the tweed one best.

   _____

3. That Hitchcock movie was one of the most frightening films I have ever seen.

   _____

4. It was hard to say which of the two children looked youngest.

   _____

5. Joyce's words became even more louder when Ted refused to explain his actions.

   _____

6. Which of these three letterheads looks more informal to you?

   _____

7. Hank was the most diligent of the twins, but Holly was the smartest.

   _____

8. The mezzo soprano's voice carried better on high notes than on low notes.

   _____

9. That book would head my list of the ten most worst novels of all time.

   _____

10. Which of your parents do you and your brother resemble most?

   _____

▶ **Writing Application** **Using the Comparative and Superlative Degrees.** Write two sentences for each of the following modifiers, one using the comparative degree and one using the superlative degree.

EXAMPLE: slowly

   The molasses dripped more slowly than the maple syrup.
   However, the honey dripped most slowly of the three.

1. tall _____

   _____

2. ancient _____

   _____

3. difficult _____

   _____

4. fearful _____

   _____

5. beautiful _____

   _____

25.1 Making Logical Comparisons • Practice 1

Balanced Comparisons Compare only items of a similar kind.

CORRECTING UNBALANCED COMPARISONS	
Unbalanced	**Balanced**
My essay is longer than *Nora*. *His tennis racket* is heavier than *the instructor*.	*My essay* is longer than *Nora's essay*. *His tennis racket* is heavier than *the instructor's tennis racket*.

***Other* and *Else* in Comparisons** When comparing one of a group with the rest of the group, use the word *other* or *else*.

USING *OTHER* OR *ELSE*	
Incorrect	**Correct**
Patrick has attended *more* meetings *than any* club member. My father reads *more than anyone* in our family.	Patrick has attended *more* meetings *than any other* club member. My father reads *more than anyone else* in our family.

▶ **Exercise 1** **Writing Balanced Comparisons.** Rewrite each sentence below, correcting each unbalanced comparison.

EXAMPLE: Andrea's notes are neater than Michael.
          Andrea's notes are neater than Michael's notes.

1. George's diagram is more exact than Henry.

   _____

2. Charles's directions are as simple to follow as Randy.

   _____

3. Martin's computer has more memory than Philip.

   _____

4. My math teacher's tests are longer than my English teacher.

   _____

▶ **Exercise 2** **Forming Comparisons with *Other* or *Else*.** Rewrite each sentence, adding *other* or *else* to make the comparison clear.

EXAMPLE: My sister Eva likes to ski more than anyone in our family.
          My sister Eva likes to ski more than anyone else in our family.

1. Mayor Powell gives more speeches than any city politician.

   _____

2. I like to play baseball more than any sport.

   _____

3. Detective Harris has solved more cases than any investigator.

   _____

4. Dr. Parker treats more patients than anyone on the hospital staff.

   _____

25.1 Making Logical Comparisons • Practice 2

▷ **Exercise 1** **Making Balanced Comparisons.**   Rewrite each of the following sentences, making the illogical comparisons more balanced.

EXAMPLE: This dog's coat is shinier than that dog.
　　　　　This dog's coat is shinier than that dog's coat.

1. Bernie's roller skates look newer than Jodie.
_____

2. This year's fair was better attended than last year.
_____

3. Our morning newspaper's circulation is much larger than our afternoon newspaper.
_____

4. Pia's project covered more material than Eddie.
_____

5. Because this painter is dead, his work is more valuable than that painter.
_____

▷ **Exercise 2**   **Using *Other* and *Else* in Comparisons.**   Rewrite each of the following sentences, adding *other* or *else* to make the comparisons more logical.

EXAMPLE: George types faster than any student in his class.
　　　　　George types faster than any other student in his class.

1. My mother sings more beautifully than any member of my family.
_____

2. Theodore Roosevelt took office at a younger age than any American President.
_____

3. Our English teacher is stricter than anyone on the faculty.
_____

4. I like chocolate better than any food.
_____

5. Julie was funnier than anyone in the stunt show.
_____

▷ **Writing Application**   **Writing Logical Comparisons.**   Write a sentence that makes the comparison specified in each of the following items. Make sure that your comparisons are balanced and logical.

EXAMPLE: Compare the records of two basketball teams.
　　　　　Our basketball team's record is much better than their basketball team's record.

1. Compare the events in two different books.
_____

2. Compare the humor on two television shows.
_____

3. Compare one President with all the rest, using the word *better*.
_____

4. Compare one popular singer with all the rest, using the word *worse*.
_____

5. Compare one city with all the rest.
_____

25.2 Glossary of Troublesome Adjectives and Adverbs • Practice 1

Troublesome Adjectives and Adverbs   Learn how to use troublesome modifiers.

TROUBLESOME MODIFIERS		
Word	**Part of Speech**	**Example**
bad	adjective	I felt *bad* when I heard the news.
badly	adverb	She performed *badly* during the audition.
fewer	adjective	This beverage has *fewer* calories.
less	adjective	They asked us to make *less* noise.
good	adjective	Bill has *good* ideas.
well	adjective or	I didn't feel *well* this morning.
	adverb	Betsy swims *well*.
just	adverb	Pour me *just* half a cup of juice.

▷ Exercise 1   **Using Troublesome Adjectives and Adverbs.**   Underline the word in parentheses that correctly completes each sentence.

EXAMPLE: this stew tastes extremely (<u>good</u>, well).

1. Carol draws (good, well).

2. This milk tastes (bad, badly).

3. I play tennis (bad, badly).

4. There were (fewer, less) people on line an hour ago.

5. The bread you are baking smells (good, well).

6. Although he is out of the hospital, he still doesn't feel (good, well).

7. I eat (less, fewer) sugar than I used to.

8. Why are you reading with (fewer, less) expression?

9. The orchestra played (bad, badly).

10. The first part of your speech sounds (good, well).

▷ Exercise 2   **Using Troublesome Modifiers in Sentences.**   Use each word listed below as a modifier in an original sentence.

EXAMPLE: less

    This machine uses less energy than our older model.

1. fewer

   _____

2. badly

   _____

3. good

   _____

4. well

   _____

5. bad

   _____

25.2 Glossary of Troublesome Adjectives and Adverbs • Practice 2

▶ **Exercise 1** **Correcting Errors Caused by Troublesome Adjectives and Adverbs.** Some of the following sentences contain errors in the use of the modifiers. Rewrite the faulty sentences, writing *correct* if a sentence contains no errors.

EXAMPLE: They sang good together.
            They sang well together.

1. We found less seashells on the beach this year.

   _____

2. Greg looked badly after running the marathon.

   _____

3. Our vacation begins in just two weeks.

   _____

4. Ellen did good in the auditions, but Kathryn did better and won the role.

   _____

5. I only want three things for my birthday this year.

   _____

6. The pineapple tasted especially well served with bananas and ice cream.

   _____

7. Gramps has been responding well to treatment for arthritis.

   _____

8. Mort just needs three more points to beat the scoring record in our league.

   _____

9. Unfortunately, Roger is taking the news very bad.

   _____

10. Less than a hundred people came to the auction.

   _____

▶ **Writing Application** **Using Troublesome Adjectives and Adverbs Correctly.** Write a sentence according to the directions given in each of the following items.

EXAMPLE: Use *badly* to describe some action.
            Because his arm hurt, he threw the ball badly.

1. Use *Only* at the beginning of a sentence.

   _____

2. Use *bad* with a linking verb.

   _____

3. Use *fewer* to compare two sets of items.

   _____

4. Use *less* to compare two sets of items.

   _____

5. Use *well* as an adverb.

   _____

26.1 # End Marks • Practice 1

Uses of the Period Use a period to end a declarative sentence, an imperative sentence, and an indirect question. Use a period to end most abbreviations.

PERIODS
Declarative Sentence: Theodore Roosevelt was president of the United States. *Imperative Sentence:* Drive straight ahead. *Indirect Question:* I asked where we were going. *Abbreviations:* Mr. Rd. Tenn. Mt.

Uses of the Question Mark Use a question mark to end an interrogative sentence. Use a question mark to end an incomplete question in which the rest of the question is understood. Use a question mark to end a statement that is intended as a question.

QUESTION MARKS
Interrogative Sentence: Who are you? *Incomplete Question:* Certainly, we should have lunch. Where? *Statement Intended as a Question:* We are early?

Uses of the Exclamation Mark Use an exclamation mark to end an exclamatory sentence or an imperative sentence if the command is urgent and forceful. Use an exclamation mark after an interjection expressing strong emotion.

EXCLAMATION MARKS
Exclamatory Sentence: That was a wonderful trip! *Imperative Sentence:* Be quiet! *Interjection:* Wow! This is fun.

▷ **Exercise 1** **Using End Marks Correctly.** Add the proper end mark to each item.

EXAMPLE: What a great name for a dog _____.____

1. The Egyptians wrote on papyrus _____
2. Which way is the stadium _____
3. Ouch _____ That hurts.
4. Tell me your name _____
5. Where did you find this _____
6. We asked why she left _____
7. L _____ Butterfield
8. Look out _____
9. Austria is in central Europe _____
10. Who is the Prime Minister _____

▷ **Exercise 2** **Supplying End Marks.** Write the kinds of sentences listed below. Be sure to use correct end marks.

EXAMPLE: Question _____*Which briefcase is mine?*_____

1. Question _____
2. Indirect Question _____
3. Declarative Sentence _____
4. Exclamatory Sentence _____
5. Imperative Sentence _____

26.1 End Marks • Practice 2

Exercise 1 **Using the Period.** The following sentences do not have periods. Add periods where they are needed.

EXAMPLE: Jacob Jones, Sr, was not pleased when his son ran off to join the circus
      Jacob Jones, Sr., was not pleased when his son ran off to join the circus.

1. Straighten your tie and comb your hair
2. I think Mrs Berg gave the message to her son, Chris Berg, Jr
3. Sgt S P Casey wrote the speeding ticket that Mr Gillespie received
4. Fill out the form and sign it at the bottom
5. Dr Birch asked me if Sally Ryan, R N, works at the hospital in Coral Springs

Exercise 2 **Using the Question Mark.** The following sentences do not have end marks. Some sentences are direct questions requiring question marks. Others are indirect questions requiring periods. Still others are statements intended as questions. Add the correct punctuation mark.

EXAMPLE: She wondered if she would ever be famous
      She wondered if she would ever be famous.

1. How many people attended the play the first night The second night
2. I wondered why my car would not start
3. You lost the ten dollars I gave you for the tickets to the concert
4. The students asked if any more assemblies would be scheduled
5. Which doctor developed a successful vaccine for smallpox When
6. The children asked whether any refreshments would be served
7. Which planet is the red one
8. A stork built its nest on your chimney
9. Would you repeat that
10. The puppy scratched you

Exercise 3 **Using the Exclamation Mark.** Exclamation marks have been left out of each of the following items. Add exclamation marks as needed. Then identify each item that requires an exclamation mark as an *exclamatory sentence*, an *imperative sentence*, or an *interjection*.

EXAMPLE: Watch out
      Watch out!   *imperative sentence*

1. Surprise We tricked you. _____
2. We broke the record for having the most people in a telephone booth _____
3. That's impossible _____
4. Don't touch Those vases are priceless. _____
5. If only I could remember _____
6. Well This is a deliberate insult. _____
7. He repaired the television in less than five minutes _____
8. I haven't eaten since yesterday _____
9. Foul That was a double dribble. _____
10. Stop dragging your feet _____

26.2 Commas That Separate Basic Elements
• Practice 1

Commas With Compound Sentences   Use a comma before the conjunction to separate two independent clauses in a compound sentence.

COMPOUND SENTENCES
I cooked dinner, and Glenda set the table. We waited for John, but he never arrived.

Commas Between Items in a Series   Use commas to separate three or more words, phrases, or clauses in a series.

SERIES
Firs, spruces, and pines are evergreen trees. They traveled out of New York, through Pennsylvania, and into Ohio.

Commas Between Adjectives   Use commas to separate adjectives of equal rank. Do not use commas to separate adjectives that must stay in a specific order.

ADJECTIVES
With Commas: He drove a shiny, green sedan. *Without Commas:* The attic was filled with many old clothes.

▶ **Exercise 1**   **Using Commas Correctly.**   Add commas where they are required.

EXAMPLE: Bill left the party and he went home.
                       Bill left the party, and he went home.

1. Native Americans grew corn beans and tomatoes.
2. The sleek powerful leopard raced toward its prey.
3. The road ran around the mountain across the river and into the town.
4. We approached the medieval castle with its old drawbridge huge towers and broad moat.
5. Following the directions thinking carefully and taking your time will ensure success on the project.
6. The California condor the Wyoming toad and the red fox are endangered species.
7. Charles did his best but he still lost the race.
8. Claire saw two of her friends in the grandstand so she went to sit with them.
9. That large heavy bag is mine.
10. California Oregon and Washington border the Pacific Ocean.

▶ **Exercise 2**   **Understanding the Use of Commas.**   These sentences are punctuated correctly. Identify the use of commas by writing the words *compound sentence*, *series*, or *adjectives*.

EXAMPLE: Ed wrote letters, and then he listened to music.   _____*compound sentence*_____

1. Alberta, Ontario, and Quebec are Canadian provinces. _____
2. The quick, brown fox outran the shaggy dog. _____
3. With hard work, with the right skills, and with a little luck you can be successful. _____
4. Dad and I left for the airport at noon, yet we were still late for Mom's plane. _____
5. Several noisy squirrels lived in the oak tree. _____

26.2 # Commas That Separate Basic Elements
• Practice 2

▶ **Exercise 1** **Using Commas with Compound Sentences.** Commas have been left out of the following compound sentences. Read each sentence and add commas where they are needed.

EXAMPLE: She was tired yet she was determined to finish the race.
She was tired, yet she was determined to finish the race.

1. The sheep bleated fearfully but the shears never cut their skin.
2. The freshly painted walls and newly waxed floors made the apartment pleasant yet major repairs were still needed.
3. Lin is inclined to exaggerate but her stories are entertaining.
4. Mr. Klein's kitchen has been remodeled and it now contains many modern conveniences.
5. There were no trees growing on the desert island nor was there any water.
6. We could hear music blaring inside the house but no one answered when we knocked.
7. Tom hoed the soil and Eliza trimmed the branches.
8. Wind rattled the windows of the cabin yet the campers slept soundly.
9. She was forced to dismount for her horse was lame.
10. Many people have reptiles as pets but few of them know how to care for reptiles properly.

▶ **Exercise 2** **Using Commas Between Items in a Series.** In each of the following sentences, add commas as needed.

EXAMPLE: Alex threw back the covers stomped across the room and pounced on the alarm clock.
Alex threw back the covers, stomped across the room, and pounced on the alarm clock.

1. The pioneers crossed deserts scaled mountains and waded through rivers before they reached the West.
2. Silk cotton and wool are natural fibers.
3. I must mow the lawn trim the hedges and weed the garden.
4. Studying your notes listening to directions and feeling confident can help you do well on the exam.
5. The performers ran off the stage down the aisles and through the exit doors.
6. For dinner Lauren wanted spaghetti and meatballs bread and butter and cake and ice cream.
7. Becky first requested then insisted on and finally pleaded for permission to visit her cousin for the weekend.
8. Bring a wrench a pair of pliers and a hammer and nails out to the garage.
9. Elizabeth polished the silverware set the table and lit the candles.
10. Ted walked to the end of the diving board leaped into the air and dived gracefully into the pool.

▶ **Exercise 3** **Using Commas Between Adjectives.** In each of the following sentences, two adjectives have been underlined. Add commas between the two adjectives only where necessary.

EXAMPLE: The two little girls were playing jacks. (no comma needed)

1. Thomas and I noticed an <u>unfamiliar musky</u> odor inside the cave.
2. <u>Many shallow</u> pools formed on the beach after the light rain.
3. <u>Several faint</u> giggles brought the librarian to his feet.
4. On the door was a <u>heavy ornate</u> knocker in the shape of a wreath.
5. <u>Slow steady</u> rowing soon brought all of the team's boats to shore.

26.2 Commas That Set Off Added Elements
(Introductory Material, Parenthetical Expressions)
• Practice 1

Commas After Introductory Material   Use a comma after an introductory word, phrase, or clause.

INTRODUCTORY MATERIAL
Introductory Word: Yes, Jim is our best debater.
Introductory Phrase: With very little money, she left home for the big city.
Introductory Clause: After he finished school, Dick joined the Army.

Commas with Parenthetical Expressions   Use commas to set off parenthetical expressions.

PARENTHETICAL EXPRESSIONS
Names of People Being Addressed: That's the right answer, *Doug.*
Certain Adverbs: We chose, *therefore,* not to go.
Common Expressions: This solution, *I think,* is the best.
Contrasting Expressions: The river is long, *not deep.*

> **Exercise 1**   **Using Commas After Introductory Material.**   Write the introductory word, phrase, or clause in each sentence, and add the needed comma.

EXAMPLE: Remember you have only thirty minutes for this section of the test. _____*Remember,*_____

1. After the brief rain shower had ended the sun began to shine. _____

2. No this is the wrong answer. _____

3. With all the energy he could muster the old man tried to speak. _____

4. To win the district championship we practiced day and night. _____

5. Please isn't there someone who can help me? _____

6. With only a compass and a canteen of water he set out across the desert. _____

_____

7. Sarah stop talking and listen to me. _____

8. To escape capture by the police the fugitive hid in an abandoned cave. _____

_____

9. Certainly we should begin to plan the school fair as soon as possible. _____

10. After I saw that movie I could understand why it won an Oscar. _____

> **Exercise 2**   **Using Commas with Parenthetical Expressions.**   Use the following parenthetical expressions in sentences. Correctly punctuate these expressions with commas.

EXAMPLE: however _____*This dog, however, is not ours.*_____

1. nevertheless _____

2. I believe _____

3. of course _____

4. therefore _____

5. not yours _____

26.2 Commas That Set Off Added Elements
(Introductory Material, Parenthetical Expressions)
• Practice 2

▶ **Exercise 1** **Using Commas After Introductory Material.** Each of the following sentences needs a comma to set off introductory material. Write the introductory word or words, the comma, and the word following the comma.

EXAMPLE: To get a better view Fran climbed to the top of the hill.
            To get a better view, Fran

1. For better or for worse we were committed to the task.

   _____

2. If you are easily frightened don't see that movie.

   _____

3. Gripping the man's cuff in his jaws the bulldog braced his legs and pulled.

   _____

4. Yes these plastic treads should make the stairs safer.

   _____

5. To calm the jittery horse Irene stroked its neck and spoke quietly.

   _____

6. Please isn't there any way you could make an exception?

   _____

7. Remember no one is admitted beyond this point.

   _____

8. With dry clothing and warm food the climbers soon recovered.

   _____

9. After the brief intermission we returned to our seats.

   _____

10. Marsha and Bill will you please stop arguing?

    _____

▶ **Exercise 2** **Using Commas with Parenthetical Expressions.** Add commas as needed to set off the parenthetical expressions in each of the following sentences.

1. Check the yellow pages of the telephone directory Melissa.
2. Charles we believe is the right man for the job.
3. Audrey's hair is black not red.
4. We assumed nevertheless that you would still come to the party.
5. This kitten however believes your hen is its mother.
6. If you bring in the painting Mr. Curtis we can help you choose a frame.
7. Beth's grades therefore need improvement.
8. Hurry up Armando or we'll miss our bus.
9. Their younger son not the older showed an interest in the family business.
10. Everyone is eagerly anticipating the holiday of course.

26.2 Commas That Set Off Added Elements
(Nonessential Expressions) • Practice 1

Commas with Nonessential Expressions Use commas to set off nonessential expressions. These expressions are additional phrases or clauses that can be left out. Expressions that are essential cannot be left out without changing the meaning of the sentence.

ESSENTIAL AND NONESSENTIAL EXPRESSIONS
Essential: The Hollywood star *Clark Gable* appeared in this film.
Nonessential: Clark Gable, *the Hollywood star*, appeared in this film.
Essential: The old man *smiling broadly* is my grandfather.
Nonessential: The old man, *smiling broadly*, took the little boy in his arms.
Essential: I am looking for a beautiful gift *that is inexpensive.*
Nonessential: I bought this beautiful gift, *which was inexpensive*, at the local boutique.

▶ **Exercise 1** **Using Commas with Nonessential Expressions.** Add commas to set off nonessential expressions. Not every sentence contains a nonessential expression.

EXAMPLE: That house which was built in 1802 belonged to the first mayor of our town.
That house, which was built in 1802, belonged to the first mayor of our town.

1. Ernest Hemingway the famous author wrote *The Old Man and the Sea.*
2. The two soldiers eager to join their battalion were unaware that the enemy followed them.
3. The table that you gave your brother must have been difficult to build.
4. Captain Wilson standing on the deck of his ship looked out toward the horizon.
5. My sister staring absentmindedly out the window didn't hear me speak to her.
6. The harvest moon which shone brightly that evening illuminated the entire countryside.
7. Jimmy Carter the former president was also governor of Georgia.
8. We are hiring only people who have computer skills.
9. Karl who is graduating this year has been a tremendous asset to the school.
10. The play that we are planning to see has received very favorable reviews.

▶ **Exercise 2** **Writing Essential and Nonessential Expressions.** Complete each sentence with an appropriate expression. Set off the nonessential expressions with commas.

EXAMPLE: The dog, _____a Labrador retriever,_____ was very friendly.

1. The British soldiers _____ began to fire on the enemy.
2. This coat _____ is extremely warm.
3. Willa Cather _____ wrote *My Antonia.*
4. The Romans _____ were great builders.
5. The song _____ is very popular in England.
6. The binoculars _____ are excellent for birdwatching.
7. This year we are taking our vacation at Nature Lake _____.
8. That cat _____ belongs to my brother.
9. The man _____ is our history teacher.
10. This is a painting of Paul Revere _____.

26.2 Commas That Set Off Added Elements
(Nonessential Expressions) • Practice 2

▶ **Exercise 1** **Using Commas with Unessential Expressions.** Read each of the sentences carefully to determine whether the underlined expression is essential or nonessential. If the material is essential, write *E.* If the material is nonessential, add any commas needed.

EXAMPLE: The New England poet <u>Emily Dickinson</u> lived a very quiet life. ____*E*____

1. Our new kittens <u>which could not find their mother</u> meowed loudly. _____
2. Grandmother's old quilt <u>filled with soft eiderdown</u> was a family heirloom. _____
3. My favorite book is a spellbinding story written by the famous author <u>Robert Louis Stevenson.</u> _____
4. My favorite author <u>Robert Louis Stevenson</u> wrote *Treasure Island.* _____
5. Only a person <u>who was a genius</u> could have formulated this theory. _____
6. Albert Einstein <u>who was a genius</u> formulated the theory of relativity. _____
7. Our school newspaper <u>published twice a month</u> won an award. _____
8. The person <u>wearing a new red coat</u> boarded the plane. _____
9. Fred <u>my younger brother</u> has just learned to swim. _____
10. I would like you to meet Miss Jorgenson <u>my new neighbor.</u> _____
11. Alice Waters <u>the owner of a famous restaurant</u> uses only the freshest ingredients in her recipes. _____
12. The hat <u>with the red feather</u> is the one she wore to the wedding. _____
13. Janice <u>the girl who designed the posters</u> won a prize for her art. _____
14. The baby <u>resting in the nearest crib</u> was born today. _____
15. Mrs. Brown's baby <u>the one whose eyes are open</u> weighed eight pounds. _____

▶ **Exercise 2** **Adding Nonessential Expressions to Sentences.** Complete each sentence with an appropriate nonessential expression. Set off the nonessential expression with commas.

EXAMPLE: The kittens _____ were very friendly.
The kittens, which Martin kept in the garage, were very friendly.

1. Donald _____ has been saving for a snowboard.
2. My sister _____ wants to get another dog.
3. That airport _____ has very modern terminals now.
4. My beach blanket _____ is the one with blue and white stripes.
5. These shoes _____ gave me a blister.
6. The campers gathered around the bonfire _____.
7. The American buffalo _____ was hunted almost to extinction.
8. The chicken coop _____ is in need of repairs.
9. Fresh swordfish _____ is on the menu at that restaurant.
10. My grandmother _____ makes her own tortillas.
11. Uncle Tobias _____ had all his suits made by a tailor.
12. Perry and Angela _____ watched as the tornado approached.
13. At the fair, Jake got a temporary tattoo _____.
14. The thermostat _____ is set at seventy-two degrees.
15. Brett _____ made the first touchdown of the game.

26.2 Commas That Set Off Added Elements
(Dates and Geographical Names, Other Uses of the Comma) • Practice 1

Commas with Dates and Geographical Names   When a date is made up of two or more parts, use a comma after each item except when a month is followed by a day or a year. When a geographical name is made up of two or more parts, use a comma after each item.

DATES AND GEOGRAPHICAL NAMES

Date: Thursday, March 14, 1988, is my date of birth.
         March 14 is my birthday.
         I was born in March 1988.
Geographical Name: My family is moving to Cleveland, Ohio, tomorrow.

Other Uses of the Comma   Use commas in the situations shown in the chart below.

OTHER USES OF THE COMMA
Address: Send the letter to Robert Brown, 16 Sun Lane, Lima, Ohio 45801. *Salutation and Closing:* Dear Bob, Sincerely, *Numbers:* 69,486 miles *Direct Quotations:* "I'll see you tonight," Gail said, "after the play is over." *To Prevent Confusion:* After studying, Peter went outside to play ball.

▷ **Exercise 1**   **Using Commas with Dates and Geographical Names.**   Insert commas where they are needed.

1. The Battle of Gettysburg began on July 1 1863.

2. Montgomery Alabama was the first capital of the Confederacy.

3. My grandparents moved from Hartford Connecticut to Tampa Florida.

4. On April 14 1985 our community held its bicentennial.

5. The English nobles forced King John to sign the Magna Carta in June 1215.

6. My parents celebrated their fifteenth wedding anniversary on August 18 1984.

7. John's ancestors come from Warsaw Poland.

8. America had only forty-nine states before August 1959.

9. On October 19 1781 the British surrendered at Yorktown.

10. We have moved to Eureka California from Salem Oregon.

▷ **Exercise 2**   **Using Commas in Other Situations.**   Add commas where they are needed.

1. Mail this letter to Brian Johnson 110 Merton Street Fairfield Connecticut 06430.

2. Sincerely
    Bill

3. Outside Bob breathed a sigh of relief.

4. "These are the times that try men's souls" wrote Thomas Paine.

5. The state of New Mexico has an area of 122666 square miles.

6. Dear Susan

7. "Let's go to the park" Laura suggested "and have a picnic."

8. Their office is located at 150 Main Street Wilbraham Massachusetts.

9. The general had 45000 men in his army.

10. My new address is 2840 Haskell Avenue Dallas Texas 75221.

26.2 Commas That Set Off Added Elements
(Dates and Geographical Names, Other Uses of the Comma) • Practice 2

▷ **Exercise 1** **Using Commas with Dates or Geographical Names.** Add commas where they are needed in each of the following sentences.

EXAMPLE: The new student had come from San Juan Puerto Rico in March.
   The new student had come from San Juan, Puerto Rico, in March.

1. On March 15 1917 the Czar of Russia gave up his throne.

2. The exchange student explained that Nairobi Kenya is located almost directly on the Equator.

3. This recipe for clam sauce comes from a restaurant in Milan Italy.

4. On Thursday March 15 Lynn will give a party to celebrate her birthday.

5. Alexandra will leave for Geneva Switzerland on Monday October 10.

▷ **Exercise 2** **Using Commas in Other Situations.** Commas have been left out of the following sentences and groups of words. Add commas where they are needed.

EXAMPLE: There were 1407 people in the audience, all demanding an encore.
   There were 1,407 people in the audience, all demanding an encore.

1. Send this postcard to Jimmy Murphy 509 Cliff Street Newfield New York 14867.

2. The Zambian census taken in 1963 indicated a population of 3405788 Africans and 84370 non-Africans.

3. In the spring Mandy planted 3000 flowers.

4. Arlene advised "Take the train instead of the bus."

5. While racing John's dog developed a limp.

6. Maryann's permanent residence is 3 Hill Drive Apartment 3E New Milford Connecticut 06776.

7. Inside Mr. Martin took off his coat and warmed himself by the fire.

8. "Your request is unreasonable" Barry stated.

9. My dear Patricia
   Sincerely
   Nathaniel

10. "The serial number" said Sue "is 101, 27, 304."

▷ **Writing Application** **Using Commas to Set Off Elements in Your Writing.** Write five original sentences, each containing the material described in the following directions. Use commas when necessary.

EXAMPLE: Use the word *however*.
   Nothing, however, could have pleased them more.

1. Use your area code and telephone number.

   _____

2. Use the expression *not the green one.*

   _____

3. Use the phrase *Under the surface of the crystal-clear water* to begin a sentence.

   _____

4. Directly address *Cindy*, asking her a question.

   _____

5. Use the name and complete address of a friend.

   _____

Name _____ Date _____

Semicolons Used to Join Independent Clauses   Use a semicolon to join independent clauses that are not already joined by the conjunctions *and, or, nor, for, but, so,* or *yet.* Semicolons may also be used to join independent clauses separated by either a conjunctive adverb or a transitional expression.

SEMICOLONS AND INDEPENDENT CLAUSES
No Conjunction: Sarah's best subject is math; John's is science.
Conjunctive Adverb: We expect to win easily; nevertheless, we are still practicing very hard.
Transitional Expression: His sister is an outstanding poet; as a result, she won the school poetry contest.

Semicolons Used to Avoid Confusion   A semicolon may be used to avoid confusion when independent clauses or items in a series already contain commas.

SEMICOLON TO AVOID CONFUSION
I've been to San Francisco, California; Denver, Colorado; and Boston, Massachusetts; but I've never been to New Orleans, Louisiana.

▶ **Exercise 1**   **Using Semicolons Correctly.**   In each sentence a comma is used instead of a semicolon. Circle the comma to show that a semicolon is needed.

EXAMPLE: Ken slept late (,) as a result, he missed his bus.

1. George decided not to walk to work, it was too far, and he had too little time.

2. Running through the park, Gail tripped, she scraped her knee badly.

3. I thought Barry's painting was excellent, in fact, it was the best in the show.

4. Pack a warm sweater for the trip, otherwise, you will be cold at night.

5. The tulips, which looked so beautiful this spring, were planted only last fall, however, we will have to move them when we build the new garage.

6. During the Golden Age of Greece, playwrights wrote great tragedies, they also wrote brilliant comedies.

7. If we expect to have this paper finished by May 15, we can't waste any time, therefore, let's begin planning it today.

8. After the plane had landed, mechanics checked its engines, as a result, they decided to ground the aircraft for three days.

9. If I am not awake by five o'clock, call me, otherwise, I will be late for work.

10. The man did not show up for his appointment that morning, instead, he left town.

▶ **Exercise 2**   **Writing Compound Sentences with Semicolons.**   Complete these sentences.

EXAMPLE: _____*I like to fish*_____ ; however, _____*I do not enjoy baiting the hook.*_____

1. _____ ; however, _____

2. _____ ; instead, _____

3. _____ ; for instance, _____

4. _____ ; in fact, _____

5. _____ ; moreover, _____

26.3 The Semicolon • Practice 2

▶ **Exercise 1** Using Semicolons to Join Independent Clauses. Read each sentence, and insert any necessary semicolons.

1. Jeb hurried to finish his project as a result, his work was slipshod and unacceptable.

2. Some of the volunteers were assigned the task of painting others were responsible for repairing the playground equipment.

3. Lester sent the hamburger back it was too rare.

4. The soup was cold the salad was limp the chicken was burned.

5. The prairie dog barked a warning immediately, all the rodents scampered for safety.

6. Marge had a cast on her leg nevertheless, she was the first one on the dance floor.

7. I expect you to be on time furthermore, be ready to work hard.

8. Ornamental fans were arranged on the walls large, comfortable cushions were scattered on the rug.

9. Mrs. Walker forgot to mail the payment consequently, the electricity was turned off.

10. The fans droned overhead the temperature rose steadily the students sat listlessly at their desks.

▶ **Exercise 2** Using Semicolons and Commas to Avoid Confusion. Read the following sentences, and circle any commas that should be semicolons.

EXAMPLE: Heather, who was eight, had always loved living in Aspen Park, a suburb of Detroit (,) but she faced the move without fear.

1. You can lower fuel bills by insulating your house with such materials as batts, which are made of fiber glass and fit in your walls or ceilings, rolls, also made of fiber glass, which can be laid over an attic floor, and rigid foam boards, which can be used in small spaces.

2. The three puppies that we kept from our poodle's first litter were Coco, a light brown female, Snowflake, a white female, and Tippy, a gray male.

3. The neglect of the area was evident in its crumbling buildings, which had been abandoned, the vacant lots, which were littered with trash, and the rutted streets filled with numerous potholes.

4. In our family, Christine, who is seventeen, plays the guitar, Julie, who is fifteen, plays the trombone, and Maxine, who is only nine, plays the bassoon.

▶ **Writing Application** Using Semicolons in Your Writing. Write three original sentences, each using semicolons as indicated in the following directions.

EXAMPLE: Use a semicolon in a sentence with a conjunctive adverb.

The Johnsons were pet lovers; indeed, they had three cats, six dogs, and a dozen hamsters.

1. Use two semicolons to join three independent clauses in the same sentence.

_____

2. Use a semicolon to join two independent clauses separated by *on the other hand.*

_____

3. Use a semicolon with two independent clauses that already contain commas.

_____

26.3 # The Colon • Practice 1

The Colon as an Introductory Device   Use a colon before a list of items following an independent clause.

COLON BEFORE A LIST
We traveled to three cities: Chicago, St. Louis, and Kansas City.

Special Uses of the Colon   Use a colon in a number of special writing situations.

SPECIAL USES OF THE COLON	
Numerals Giving the Time	4:30 P.M. 8:00 A.M.
Salutations in Business Letters	Dear Sir:
Labels Used to Signal Important Ideas	Warning: Keep this medication out of the reach of children.

▶ **Exercise 1**   **Using Colons as Introductory Devices.**   Add colons where they are needed. Not every sentence needs a colon.

EXAMPLE: We bought three items a pencil, a pen, and an eraser.
          We bought three items: a pencil, a pen, and an eraser.

1. This semester we are studying several civilizations Egyptian, Greek, and Roman.

2. My list for camp includes the following items of clothing shirts, shorts, sneakers, socks, sweaters, and swimming suits.

3. We saw many types of dogs at the show collies, setters, poodles, beagles, and boxers.

4. Dad and I planted three trees a pine, a birch, and a red maple.

5. Barbara's favorite colors were blue, yellow, and pink.

▶ **Exercise 2**   **Using Colons in Special Situations.**   Add colons where necessary in the items below.

EXAMPLE: 600 A.M.
          6:00 A.M.

1. Dear Mr. Harper

2. Notice This building is closed until September 15.

3. Caution Wash hands after use.

4. Dear Taxpayer

5. 1140 P.M.

6. Gentlemen

7. Warning substance is harmful if swallowed.

8. 1219 A.M.

9. Dosage Two tablets three or four times daily.

10. Dear Madam/Sir

26.3 The Colon • Practice 2

▶ **Exercise 1**   **Using Colons as Introductory Devices.**   Colons have been left out of some of the following sentences. Insert any necessary colons. Write *correct* for any sentence that does not need a colon.

1. We finally located several constellations Orion, Taurus, Pisces, and Virgo. _____

2. Merry carried the following items on her first day of class a pencil sharpener, an eraser, a box of crayons, and a lunch box. _____

3. It was once believed that the universe was made up of four elements earth, water, air, and fire. _____

4. My favorite movies include *North by Northwest, The Best Years of Our Lives*, and *Mr. Smith Goes to Washington.* _____

5. The value of our property increased because of several improvements landscaping the yard, blacktopping the driveway, and insulating the house. _____

6. Follow these rules for healthy teeth brush at least twice a day, floss regularly, eat healthful foods, and visit your dentist twice a year. _____

7. Andrew has sailed in each of these oceans the Pacific, the Atlantic, the Indian, and the Arctic. _____

8. Ninety-nine percent of the air we breathe is made of the gases nitrogen and oxygen. _____

9. From recycled paper, we can get these things newspapers, cereal boxes, wrapping paper, cardboard containers, and insulation. _____

10. From recycled glass we get glass jars and tiles. _____

▶ **Exercise 2**   **Using Colons in Special Situations.**   Colons have been left out of the following expressions. Add the necessary colons.

1. Dear Colonel Landstrom

2. 400 A.M.

3. Caution Proceed at your own risk.

4. Dear Voter

5. Warning The Surgeon General has determined that cigarette smoking is dangerous to your health.

6. Danger Jellyfish are in these waters.

7. Dear Sir or Madam

8. 1225 P.M.

9. Notice Trespassers will be prosecuted.

10. My dear Ms. Hedden

▶ **Writing Application**   **Using Colons in Your Writing.**   Write five original sentences or examples according to the following directions, using colons as needed.

EXAMPLE: Write a salutation of a business letter.   *Dear Senator Craig:*

1. Write a list of items following an independent clause.

    _____

2. Write a list of items following a verb.

    _____

3. Write a list of items following a preposition.

    _____

4. Write a sentence containing a numeral and an abbreviation giving the time.

    _____

5. Write a label and an important idea it signals.

    _____

Name _____ Date _____

Quotation Marks With Direct Quotations

(Direct and Indirect Quotations; Direct Quotations with Introductory, Concluding, and Interrupting Expressions)

• Practice 1

Direct and Indirect Quotations A direct quotation represents a person's exact speech or thoughts and is enclosed in quotation marks (" "). An indirect quotation reports the general meaning of what a person said or thought and does not require quotation marks.

DIRECT AND INDIRECT QUOTATIONS	
Direct Quotations:	"Set the table for breakfast," Dad said.
	"Are you ready?" she asked.
Indirect Quotations:	Bill said that he would help me.
	Carol asked why we were going.

Direct Quotations With Introductory, Concluding, and Interrupting Expressions

Expressions such as *he asked* are often used to identify the speaker in a direct quotation. These expressions can begin, conclude, or interrupt a quotation. Note that punctuation marks are usually placed inside the quotation marks.

PUNCTUATING DIRECT QUOTATIONS	
Introductory Expression	Barbara said, "Let's shovel the snow."
Concluding Expression	"I am happy," said Bill. "Hurry!" everyone yelled.
	"Will you join us tomorrow?" we asked.
Interrupting Expression	"That," we were informed, "is a snow leopard."
Two Sentences	"This is not the right way," George said. "Let's turn back."

▶ **Exercise 1** **Punctuating Direct Quotations.** Place quotation marks, commas, and other punctuation marks where they are required.

1. The parakeet in that cage Walter explained is named Polly.

2. I wonder if you sell tape Pam asked.

3. We asked when Halley's comet would appear.

4. This book he said was written by Barbara Tuchman.

5. Pass me the ball Sam yelled. I can score a touchdown.

6. Let's go they shouted.

7. The dentist said you have no cavities.

8. This play Claire announced has been canceled.

9. Will you show me your pottery I asked the clerk. I would like to buy a gift for someone.

10. These Native American villages the guide explained were abandoned centuries ago.

▶ **Exercise 2** **Writing Direct Quotations.** Complete these sentences.

EXAMPLE: I asked, _____*"When was this museum opened?"*_____

1. Carol said, "_____."

2. "_____," he explained, "_____."

3. "_____?" we asked.

4. "_____!" they exclaimed.

5. "_____," he announced.

26.4 Quotation Marks with Direct Quotations

(Direct and Indirect Quotations; Direct Quotations with Introductory, Concluding, and Interrupting Expressions)
• **Practice 2**

▶ **Exercise 1**   **Distinguishing Between Direct and Indirect Quotations.**   Read each of the following sentences carefully to determine whether it contains a direct quotation, which requires quotation marks, or an indirect quotation. If the sentence contains a direct quotation, write *D* in the blank. If it contains an indirect quotation, write *I*.

EXAMPLE: It was the same old story repeating itself, thought Bruce. _____*D*_____

1. Carol complained that her sister was never on time. _____
2. I have noticed that, commented Bruce. _____
3. I wish she would hurry, continued Carol. _____
4. Bruce thought that the delay might make them miss the movie. _____
5. He said that they should probably leave without her. _____
6. Maybe she has a reason, said Carol. _____
7. I, however, object to the casual way she operates, she added. _____
8. Beginning to worry, Bruce decided that he should try to remain calm. _____
9. Let's give her five more minutes, he suggested. _____
10. That's a good idea, Carol agreed. _____
11. Justine asked Ramon if he would like to stay for dinner. _____
12. I hope the weather cooperates on the day of the party, whined Martha. _____
13. The teacher explained, Acid rain is harmful to water in lakes, often killing fish and plants that live there. _____
14. Oliver wondered if he could have some more porridge. _____
15. Our highways could be much safer, declared Bob. _____

▶ **Exercise 2**   **Using Direct Quotations with Introductory, Concluding, and Interrupting Expressions.**   The following direct quotations have not been correctly punctuated or capitalized. Rewrite each sentence, making the necessary corrections.

EXAMPLE: Elena said we will need at least twelve more
Elena said, "We will need at least twelve more."

1. There will be no exceptions to this rule the teacher announced

_____

2. Brian added after the wood is sanded, apply a thin coat of varnish

_____

3. Two heads are better than one said Sandra

_____

4. Have you ever considered a permanent the hairdresser politely inquired

_____

5. Do it now shouted Jake

_____

26.4 Quotation Marks With Direct Quotations
(Quotation Marks With Other Punctuation Marks,
Quotation Marks for Dialogue) • Practice 1

Quotation Marks With Other Punctuation Marks   Place a comma or a period inside the final quotation mark. Place a question mark or exclamation mark inside the final quotation mark if the end mark is part of the quotation and outside if the end mark is part of the entire sentence, not the quotation.

QUOTATION MARKS AND OTHER PUNCTUATION MARKS	
Commas and Periods:	"This car has a flat tire," Dad said.
Question Marks and Exclamation Marks **Inside Final Quotation Marks:**	Karl asked, "What is the homework assignment for today?"
Question Marks and Exclamation Marks **Outside Final Quotation Marks:**	I'm surprised that you can say, "I'm guilty"!

Quotation Marks for Dialogue   When writing dialogue, begin a new paragraph with each change of speaker.

DIALOGUE
"Where are you traveling?" the old man in the gray overcoat asked me. He continued to look at me with great curiosity. "I'm visiting my aunt and uncle in Los Angeles," I announced.

▶ **Exercise 1**   **Punctuating Direct Quotations.**   One or two punctuation marks have been left out of each sentence. Add them correctly to the sentences.

EXAMPLE: Ken asked, "What am I supposed to do"
          Ken asked, "What am I supposed to do?"

1. The umpire shouted, "Play ball"

2. "There will be a full moon tonight" he said.

3. "How are we going to explain this to Mom" Connie asked.

4. Bill announced, "The library is closing in fifteen minutes"

5. Has everyone said, "You are lying"

6. He screamed, "Stop the car"

7. "Wait a minute" I shouted.

8. "I need a new pair of sneakers for track" Clara said.

9. Bob asked "When does the planetarium show begin"

10. "Do these math problems ever become any easier" I wondered.

▶ **Exercise 2**   **Paragraphing Dialogue.**   Circle the first word in each sentence that requires indentation for a new paragraph.

"This library is enormous," Jim said. "Where should we begin?" "I think the best place to start is the library catalog," Kathy suggested. "Yes," Jim agreed, "we can search for books on our subject, *Sioux Indians*." "We'll find all the books in the library that might help us," Kathy said. "Then we can look in the periodical section," Jim added. Kathy smiled. "That will give us plenty of information for our paper."

26.4 Quotation Marks With Direct Quotations
(Quotation Marks With Other Punctuation Marks,
Quotation Marks for Dialogue) • Practice 2

▶ **Exercise 1** Using End Marks with Direct Quotations. End marks have been left out of the following sentences. Read each sentence and decide if the missing punctuation goes inside or outside the quotation marks. Then, add the necessary punctuation.

EXAMPLE: Has anyone said, "Please"
Has anyone said, "Please"?

1. Noel commented, "I can't think of a better reason"

2. Who said, "Waste not, want not"

3. How could the owner have said, "My dog is friendly"

4. How dare you say, "You weren't invited"

5. My friend asked, "Why does firing a pistol start the race"

6. The pilot continued, "Is this your first flight"

7. Zelda excitedly announced, "I got the job"

8. Ben said, "All he had ever asked for was a fair chance"

9. Will anyone say, "That is not what I meant"

10. As the artist sketched, he muttered, "This still isn't right"

▶ **Writing Application** Using Quotation Marks in Your Writing. Choose one of the following topics or make up a topic of your own. Then write a dialogue consisting of at least fifteen sentences. Use as many different quotation rules as possible, and remember to punctuate and indent correctly.

A day at the beach
A broken promise
A moment of anger

A situation to be avoided
A change of opinion

_____

_____

_____

_____

_____

_____

_____

_____

_____

_____

_____

_____

_____

_____

_____

_____

_____

26.4 Underlining, and Other Uses of Quotation Marks • Practice 1

When to Underline Underline the titles of long written works, publications published as a single work, movies, television and radio series, and works of music and art. Underline the names of individual air, sea, space, and land craft.

WORKS THAT ARE UNDERLINED	
Title of a Book:	The Deerslayer
Title of a Play:	King Lear
Title of a Movie:	Star Wars
Title of a Television Series:	Victory at Sea
Title of a Painting:	Night Watch
Name of Sea Craft:	the Lusitania
Number Used as Name:	Thirteen is an unlucky number.

When to Use Quotation Marks Use quotation marks around the titles of short written works, episodes in a series, songs, parts of a long musical composition, and the title of a work that is mentioned as part of a collection.

WORKS WITH QUOTATION MARKS	
Title of a Short Story:	"The Purloined Letter"
Title of an Article:	"How to Train Your Dog"
Title of a Song:	"Night and Day"

▷ **Exercise 1** **Punctuating Different Types of Works.** Use underlining or quotation marks with the works in each sentence.

EXAMPLE: I went to see the play Cats.
　　　　　　 I went to see the play Cats.

1. Carol read that article in News Magazine.
2. Dad enjoys Cole Porter's song I Get a Kick Out of You.
3. We heard Appalachian Spring performed by the local symphony orchestra.
4. The President quoted The New York Tribune.
5. Mom's article, Balancing Your Career and Your Family, will be published next month.
6. The movie Schindler's List deserved to win its many Oscar awards.
7. My uncle has a leading role in the play Kiss Me, Kate.
8. In his book, The American Family, I enjoyed chapter six, Family Vacations.
9. The television series The Honeymooners was extremely popular many years ago.
10. Fifteen has always been my lucky number.

▷ **Exercise 2** **Choosing the Correct Form.** Circle the correct form below.

EXAMPLE: The magazine "Modern World" or ⟨Modern World⟩

1. Chekov's play The Seagull or "The Seagull"
2. An article titled My Life or "My Life"
3. Longfellow's long poem The Song of Hiawatha or "The Song of Hiawatha"
4. The Apollo 8 spacecraft or the "Apollo 8" spacecraft
5. A chapter entitled "The Ageless Ones" or The Ageless Ones

26.4 Underlining and Other Uses of Quotation Marks • Practice 2

▶ **Exercise 1** **Underlining Titles, Names, and Words.**   Each of the following sentences contains a title, name, or word that needs underlining. Underline them.

EXAMPLE: The <u>Lusitania</u> sank in 1915 off the coast of Ireland.

1. I've seen Doctor Zhivago twice at the movies and once on television.
2. One of the three ships that brought Columbus to the New World was the Santa Maria.
3. Njal's Saga is a long epic poem written in Icelandic.
4. Grant Wood's American Gothic can be seen in the Art Institute of Chicago.
5. Lydia wanted to play the part of Helen Keller in the production of The Miracle Worker done at our school.
6. In the novel The Yearling, Jody learns that he cannot run away from his grief.
7. Many people think the number thirteen is unlucky.
8. Howdy Doody was one of the first television shows for children.
9. The librarian explained that back issues of the Herald Tribune were on microfilm in the periodical room.
10. Charles Lindbergh flew the famous Spirit of St. Louis.

▶ **Exercise 2** **Using Quotation Marks with Titles.**   Each of the following sentences contains a title that needs quotation marks. Some of the sentences also contain titles that need underlining. Either enclose the titles in quotation marks or underline them.

EXAMPLE: My favorite song is Getting to Know You from The King and I.
   My favorite song is "Getting to Know You" from <u>The King and I</u>.

1. Song of High Cuisine is a brief poem by Phyllis McGinley that ridicules such delicacies as snails and nightingales' tongues.
2. My favorite song from the musical Brigadoon is There But For You Go I.
3. Did you see The Battle of the Klingons on Star Trek?
4. As do most of Ray Bradbury's short stories, The Whole Town's Sleeping has a startling conclusion.
5. While listening to Sunrise, the first movement of the Grand Canyon Suite, we could almost see the morning light.

▶ **Writing Application** **Using Underlining and Quotation Marks.**   Write five original sentences, each including a specific example of one of the following items. Be sure to punctuate and capitalize correctly.

EXAMPLE: The title of a short poem
   Reading the poem "Little Boy Blue" always makes me cry.

1. The title of a painting _____
2. A book title _____
3. The name of a specific ship or airplane _____
4. A song title _____
5. A magazine title _____

26.5 The Hyphen • Practice 1

When to Use the Hyphen   A hyphen is used to form numbers from twenty-one to ninety-nine and with fractions that are used as adjectives. Hyphens are also used with certain prefixes and suffixes, and with certain compound nouns and modifiers. Do not use hyphens with compound proper adjectives or modifiers that include a word ending in *ly*.

USES OF THE HYPHEN	
With Numbers:	seventy-five books
With Fractions Used as Adjectives:	the three-fifths rule
Prefixes and Suffixes:	post-season game
	ex-senator
Compound Nouns:	great-grandmother
Compound Modifiers:	once-a-month meeting

Rules for Dividing Words at the End of a Line   Divide words only between syllables. Do not divide a word so that a single letter stands alone and do not divide proper nouns or project adjectives. Divide a hyphenated word only after the hyphen.

DIVIDING WORDS	
Correct	**Incorrect**
mid-dle	midd-le
afar	a-far
Henry	Hen-ry
empty-hand-ed	emp-ty-handed

▶**Exercise 1**   **Using Hyphens.**   Put hyphens where they are necessary.

EXAMPLE: We have thirty three volunteers.
             We have thirty-three volunteers.

1. Our team won the pre season contest.

2. The president elect spoke to our school.

3. A long awaited opportunity had finally presented itself.

4. We visited my great grandfather over the holiday.

5. A terrible mid air collision occurred on Saturday.

6. The candidate's pro union sympathies were very obvious.

7. His success in school helped build Roger's self confidence.

8. Calvin was a mean spirited man.

9. The ex governor has decided to run for the Senate.

10. I watched the slow motion pictures of the game.

▶**Exercise 2**   **Hyphenating Words.**   Draw vertical lines between syllables that can be divided at the end of a line. Do nothing to words that cannot be divided.

EXAMPLE: butter   but|ter
             lane   _____

1.	adopt	6.	bookstore
2.	helpful	7.	glass
3.	rooted	8.	football
4.	carpet	9.	among
5.	harbor	10.	birthday

26.5 The Hyphen • Practice 2

▶ **Exercise 1**   **Using Hyphens in Numbers, Word Parts, and Compound Words.**   Examine the following items and add hyphens where needed. If an item does not require a hyphen, write *correct*.

EXAMPLE: A newly minted coin ___*correct*___

1. nine tenths of the population _____
2. anti smoking campaign _____
3. self explanatory letters _____
4. a never to be forgotten day _____
5. a jack in the box _____
6. newly appointed officials _____
7. mid Victorian ideas _____
8. an all encompassing study _____
9. A pre Babylonian civilization _____
10. star shaped designs _____

▶ **Exercise 2**   **Using Hyphens to Divide Words.**   Imagine that you have to decide either to hyphenate each of the following words at the end of a line or to write the complete word on the next line. If you can divide a word, write in the blank the part of the word that would appear at the end of the first line. If you cannot divide the word, write the complete word.

EXAMPLE: old-fashioned ___*old-*___

1. ready _____
2. laugh _____
3. promised _____
4. Thailand _____
5. under-rated _____

6. grocery _____
7. Maryann _____
8. over _____
9. forty _____
10. evasive _____

▶ **Writing Application**   **Using Hyphens in Your Writing.**   Write five original sentences, each including a hyphenated word. Divide at least four words at the ends of lines. Try to apply as many of the different rules for hyphenation as you can.

EXAMPLE: ___*The ex-governor had once been all-powerful.*___

1. _____

_____

2. _____

_____

3. _____

_____

4. _____

_____

5. _____

_____

26.5 The Apostrophe (with Possessive Nouns, with Pronouns) • Practice 1

Apostrophes with Possessive Nouns Form the possessive of nouns according to the following rules.

FORMING POSSESSIVE NOUNS	
Add an apostrophe and an *-s* to show the possessive of most singular nouns.	father's car Dave's book boss's office
Add just an apostrophe to show the possessive case of plural nouns ending in *-s* or *-es.*	dogs' owner churches' congregations
Add an apostrophe and *-s* to show the possessive case of plural nouns that do not end in *-s* or *-es.*	the four men's cars the geese's honking
Add an apostrophe and *-s* (or just an apostrophe if the word is a plural ending in *-s*) to the last word of a compound noun to form the possessive.	high school's mascot Boy Scouts' trip president-elect's speech

Apostrophes with Pronouns Use an apostrophe and *-s* with indefinite pronouns to show possession. Do not use an apostrophe with possessive personal pronouns.

POSSESSIVE FORMS OF PRONOUNS		
Indefinite		**Personal**
another's	one another's	my, mine, our
anybody's	somebody's	ours, your, yours
each other's	no one's	his, her, hers, its, their, theirs

▶ **Exercise 1** **Writing Possessive Forms.** In the space at the right of each phrase write the possessive form of the item.

EXAMPLE: the money of his father _____*his father's money*_____

1. the toys of the children _____
2. the tents of the circus _____
3. the barn of the horses _____
4. the business of no one _____
5. the house of our sister-in-law _____

▶ **Exercise 2** **Using Possessives.** Complete each sentence with a possessive noun or pronoun.

EXAMPLE: _____*Ken's*_____ paper is excellent.

1. _____ footprints were in the snow.
2. _____ book was a bestseller.
3. _____ party was the most successful of the year.
4. He owns a store that sells _____ clothes.
5. The _____ secretary is on vacation this week.

26.5 The Apostrophe (with Possessive Nouns, with Pronouns) • Practice 2

▶ **Exercise 1** **Using Apostrophes to Form the Possessives of Nouns.** The following sentences contain underlined singular or plural nouns. Write each underlined noun in the blank, putting it into the possessive form by adding an apostrophe and -s, or only an apostrophe, as needed.

EXAMPLE: The <u>children</u> hour at the public library has been a great success. _____*children's*_____

1. According to legend, a <u>dragon</u> breath was quite dangerous. _____
2. All of the <u>pencils</u> points were broken. _____
3. The pond became the <u>geese</u> home for the summer. _____
4. Many have benefited from reading <u>Do-It-Yourself</u> advice in the newspaper _____
5. Most designers believe that <u>garments</u> colors attract buyers. _____
6. This yarn was purchased at the <u>Jack and Jill Craft Store</u> sale. _____
7. <u>Ross</u> lizard must be kept on a leash at all times. _____
8. Elected officials represent the <u>people</u> choice. _____
9. <u>Chancellor Helmut Schmidt</u> reelection seemed likely. _____
10. Discard the <u>lettuce</u> outer leaves. _____
11. The <u>mushrooms</u> condition made them impossible to sell. _____
12. My <u>sister</u> new bathing suit fit me perfectly. _____
13. Did you know that <u>James</u> dog went to obedience school? _____
14. The <u>geese</u> honking as they flew overhead was a sound Leroy always enjoyed. _____
15. The sale at <u>Jackson and Son</u> downtown store begins today. _____

▶ **Exercise 2** **Using Apostrophes with Pronouns.** The following sentences contain pronouns used as possessives. If all pronouns in a sentence are used correctly, write *correct*. If one or more pronouns are used incorrectly, write them correctly in the blank.

EXAMPLE: When they divided up the property, the lake became his and the island became their's.

_____*theirs*_____

1. Everybody else's favorite dessert is not necessarily yours' or mine. _____
2. The tools in your garage are our's, not your's. _____
3. Someones' cat was howling in the alley while our's was sleeping peacefully. _____
4. The veterinarian examined her' parakeet and said it's wing was broken. _____
5. Ours is the preferred method, even though their's is almost as good. _____
6. Listen to his' idea for a solution before you decide to accept hers. _____
7. Her's is the best solution to our problem. _____
8. I will help you finish your math work if you will help Leon with his. _____
9. It is still not too late to file your' tax return. _____
10. Their's is always the first yard on the block to have its' leaves raked. _____
11. Is this your baseball cap, or is it someone elses'? _____
12. The two cats helped with each others' grooming. _____
13. Henry brought his' new bow and arrow to the archery class. _____
14. Shall we go to my house after school, or would you rather go to your's? _____
15. Of all the presentations, hers was the most interesting. _____

26.5 The Apostrophe (with Contractions, Special Uses)
• Practice 1

Apostrophes with Contractions   Use an apostrophe in a contraction to show the position of the missing letter or letters. The most common contractions are formed with verbs.

COMMON CONTRACTIONS WITH VERBS		
Verb + *not*	aren't (are not)	isn't (is not)
	didn't (did not)	can't (cannot)
Pronoun + the verb *will*	I'll (I will)	they'll (they will)
Pronoun or noun + the verb *be*	it's (it is)	Bob's (Bob is)
Pronoun or noun + the verb *would*	she'd (she would)	Betsy'd (Betsy would)

Special Uses of the Apostrophe   Use an apostrophe and -s to write the plurals of numbers, symbols, letters, and words used to name themselves.

SPECIAL USES OF THE APOSTROPHE	
three *6* 's	four *?* 's
Roll your *r* 's.	
Always capitalize *I* 's in sentences.	

▶ **Exercise 1**   **Using Contractions Correctly.**   Each sentence contains a word group that can be written as a contraction. Write each contraction in the space at the right.

EXAMPLE: We are not leaving now. _____*aren't*_____

1. Carol is singing in the choir. _____

2. Who is your homeroom teacher? _____

3. You should not leave your roller skates in the driveway. _____

4. Where is my cookbook? _____

5. I would not do that if I were you. _____

6. He would do that for you. _____

7. They were not expected home until 6:00 P.M. _____

8. You will be late for school. _____

9. Who will help me with this problem? _____

10. Roger is selling his crafts at the fair. _____

▶ **Exercise 2**   **Using Contractions in Sentences.**   Fill in each blank with an appropriate contraction.

EXAMPLE: _____*She's*_____ at college this year.

1. _____ the cap for the bottle of mayonnaise?

2. My phone number has two _____ in it.

3. There are three _____ in banana.

4. She _____ my choice for class president.

5. _____ see me in the morning.

26.5 The Apostrophe (with Contractions, Special Uses)
• Practice 2

▶ **Exercise 1** Using Contractions in Informal Writing. Each of the following sentences contains one or more word groups that can be written as contractions. On the line write each of these word groups as a contraction.

EXAMPLE: Where is the new science-fiction book I ordered? _____*Where's*_____

1. Who is the new student representative? _____
2. I am not certain whether he is upstairs or downstairs. _____
3. This pen will write if you will just keep shaking it. _____
4. You are ignoring what I am saying. _____
5. Glenda is the one I would like to invite. _____
6. There cannot be any doubt about who will be invited.
7. You will enjoy looking at these old pictures of the class of 1956.
8. They were not sure who would be on the committee. _____
9. The school library does not have the book I need. _____
10. Where is the one who said she would be here early? _____

▶ **Exercise 2** Recognizing Special Uses of the Apostrophe. Write five original sentences, each using the plural of one of the following numbers, symbols, letters, or words. Be sure to underline each plural form and use apostrophes where they are needed.

EXAMPLE: t
        Please take greater care in crossing your t's.

1. 9 _____
2. m _____
3. huh _____
4. ? _____
5. please _____

▶ **Writing Application** Using Apostrophes in Your Writing. Write a brief dialogue between two friends. You can use one of the following topics or make up your own. Apply as many of the rules for apostrophes as you can.

   A discussion of math homework
   A discussion of a movie, a book, or a television show

_____
_____
_____
_____
_____
_____
_____
_____

27 Capitals for First Words and *I* • Practice 1

Sentences   Capitalize the first word in declarative, interrogative, imperative, and exclamatory sentences.

SENTENCES	
Declarative:	She is losing the race.
Interrogative:	Where is the milk?
Imperative:	Bring me that pen.
Exclamatory:	What a surprise you gave me!

Quotations   Capitalize the first word in a quotation if the quotation is a complete sentence.

QUOTATIONS
"Let's go now" Sandy suggested.
"Let's go now," Sandy suggested, "before it is too late."

The Word *I*   Capitalize the word *I* whenever it appears in a sentence.

▶ **Exercise 1**   **Using Capitals to Begin Sentences.**   On the lines, write the words in these sentences that should be capitalized, adding the missing capitals.

EXAMPLE: we are having a party tomorrow.   _We_

1. what is the topic of your paper? _What_
2. do research for your project in the library. _Do_
3. oh! this is wonderful! _Oh, This_
4. i am the captain of this ship. _I_
5. your kidneys remove wastes from your body. _Yain_
6. who is the star of that movie? _Who_
7. ouch! i hit my shoulder! _Ouch,_
8. this piece of pottery was made centuries ago. _____
9. an airplane circled the field. _____
10. where is the key for the door? _____

▶ **Exercise 2**   **Using Capitals in Sentences.**   On the lines, write the word or words in each sentence that should be capitalized, adding the missing capitals.

EXAMPLE: She and i are doing the science experiment together.   _I_

1. Patrick Henry said, "give me liberty or give me death!" _____
2. Carl and i are first cousins. _____
3. Mom said, "i think we made a mistake." _____
4. "this coat," Kevin explained, "belongs to my sister." _____
5. Sally, Jim, and i spent all our money at the fair. _____
6. "please listen to me," Carol said. "we must act quickly." _____
7. "this test," Jim thought, "is extremely difficult." _____
8. she and i will arrive at your house by 6:00 P.M. _____
9. "what time is it?" she asked. _____
10. "all the ingredients are here," he said. "now we can begin cooking." _____

27 Capitals for First Words and *I* • Practice 2

▶ **Exercise 1**   **Using Capitals to Begin Sentences.**   On the lines, write the word or words in each sentence that should be capitalized, adding the missing capitals.

EXAMPLE: great! when will we leave? _____*Great/When*_____

1. few students have shown more determination than she. _____

2. i left my book somewhere. but where? _____

3. what? would you repeat that? _____

4. please refer to an encyclopedia for a more detailed explanation. _____

5. next weekend? we thought the play opened tonight. _____

6. how talented you are! _____

7. stand at attention during the inspection. _____

8. when is the science project due? _____

9. wow! that was a surprise! _____

10. his bicycle is considerably older than he is. _____

▶ **Exercise 2**   **Using Capitals for Quotations.**   On the lines, write the word or words in each sentence that should be capitalized, adding the missing capitals.

EXAMPLE: "where did you find this one?" he asked. _____*Where*_____

1. "begin tuning your instruments," the conductor told the musicians. _____

2. the telephone operator asked, "what number did you want?" _____

3. "let me do the driving," said Earl. "sit back and relax." _____

4. "turnips are good for you," he stated as he served the steaming dish. _____

5. "cardinals devour the birdseed," she explained, "but woodpeckers prefer suet." _____

6. after an hour the audience began to shout, "we want Joe! we want Joe!" _____

7. "all the important documents are in the filing cabinet," the secretary explained. "notice, however, that they are not in alphabetical order." _____

8. Marty whispered, "let me borrow some paper." _____

9. "collecting rock samples," Jill told the class, "is a fascinating hobby." _____

10. "dependable equipment is a must," the instructor noted. _____

▶ **Exercise 3**   **Using the Pronoun *I*.**   Rewrite the following sentences, adding the missing capitals.

EXAMPLE: she and i were the last to arrive.
_____*She and I were the last to arrive.*_____

1. am i late?

_____

2. i hope i answered the question correctly.

_____

3. "sometimes," i told her, "i feel as discouraged as you do."

_____

4. when they finally announced the winner, it was i.

_____

5. the following pronouns are singular: *i*, *she*, and *he*.

_____

Name _____   Date _____

27 Capitals for Proper Nouns (Names of People, Geographical Places) • Practice 1

Names of People   Capitalize each part of a person's full name.

PEOPLE	
Barbara	R. A. Johnson
John P. Smith	Kathy O'Brien

Geographical Places   Capitalize geographical names.

GEOGRAPHICAL NAMES	
Streets:	Pine Avenue, Main Street
Towns and Cities:	Fairfield, London
States:	Nevada, Florida
Nations:	Belgium, Burma
Continents:	Antarctica, North America
Valleys and Deserts:	the Connecticut Valley, the Sahara Desert
Mountains:	the Alps, the Andes Mountains
Sections of a Country:	New England, the Northwest
Islands:	Mackinac Island, Padre Island
Scenic Spots:	the Grand Canyon, Sequoia National Park
Rivers and Falls:	the Mississippi River, Niagara Falls
Lakes and Bays:	Lake Michigan, Chesapeake Bay
Seas and Oceans:	the Red Sea, the Pacific Ocean

▶ **Exercise 1**   Using Capitals for Names of People and Geographical Places.   On the line, write the words that should be capitalized, adding the missing capitals.

EXAMPLE: We are reading poems by emily dickenson. _____*Emily Dickenson*_____

1. I walked home with cindy. _____

2. Is the old house on poplar street haunted? _____

3. Two of the thirteen original colonies were pennsylvania and virginia. _____

4. Bob and his family are moving to the southwest. _____

5. Have you heard of an author named c. p. snow? _____

6. I just received some new stamps from egypt for my collection. _____

7. We went to phoenix to see a professional basketball game. _____

8. Our house is only a few miles from the missouri river. _____

9. Have you ever seen the appalachian mountains? _____

10. The man who owns that store is james a. small. _____

▶ **Exercise 2**   Adding Names of People and Geographical Places to Sentences.   Complete each sentence with an appropriate name of a person or geographical place.

EXAMPLE: The person leading the band is _____*Roger Brown*_____ .

1. In school, I just saw a film about _____ .

2. We went sailing on _____ last weekend.

3. The person sitting behind me in English class is _____ .

4. Betty visited her aunt and uncle in _____ .

5. _____ wrote that book, didn't he?

Capitals for Proper Nouns (Names of People, Geographical Places) • **Practice 2**

▷ **Exercise 1**   **Using Capitals for Names of People.**   On the line, write each name that you find in the following sentences, adding the missing capitals.

EXAMPLE: Her best friend was andrea mcmahon.
  Andrea McMahon

1. We asked nilda to join us on our class trip. _____

2. This book by e. b. white is a children's classic. _____

3. My cousin, paul mcbride, is a talented trumpet player. _____

4. helen st. james invited us to her graduation party. _____

5. The firm is managed by t. l. jackson. _____

6. She usually listens to the music of brahms or beethoven. _____

7. Short stories by o. henry were among his favorites. _____

8. The convention was organized by susan b. anthony. _____

9. With a friendly smile, maria lopez invited the unexpected visitors to enter. _____

10. The patriot paul revere was an expert silversmith. _____

11. I wonder if alphonse likes his name. _____

12. I think paul would go to any movie directed by steven spielberg. _____

13. She was introduced to the group as colleen o'connor. _____

14. The father of henry david thoreau was a pencil maker. _____

15. When kathleen mcnamara married danny mcgovern, she started using the hyphenated name mcnamara-mcgovern.

_____

▷ **Exercise 2**   **Using Capitals for Geographical Places.**   On the line, write each geographical place name that you find in the following sentences, adding all the capitals that are missing.

EXAMPLE: They had seen niagara falls in 2000.
  Niagara Falls

1. A few miles south of buckhorn lake is the cumberland national park.

_____

2. The Blakes bought a cottage on lake drive in schuyler county.

_____

3. Our tour included a visit to india, china, and neighboring countries in asia.

_____

4. The trip was extended to include a week's stay in ceylon, an island in the indian ocean.

_____

5. The st. johns river flows into the atlantic ocean near jacksonville, florida.

_____

27 Capitals for Proper Nouns (Other Proper Nouns) • Practice 1

Other Proper Nouns Capitalize the names of specific events and periods of time. Capitalize the names of various organizations, government bodies, political parties, and nationalities, as well as the languages spoken by different groups. Capitalize references to religions, deities, and religious scriptures. Capitalize the names of other special places and items.

SPECIFIC EVENTS AND TIMES	
Historical Periods:	the Middle Ages
Historical Events:	World War II
Days and Months:	Monday, August
SPECIFIC GROUPS	
Organizations:	the Girl Scouts
Government Bodies:	the House of Representatives
Nationalities:	Chinese, American
RELIGIOUS REFERENCES	
Christianity:	the Holy Ghost, the Bible
Judaism:	the Prophets, the Torah
OTHER SPECIAL PLACES AND ITEMS	
Monuments:	the Washington Monument
Buildings:	the Museum of Modern Art
Celestial Bodies:	Mars, the Big Dipper

▶ **Exercise 1** **Using Capitals for Specific Events, Times, and Groups.** On the line, write the words in these sentences that should be capitalized, adding the missing capitals.

EXAMPLE: In 1914, world war I begin. _____World War_____

1. My father is speaking at the rotary club. _____

2. Abraham Lincoln was a member of the republican party. _____

3. labor day always occurs in september. _____

4. My brother wants to attend yale university. _____

5. Richard's mother has just started working for eastman kodak co. _____

6. Some day I hope to speak french and russian fluently. _____

7. The american revolution ended in 1783. _____

8. Each year a large group of people watches the super bowl at my house. _____

9. Yesterday we had a speaker from the defense department. _____

10. Americans held a constitutional convention in 1787. _____

▶ **Exercise 2** **Using Capitals for Religious References, Special Places, and Special Items.** On the line, write each word that should be capitalized, adding the missing capitals.

EXAMPLE: The koran is the sacred text of Islam. _____Koran_____

1. The talmud is a collection of ancient Jewish religious writings. _____

2. Someday I would like to visit the planet venus. _____

3. Sally Field won an oscar for her performance. _____

4. A popular brand of camera is photomax. _____

5. We saw the lincoln memorial last year. _____

27 Capitals for Proper Nouns (Other Proper Nouns) • Practice 2

▶ **Exercise 1** **Using Capitals for Other Proper Nouns.** On the line, write each proper noun that you find in the following sentences, adding the missing capitals.

EXAMPLE: The temple was dedicated to the goddess minerva.
            Minerva

1. The english and americans have been allied for many years. _____

2. Janet bought a box of chocolate dream to make cocoa for the ice-skating party. _____

3. Many cards sent on valentine's day picture the god cupid. _____

4. In washington Jed saw the lincoln memorial. _____

5. In our country, thanksgiving is traditionally celebrated on the last thursday in november.

   _____

6. After graduating from westchester community college, she worked for gaylord ad agency.

   _____

7. John was a republican when he was first elected to the house of representatives.

   _____

8. In the spring, christians celebrate easter.

   _____

9. Colorful fireworks blazed across the sky on that fourth of july. _____

10. The founder of the religion now known as islam was mohammed. _____

▶ **Writing Application** **Using Capitals for Proper Nouns.** Write a brief description of a real or fictional vacation area. Your description should include proper nouns from at least ten of the twelve categories in the following list. Try to make the area appeal to tourists by writing in the style of a travel brochure. Be sure to capitalize correctly.

1. A town or city and state
2. A language
3. A special event
4. A historical event or period
5. A body of water
6. A mountain

7. A building
8. A celestial body
9. A monument
10. A month
11. A religious holiday
12. A section of a country

_____
_____
_____
_____
_____
_____
_____
_____
_____
_____
_____

27 Capitals for Proper Adjectives • Practice 1

Proper Adjectives Capitalize most proper adjectives. Common nouns modified by proper adjectives, however, are not capitalized.

PROPER ADJECTIVES	
California oranges	*Canadian* history
Thanksgiving dinner	*Civil War* battlefield
Ivory soap	*Hollywood* stars

▷ **Exercise 1** **Using Capitals for Proper Adjectives.** Underline each adjective that should be capitalized.

EXAMPLE: These <u>florida</u> summers are very hot.

1. My new dog is an english setter.
2. George doesn't know much about american history.
3. Our family is moving to the chicago suburbs.
4. Walter's grandmother baked him a german chocolate cake for his birthday.
5. I took photographs of the party with my flexolens brand camera.
6. Archaeologists are studying the mayan temples in Mexico.
7. An old studebaker convertible sat next to the curb.
8. This year we are planning a large christmas party.
9. My father enjoys jamaican coffee for breakfast.
10. The california condor is a rare species of bird.

▷ **Exercise 2** **Using Proper Adjectives in Sentences.** Use each item below in a sentence. Capitalize the proper adjectives correctly.

EXAMPLE: (indian summer) _____*This year we had a brief Indian summer in October.*_____

1. (american flag) _____
2. (swiss cheese) _____
3. (caribbean cruise) _____
4. (smilebright toothpaste) _____
5. (easter vacation) _____
6. (iroquois villages) _____
7. (danish pastry) _____
8. (thanksgiving dinner) _____
9. (spanish colonies) _____
10. (mohawk sedan) _____

27 Capitals for Proper Adjectives • Practice 2

▶ **Exercise 1**   **Using Capitals for Proper Adjectives.**   Complete each of the following sentences by supplying a proper adjective that is correctly capitalized.

EXAMPLE: Her most treasured possession was an antique ____*Victorian*____ sofa.

1. Philip's dog, an _____ setter, won a prize.
2. The _____ buses run twenty-four hours a day.
3. This Sunday we will have a _____ party.
4. I asked you to buy _____ dish detergent.
5. The _____ car proved to be the best buy.
6. Saul's parrot nibbled on the _____ cracker.
7. The librarian located a translation of the _____ novel.
8. It is easier to write with a _____ pen.
9. The _____ family attended a reunion in Maryland.
10. _____ winters are usually long and cold.
11. I wish we had bought _____ cheese instead of this tasteless stuff.
12. While we were in England, we tried to follow _____ customs.
13. Don't you think Sally's _____ accent is charming?
14. Maury prefers _____ cough drops over all others.
15. Unable to use chopsticks, Carl used a fork in the _____ restaurant.

▶ **Writing Application**   **Using Capitals for Proper Adjectives.**   Use each of the following words as a proper adjective in an original sentence. Be sure to capitalize the proper adjectives correctly.

EXAMPLE: italian
_____*He returned with many stories about the friendliness of the Italian people.*_____

1. mexican	3. roman	5. california	7. canadian	9. african
2. buddhist	4. juiceking	6. danish	8. new england	10. japanese

1. _____
2. _____
3. _____
4. _____
5. _____
6. _____
7. _____
8. _____
9. _____
10. _____

27 Capitals for Titles of People • Practice 1

Social and Professional Titles Capitalize the title of a person when it is followed by a person's name or when it is used in direct address. Capitalize the titles of certain high government officials even when they are not followed by a person's name or used in direct address.

TITLES OF PEOPLE	
Before a Noun:	This class is taught by *Professor Johnson*.
Direct Address:	Pay attention, *Private Smith*.
	Pay attention, *Private*.
Titles Without a Person's Name:	The *President* is speaking tonight.

Family Titles Titles showing family relationships are capitalized when used with the person's name, in direct address, or when they refer to specific persons. A title after a possessive noun or pronoun is never capitalized.

FAMILY TITLES	
Before a Name:	We went to see *Uncle* John.
In Direct Address:	"Hello, *Grandpa*," I said.
Referring to a Specific Person:	Is *Grandmother* ill?
After a Possessive Noun:	I met Bill's *aunt*.
After a Possessive Pronoun:	His *uncle* is seventy-five.

▶ **Exercise 1** **Using Capitals for Social and Professional Titles.** Underline each word that should be capitalized.

EXAMPLE: The surgeon was <u>doctor</u> Maria Carlson.

1. The king, Henry, stood in a hillside and watched the battle in the valley below.
2. Please, sergeant, give me your help.
3. In 1862, admiral Farragut won an important victory at New Orleans.
4. Our embassy in London was run by ambassador Kennedy.
5. Has mayor Glasser decided to seek reelection?
6. The president will not run again.
7. Excuse me, mrs. Henderson, you look very tired.
8. Have you met superintendent Ritter?
9. The sermon was delivered by the reverend Peterson.
10. captain Wolfe and colonel Carlton met for dinner.

▶ **Exercise 2** **Using Capitals for Family Titles.** If the family title in each sentence is correctly capitalized, put a *C* in the blank at the right. If the title is incorrectly capitalized, write the title correctly in the blank.

EXAMPLE: I visited Uncle Fred on his farm. _____*C*_____.

1. This year, mom became thirty-five. _____
2. Carol's aunt is head of our Girl Scout troop. _____
3. I told dad you would be late. _____
4. My sister is going steady with Mike Williams. _____
5. We saw aunt Jean on television last night. _____

27 Capitals for Titles of People • Practice 2

> **Exercise 1** **Using Capitals for Social and Professional Titles.** If the title in each of the following sentences is correctly capitalized, write *correct* in the blank. If it is incorrectly capitalized, rewrite the title, correcting the error.

EXAMPLE: The president was seated in the Oval Office of the White House. _____President_____

1. Pardon me, professor, but would you repeat that quotation? _____
2. Several sermons given by the reverend Donne have been published. _____
3. After serving the school district for ten years, superintendent Mills retired. _____
4. There was limited television coverage of the President's last press conference. _____
5. All of the army's Generals agreed that a military attack was not possible. _____
6. I heard that senator Carr is widely respected. _____
7. Our teacher asked Sir Richard to speak to the class about British royalty. _____
8. The queen of England will attend the celebration next month. _____
9. Representative Wilkins voted against the revised plan. _____
10. In 1898 admiral Dewey defeated the Spanish fleet. _____

> **Exercise 2** **Using Capitals for Family Titles.** Complete each of the following sentences by filling the blank with a family title or a title with a name.

EXAMPLE: Please, _____Grandfather_____, send more pineapples.

1. My _____ likes to spend her spare time working on our car.
2. While the rest of us danced, _____ played the fiddle.
3. His _____ is now on the junior varsity soccer team.
4. "Come quickly, _____!" Rebecca cried.
5. Their _____ knits sweaters for all the children.
6. Few people are as widely traveled as Randy's _____.
7. "Let me tell you, _____, about that fish I almost caught," he said.
8. Before the race began, _____ tried to remain calm.
9. I told Jill's _____ that we would be home later than usual.
10. Slowly _____ began to shovel a narrow path through the deep snow.

> **Writing Application** **Using Capitals for Titles of People.** Write five sentences of your own, using in each sentence one title as described in the following items. Be sure to capitalize correctly.

1. a business or professional title and a specific name

   _____

2. a government title and a specific name

   _____

3. an English monarch's title

   _____

4. a military title and a specific name

   _____

5. a family member's title used in direct address

   _____

Capitals for Titles of Things • Practice 1

Works of Art   Capitalize the first word and all other important words in the titles of books, periodicals, poems, stories, plays, paintings, and other works of art.

WORKS OF ART	
Book: *The Book of Lists*	Periodical: *Art in America*
Poem: "Mending Wall"	Story: "Of Missing Persons"

School Courses   Capitalize titles of courses when they are language courses or when they are followed by a number or have a specific name.

COURSES	
French	Spanish
History 201	Math 104
Writing for Success Workshop	

▶ **Exercise 1**   **Using Capitals for Works of Art.**   Underline each word that should be capitalized in the items below.

EXAMPLE: We are reading <u>hamlet</u>.

1. I enjoy reading Robert Frost's poem "birches."
2. My parents subscribe to *american perspective magazine.*
3. Have you ever seen Winslow Homer's painting *the gulf stream.*
4. One of O. Henry's short stories is "the gift of the magi."
5. I am starting a subscription to *civil war times.*
6. The setting for *johnny tremain* is colonial America.
7. I thought *old yeller* was a heartwarming novel.
8. "christmas day in the morning" is one of Pearl S. Buck's famous short stories.
9. *A farewell to arms, for whom the bell tolls,* and *the old man and the sea* are three of Ernest Hemingway's best novels.
10. Joe likes to read *fiction international.*

▶ **Exercise 2**   **Using Capitals for Courses.**   Underline each word that should be capitalized.

EXAMPLE: I plan to take <u>french</u> next semester.

1. My favorite courses are math, chemistry, and spanish.
2. Mr. Wegmus teaches biology 101.
3. This term my sister is taking algebra II.
4. My brother is planning to take greek in college.
5. Chico is taking introduction to modern american fiction as his elective course.

27 # Capitals for Titles of Things • Practice 2

▷ **Exercise 1** Using Capitals for Works of Art. Rewrite each of the following titles, adding the missing capitals. Use underlining and quotation marks as shown.

EXAMPLE: rose in bloom _____*Rose in Bloom*_____

1. as you like it _____
2. the call of the wild _____
3. "jabberwocky" _____
4. better gardens monthly _____
5. tales of a wayside inn _____
6. the mystery of the old clock _____
7. keeping fit magazine _____
8. the old man and the sea _____
9. "the dog of pompeii" _____
10. in the rain _____
11. the thinker _____
12. computer graphics magazine _____
13. a wrinkle in time _____
14. "flowers for algernon" _____
15. "harlem night song" _____

▷ **Exercise 2** Using Capitals for Courses. For each of the following, choose the correctly written course title from the choices in parentheses and write it in the blank.

EXAMPLE: My most difficult course is _____*German*_____. (german, German)

1. I signed up for Miss Albee's _____. (earth science 201, Earth Science 201)
2. Susan is glad that she took an extra course in _____. (math, Math)
3. In _____, we are studying lyric poetry. (english, English)
4. The most popular elective course in our school is _____. (cooking, Cooking)
5. Dennis found that _____ was easier than he had thought. (algebra I, Algebra I)
6. Stuart's favorite class is _____. (french, French)
7. Jerry is taking a _____ class on Saturdays. (computer, Computer)
8. Even though Marguerite does not enjoy her _____ class, she does well in it. (social studies, Social Studies)
9. In Mr. Patrick's _____ class, we are studying Ibsen's A Doll's House. (introduction to drama, Introduction to Drama)
10. My _____ class enabled me to qualify for a good after-school job. (Typing II, typing II)

Diagraming Basic Sentence Parts (Subjects and Verbs; Adjectives, Adverbs, and Conjunctions) • Practice 1

Subjects and Verbs   In diagraming a sentence, both the subject and the verb are placed on a horizontal line. They are separated by a vertical line, with the subject on the left and the verb on the right.

SUBJECT AND VERB		
Flowers bloom.		*Dean Anderson has been invited.*
Flowers	bloom	Dean Anderson	has been invited

Adjectives, Adverbs, and Conjunctions   Adjectives are placed on slanted lines directly under the nouns or pronouns they modify. Adverbs are placed on slanted lines directly under the verbs, adjectives, or adverbs they modify. Conjunctions are placed on dotted lines between the words they connect.

ADDING ADJECTIVES AND ADVERBS	ADDING CONJUNCTIONS
An *old, angry* woman complained very *bitterly.*	A limping *but* happy runner finished first.

▷ Exercise 1   **Diagraming Subjects and Verbs.**   Diagram the subjects and verbs below.

1. Jon did agree.

2. She has been chosen.

▷ Exercise 2   **Diagraming Adjectives, Adverbs, and Conjunctions.**   Diagram each sentence below. Refer to the examples above if necessary.

1. The long, difficult race has finally begun.

2. The band played noisily but well.

Diagraming Basic Sentence Parts (Subjects and Verbs; Adjectives, Adverbs, and Conjunctions) • Practice 2

Exercise 1 **Diagraming Subjects and Verbs.** Each of the following sentences contains a subject and verb. Diagram each sentence.

1. Birds fly.

2. Mike laughed.

3. Mr. Benton has moved.

4. Braxton Library was closed.

Exercise 2 **Diagraming Subjects and Verbs With Modifiers and Conjunctions.** In addition to subjects and verbs, the following sentences contain adjectives, adverbs, and conjunctions. Diagram each sentence.

1. The young children happily played.

2. The big truck moved very slowly but extremely noisely.

3. The silver and red bicycle rides very well.

Diagraming Basic Sentence Parts (Compound Subjects and Verbs) • Practice 1

Compound Subjects and Verbs   A compound subject has its subject diagramed on two levels. A compound verb is also diagramed on two levels.

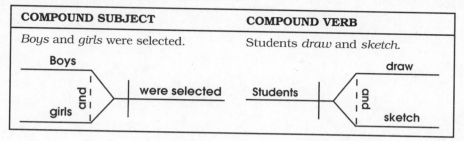

Place any adjective directly under the word it modifies. If an adjective modifies the entire compound subject, place it under the main line. Adverbs are placed directly under the words they modify. If an adverb modifies both verbs, it is placed on the main line.

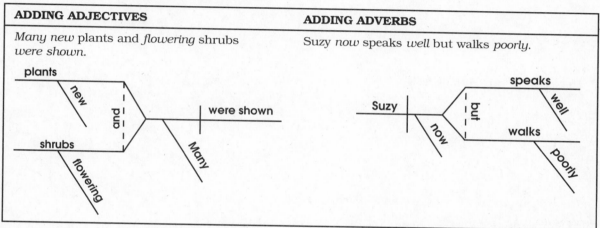

▷ **Exercise 1**   **Diagraming Compound Subjects and Verbs With Modifiers.**   Diagram the sentences below.

1.   Red roses and white asters are blooming.

2.   They meet and chat happily.

3.   Several exciting new cars and useful small trucks will be exhibited.

Diagraming Basic Sentence Parts (Compound Subjects and Verbs) • Practice 2

▶ **Exercise 1** Diagraming Compound Subjects and Compound Verbs. Correctly diagram each sentence.

1. Marigolds and zinnias are blooming.

2. The windows, tables, and shelves vibrated ominously.

3. These people can work or resign.

4. The old car groaned, sputtered, and stalled.

5. The waiter and the chef spoke softly and worked quickly.

6. Thunderstorms and tornadoes can develop rapidly.

Diagraming Basic Sentence Parts (Orders,

Sentences Beginning with *There* and *Here*, and Interjections)

• Practice 1

Orders, Sentences Beginning with *There* and *Here*, and Interjections The understood subject *you* is diagramed in the regular subject position, but in parentheses. Interjections, because they have no grammatical relationship to other words, are placed on a short line above the subject.

ORDERS	INTERJECTIONS
Wait quietly.	*Gee*, I lost quickly.

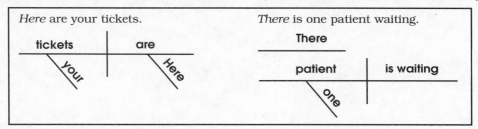

Sentences Beginning with *Here* and *There* *Here* at the beginning of a sentence is usually an adverb. It will modify the verb in the sentence. *There* is sometimes used to introduce a sentence. It has no grammatical relation to the rest of the sentence and is diagramed on a short line above the subject.

Here are your tickets.   *There* is one patient waiting.

▷ **Exercise 1** Diagraming Orders and Interjections and Sentences Beginning with *Here* and *There*. Diagram the sentences below.

1. Stand very straight.

2. Hurray, Max has arrived.

3. Here is a very detailed map.

4. There are only three girls.

Diagraming Basic Sentence Parts (Orders,
Sentences Beginning with *There* and *Here*, and Interjections)
• Practice 2

**Diagraming Orders, Sentences Beginning with *There* and *Here*, and
Interjections.**   Diagram each of the following sentences.

1. Walk now.

2. Here is your book.

3. Wow! You already finished.

4. Here is the watch.

5. Hey! Look out.

6. Proceed carefully.

7. There is the menu.

8. There are eleven players.

Diagraming Basic Sentence Parts (Complements)

• Practice 1

Complements   Direct objects, indirect objects, and subject complements are diagramed in three different ways. A direct object is placed on the same line as the verb. It follows the verb and is separated from it by a short vertical line. A compound direct object is diagramed in a way similar to compound subjects and verbs. The indirect object is placed on a short horizontal line extending from a slanted line drawn directly below the verb. A compound indirect object is diagramed below the verb.

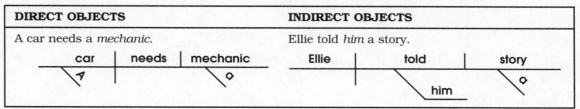

DIRECT OBJECTS	INDIRECT OBJECTS
A car needs a *mechanic.*	Ellie told *him* a story.

Predicate nouns, pronouns, and adjectives are all diagramed the same way. They are placed after the verb, separated from it by a short slanted line. A compound subject complement is diagramed in the same way as a compound subject or verb.

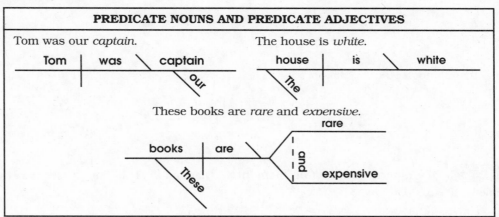

PREDICATE NOUNS AND PREDICATE ADJECTIVES

Tom was our *captain.*

The house is *white.*

These books are *rare* and *expensive.*

▶ **Exercise 1**   **Diagraming Direct and Indirect Objects and Subject Complements.**   Diagram the sentences below.

1.   Maria made her bed carefully.

2.   Joe gave Susan a new flashlight.

3.   Her new room was unusually cold.

4.   This old document seems historic and very valuable.

Diagraming Basic Sentence Parts (Complements)
• Practice 2

▶ **Exercise 1**   **Diagraming Direct Objects and Indirect Objects.**   Diagram the following
sentences. Some of the direct objects and indirect objects are compound.

1. His partner gave him a trophy.

2. The architect showed the owner and the manager the final plans.

3. Visitors often photograph deer, elk, and eagles.

▶ **Exercise 2**   **Diagraming Subject Complements.**   Diagram the following sentences. Some of the
complements are compound.

1. The new store is bright and roomy.

2. The presiding judge is a sympathetic individual.

3. Phyllis is a physician and an engineer.

Diagraming Prepositional Phrases • Practice 1

Prepositional Phrases   The diagram for a prepositional phrase is drawn under the word it modifies. The diagram has two parts: a slanted line for the preposition and a horizontal line for the object of the preposition. Adjectives that modify the object are placed beneath the object. The diagram for an adjective phrase is placed directly under the noun or pronoun that the phrase modifies. The diagram for an adverb phrase is placed directly under the verb, adjective, or adverb that the phrase modifies.

ADJECTIVE PHRASE	ADVERB PHRASE
Your table *in the restaurant* is now ready.	My aunt often walks *to our old stately library.*

▶ **Exercise 1**   **Diagraming Adjective Phrases.**   Diagram the sentences below.

1. The book in the window is quite expensive.

2. I want a room with a beautiful view.

▶ **Exercise 2**   **Diagraming Adverb Phrases.**   Diagram the sentence below.

1. Mother frequently drives to our new mall.

2. These old shoes are easier on my tired feet.

3. Sam carefully placed the blue plates on the new table.

Diagraming Prepositional Phrases • Practice 2

Diagraming Prepositional Phrases. Each of the following sentences contains one or more prepositional phrases. Diagram each sentence.

1. The train crept slowly into the station.

2. The airliner with the unusual shape is a *Stratocruiser*.

3. The woman in the blue coat ran onto the train at the last moment.

4. We shopped in the store with a book department, a magazine section, and a café.

5. Sue's father walks around the block in the evening.

6. During the storm, the rain pelted the windows with a deafening roar.

Name _____ Date _____

Diagraming Appositives • Practice 1

Appositives To diagram an appositive, place it in parentheses next to the noun or pronoun it renames. Any adjectives or adjective phrases that modify the appositive are positioned directly beneath it.

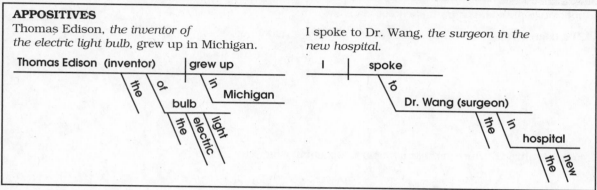

▶ **Exercise 1** **Diagraming Appositives.** Diagram the sentences below.

1. Mrs. Walters, the principal, addressed the assembly.

2. Tom Chambers, the captain of our football team, resigned.

3. This is Mabel, a true champion.

4. Our coach was Mickey, a warm, friendly, sympathetic person.

5. I spoke to Dr. Jason, a close friend.

6. I will go to Boston, one of the original colonial cities.

© Prentice-Hall, Inc.

Diagraming Appositives • 211

Diagraming Appositives • Practice 2

▶ **Exercise 1**   **Diagraming Appositive Phrases.**   Each of the following sentences contains one appositive phrase. Diagram each sentence.

1. We boarded the new train, a high-speed express streamliner.

2. Ms. Winthrop, a nurse for twenty years, is a compassionate person.

3. This highway, the Garden State Parkway, stretches along the entire length of New Jersey.

4. She will greet Ms. Daniels, the mayor of the town.

5. Mr. Peters, the principal, spoke with Mary's parents.

6. This is a jetliner, a commercial aircraft with jet engines.

Diagraming Clauses (Compound Sentences) • Practice 1

Compound Sentences   To diagram a compound sentence, begin by diagraming each clause separately, one above the other. Then join the clauses at the verbs using a dotted line shaped like a step. Place the conjunction or semicolon on the horizontal part of the step.

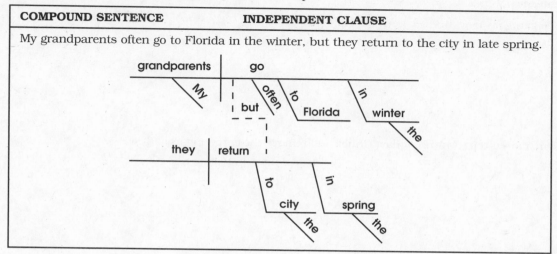

COMPOUND SENTENCE	INDEPENDENT CLAUSE

My grandparents often go to Florida in the winter, but they return to the city in late spring.

▶ **Exercise 1**   **Diagraming Compound Sentences.**   Diagram the sentences below.

1. I opened the door to my bedroom, and I found a present on my bed.

2. This is our first visit; we have never been to Chicago before.

3. Myra would not agree to our plan, but she later changed her mind.

4. I know the way to Boston, but I will probably become lost in certain parts of the city.

Diagraming Clauses (Compound Sentences) • Practice 2

▶ **Exercise 1**   **Diagraming Compound Sentences.**   Diagram each of the following compound sentences.

1. The garage is new, but the house is old.

2. Tony moved the furniture today; Chuck will remove the carpeting tomorrow.

3. They must repair the bridge; otherwise it will collapse.

4. Dorothy's father drove slowly, but he still missed the turn.

5. Three geese walked across the road, but four geese waited on the other side.

6. Ted won second prize, but, for the second straight year, Sheila won first prize.

Diagraming Clauses (Subordinate Clauses) • Practice 1

Subordinate Clauses   A complex sentence contains one independent clause and one or more subordinate clauses. In a diagram of a complex sentence, each clause is placed on a separate horizontal line. A subordinate adjective clause is placed on a horizontal line of its own beneath the independent clause. The two clauses are then connected by a dotted line from the noun or pronoun being modified to the relative pronoun in the adjective clause. A subordinate adverb clause is also written on a horizontal line of its own beneath the independent clause. The subordinate conjunction is written along a dotted line. This line extends from the modified word in the independent clause to the verb in the adverb clause.

ADJECTIVE CLAUSES

The car *that you like* is a Windstream.

ADVERB CLAUSES

My parents arrived *after the show had begun.*

▶ **Exercise 1**   **Diagraming Adjective and Adverb Clauses.**   Diagram the sentences below.

1. The book which you borrowed from the library is in our own bookcase.

2. This is the movie that we saw in Los Angeles.

3. If you buy that computer, you can use the new software.

4. The next bus leaves whenever it is filled with passengers.

Diagraming Clauses (Subordinate Clauses) • Practice 2

▷**Exercise 1**   **Diagraming Subordinate Clauses.**   Each of the following sentences contains an
adjective or an adverb clause. Diagram each sentence.

1. We found the student who had wandered from the group.

2. Margie enjoyed hot soup before the main course was served.

3. When the storm ended, people stepped outside.

4. The film that I bought was defective.

5. The box that they opened included no instructions.

6. We entered the supermarket after the sun had set.